AFRICA AND THE MODERN WORLD

IMMANUEL WALLERSTEIN

Africa World Press, Inc.
P.O. Box 1892
Trenton, New Jersey 08607

AFRICA WORLD PRESS, INC.
P.O. Box 1892
Trenton, New Jersey 08607

First Printing 1986

Copyright © Immanuel Wallerstein, 1986

All rights reserved. No part of this
publication may be reproduced, stored in a
retrieval system or transmitted in any form
or by any means electronic, mechanical,
photocopying, recording or otherwise without
the prior written permission of the publisher.

Typeset by TypeHouse of Pennington

Cover design by Adjoa Jackson-Burrowes

Library of Congress Catalog Card Number: 85-71384

ISBN: 0-86543-023-3 Cloth
 0-86543-024-1 Paper

Acknowledgement:

The essays in this volume originally appeared in various journals and books, and are reprinted here with the permission of the publishers:

Chapter 1. *Canadian Journal of African Studies*, XVII, 1, Apr. 1983, 9-16. Chapter 2. L.H. Gann & Peter Duignan, eds., *Colonialism in Africa, 1870-1960*, II: *The History and Politics of Colonialism 1914-1960*. Cambridge: at the University Press, 1970, 399-421. Chapter 3. *Africa Today*, XVIII, 3, July 1971, 62-68. Chapter 4. *Issue: A Quarterly Journal of Africanist Opinion*, III, 3, Fall 1973, 1-11. Chapter 5. Frederick S. Arkhurst, ed., *U.S. Policy Toward Africa*. New York: Praeger, 1975, 11-37. Chapter 6. Peter C.W. Gutkind & Immanuel Wallerstein, eds., *Political Economy of Contemporary Africa*. Beverly Hills: Sage, 1976, 30-57. Chapter 7. *Review*, III, 2, Fall 1979, 325-371. Chapter 8. *Monthly Review*, XXXII, 10, Mar. 1981, 47-52. Chapter 9. *Contemporary Marxism*, No. 6, 1983, 166-171. Chapter 10. Working Paper No. 9, Africa Research & Publications Project, June 1985. Chapter 11. *The Nation*, Jan. 3-10, 1976, 12-17. Chapter 12. *The Nation*, Oct. 9, 1976, 328-331. Chapter 13. *The Nation*, Nov. 12, 1977, 489-492. Chapter 14. *Issue*, VII, 4, Win. 1977, 35-37.

CONTENTS

Introduction   1

1. The Evolving Role of the Africa Scholar in African Studies (1983)   3

Africa and the World-Economy   11

2. The Colonial Era in Africa: Changes in the Social Structure (1970)   13

3. The Lessons of the PAIGC (1971)   37

4. Africa in a Capitalist World (1973)   47

5. Africa, the United States, and the World-Economy: The Historical Bases of American Policy (1975)   77

6. The Three Stages of African Involvement in the World-Economy (1978)   101

7. Peripheralization of Southern Africa: Changes in Household Structure and Labor-Force Formation, with William G. Martin (1979)   139

8. Race is Class? Some Reflections on South Africa Inspired by Magubane (1981)   153

9. The Integration of the National Liberation Movement in the Field of International Liberation (1983)   159

10. Africa, 100 Years After the Berlin Conference (1984)   165

The U.S. Role in Africa: Kissinger, Carter, and Southern Africa   175

11. Kissinger's African Mischief (1976)   177
12. Luanda is Madrid (1976)   185
13. Yankee, Stay Home! South Africa and Liberal Interventionism (1977)   197
14. Why We Said No to AID, with Sean Gervasi, Ann Seidman, and David Wiley (1977)   205

Introduction

I am grateful for the opportunity to present in one volume what I hope to be a set of reasoned, relatively consistent views on Africa and the modern world.

I have organized the papers in a very simple manner. I start with a paper I wrote for the 25th Anniversary Meetings of the African Studies Association, in which I reflected on the evolving role of the Africa scholar, and in which I indicated what role I thought he/she might most fruitfully now play. I hope my own essays reflect my implicit prescriptions.

These essays are then in two sections. The first and longer section develops my arguments about how Africa was incorporated into the capitalist world-economy, how it developed within that framework, and what interpretation one might give to the interwoven fabric of race, class, and nation in contemporary Africa.

Finally I include a brief section of four polemical articles which may seem curiously dated. They were all written in 1976 and 1977. But that was a very critical moment. The blockage in Africa's drive for political liberation that characterized the decade 1965-75 had just been broken by the collapse of Portugal's fascist regime, in which the struggle of the African movements in the Portuguese colonies had been critical. The world had to take account of the renewed African political thrust, and take account it did. The U.S. refurbished "liberal interventionism" under Kissinger and Carter. "Constructive engagement" is merely a variant on a theme. It seems to me important, even now, to look back to 1976-77 to see what was wrong with U.S. African policy, even in its most "liberal" veneer. The details are perhaps remote, but I believe the analytic framework of the polemics remains as pertinent as ever.

Immanuel Wallerstein
Binghamton
September, 1985

The Evolving Role of the Africa Scholar in African Studies

This paper was originally written for a panel on the major paradigms dealing with change in Africa. But I wish to deal less with the evolution of so-called paradigms than with evolution of the role of the specialized student of change in Africa. One cannot dissociate the two, and I do not intend to do so. But in discussions on theorizing, there occurs too often a neglect of the theorizers, which in turn may lead to misinterpretations of what is and was going on.

As we all know, before *circa* 1950 the study of Africa was confined very largely to the domain of anthropology. True, there were some partial exceptions. In the case of South Africa, the large white population and the relative importance of its participation in the world-economy meant that some economists studied it as well. And in the case of North Africa, what might be called "Islamics" also played a role.

Nonetheless, anthropology dominated the scene. The fact that the study of Africa was thus limited of course reflected the division of intellectual labor that had been carved out of the late nineteenth century, among whose features was the division of the world into three geographical zones: modern European and European-settler states, which were studied by economists, historians, political scientists, and sociologists; non-Western areas with a long-standing written culture and preferably a so-called "world religion," which were studied by so-called Orientalists; and backward peoples, which were studied by anthropologists.

Furthermore, the anthropology of which we are speaking, and which emerged as a serious corpus of work between the two World Wars, was strongly antihistorical in orientation. It centered on two concepts. One was the existence of some original pattern of social behavior of some entity usually designated a "tribe" which was thought to be internally unchanging and whose processes, in the post-"contact" situation that had caused change, had to be recaptured by careful field work. Once recaptured, these processes were described in the famous "ethnographic present." The second concept was precisely that of "cultural contact" or "acculturation." At some point, it was said, the unchanging traditional entity had come into "contact" with some outside force and changes had occurred in the "culture." These changes, too, could be studied by contemporary observation. This was considered more "applied" research than that of recapturing the "disappearing culture."

Behind these two concepts lay a rather strong ideological bias: that the "cultures" of these "tribes," *even if they were not Western cultures*, were still legitimate objects of study. There were two different explanations for this view. One was based on the premise of evolution. Since all peoples pass through identical (or at least very similar) stages, tribal cultures were merely located somewhere on a continuum. They were further back to be sure than European cultures, but this in itself made them of interest. The alternative explanation was that of cultural relativism. Since all cultures represented equally worthy solutions for the basic human problems of adaptation to the environment, what seemed strange would seem less so, once the anthropologist uncovered the code and translated it into Western terminology.

Who were these anthropologists? They were almost all either university-trained scholars on the one hand or colonial administrators or missionaries (with a scholarly bent) on the other. By and large, they all did field work in the same basic way. They lived in a given area for some time, learned the local language more or less, and utilized indigenous assistants as informants, intermediaries, and companions.

These anthropologists were all Europeans, and almost always of the nationality of the governing colonial power. The precondition for their work was indeed the fact that these "tribes" were located in areas governed by colonial authorities. But the precondition was also a major constraint. Anthropologists needed the permission of the colonial authorities to do their work. Of course, they also needed the permission of the "tribe" to do their work. The first permission was indispensable and formal. The second was only necessary in the sense that it was believed such permission, the culmination of an effort to achieve "rapport," was required for the work to be "successful." Once such rapport was achieved, it was generally considered infradig for other anthropologists to invade the same terrain.

The Evolving Role of the Africa Scholar in African Studies

Each anthropologist had his "tribe" and there were after all enough to go around.

When the work was completed, it took the form of a monograph or a report. Its audience was other anthropologists in the Western world (but first of all in the particular metropole) and all those involved at a high level in administrative work in the colonies. The research yielded some empirical knowledge of very practical use to administrators, some additional evidence of ethnographic variation for use by scholars, and very occasionally some insight into theoretical propositions.

In political terms, the anthropologists of this period were essentially secular missionaries, liberal mediators between the tribe and the Colonial Office (plus metropolitan public opinion). The anthropologists were concerned (a) to demonstrate that "backward" did not necessarily mean "primitive" or "irrational," and (b) to ensure that the negative social consequences of "contact" be minimized and the positive ones maximized.

Anthropologists thought of themselves as sympathetic "strangers" in both cultures. To the African "tribe," they came as "strangers" who however engaged in "participant observation," and therefore combined subjective empathy with objective perspective. (This was incidentally the same stance which historians at the time used to justify their choice of double practical constraints: a lifetime specialization on a limited space-time zone which was thought to create subjective empathy, and the choice of such a zone at a distant time, thought to ensure an objective perspective.) The anthropologist however also considered himself a stranger to metropolitan culture. Indeed, the psychological roots of choosing anthropology as a career was often, as we know, a sense of partial alienation from one's own culture. The anthropologist felt that he was unlike his fellow metropolitans, in that he was exempt from "ethnocentrism" (just as the missionary felt unlike laymen in that he was exempt from "materialism" or "secularism"). There was no doubt an element of self-congratulation in this stance.

The changes that began *circa* 1950 were not the doing of the Africa scholars. They were the consequence of the rise of African nationalism in the form of political movements. Nationalist movements by their very existence challenged, both implicitly and explicitly, the two basic premises of the previous work of Africa scholars.

First, nationalist movements asserted that the primary arena of social and political action, in terms of legitimacy and hence of study, was and ought to be the colonial state/putative nation, and not the "tribe." Indeed, they went further. They argued that emphasis on "tribes" and "tribalism" was a central device of the colonial authorities to maintain the colonial rule, and as a consequence they formally deplored the study of "tribes."

Secondly, nationalist movements asserted that the relationship between Europeans and Africans had not been one of "culture contact" at all, but rather one of a "colonial situation." Culture contact could be good or bad and, as we have just noted, the anthropologists had devoted themselves politically to trying to make sure it was good rather than bad. Colonial situations could only be bad. The only thing one could do to achieve good in a colonial situation was to end it. The primary force to ensure that culture contact would be good rather than bad had been the "liberal mediator." The primary force to ensure that the colonial situation would be ended had to be an African nationalist movement. Politically, therefore the nationalist movements were advocating "African agency" in place of "European agency."

The anthropologists, of the genre that had flourished in the interwar period, were deprived of the legitimacy of their subject matter. Some drew drastic conclusions. Georges Balandier, trained as an anthropologist, invented the term "colonial situation," and became a professor of sociology at the Sorbonne.

In a world that was decolonizing, African studies became drastically redefined. African colonies-becoming-independent-states now seemed to exhibit political, economic, and social processes sufficiently similar to those of the West such that they could be seen as the normal domain of political scientists, economists, and sociologists. Africa prior to colonial rule no longer seemed some unchanging entity, but could be seen as the normal domain of historians and archaeologists. African culture no longer seemed an exoticism but could be seen as the normal domain of students of literature or art or film or music. In short, all of a sudden and quite rapidly, everyone got into the act.

There was concurrently a drastic shift in the social composition of Africa scholars. A field that previously had been composed almost exclusively of citizens of the European colonial powers was now transformed by two massive new groups. Scholars in the United States, who prior to 1945, had virtually been one man—Melville Herskovits—now began to invade every remote corner of the continent. Among these American scholars, there was an important contingent of Black American scholars. The growth of the African Studies Association (ASA) itself, from the 35 or so people who founded it in 1957 to the jamboree of 1982, attests to this phenomenon dramatically. This growth was not accidental or unplanned. It was nurtured, encouraged, and financed by the great private foundations and the U.S. government. It was the inevitable outcome of the strong political interests which the United States, as the world's new hegemonic power, had assumed after the Second World War.

The Evolving Role of the Africa Scholar in African Studies 7

There was a second massive new group of Africa scholars: the Africans. Before 1945, there had been virtually only one—Jomo Kenyatta—and how extraordinary that had seemed at the time. Now there were many Africans, trained at universities, initially in the West and later in Africa itself. For, along with the rise of African Africa scholars went the rise of the African universities. The emergence of these African Africa scholars was directly linked to the rise of the nationalist movements, not because these scholars were political activists (of course some were) but because it was the existence of these movements that created the social conditions for the educational structures that sustained the African Africa scholars.

There were of course others who became Africa scholars in this period—in the U.S.S.R., in non-colonizing European countries, in Canada and Australia, in India and Japan, and in Brazil. In short, when we say that everybody got into the act, we mean not only the range of university-recognized disciplines but the geographical range of world scholarship.

The basic premises of the new collective work were, in dialectical response to the earlier scholarship, the inverse of the previous premises. The state/nation was now the locus of social action, and African agency provided the dynamic focus of the analysis. For a while, the center of much analysis was on such phenomena as the nationalist movements, state-building (both pre-colonial and post-colonial), so-called primary resistance, and Negritude.

Despite this massive social restructuring of the personnel engaging in Africa studies, their basic political stance in the period 1950-1970 was not as different from that of the pre-1950 anthropologists as one might have expected. I have suggested that the pre-1950 anthroplogists could be seen as "liberal mediators" and "secular missionaries." In various ways, the 1950-1970 Africa scholars continued to act in these roles.

Prior to 1950, Africa scholars mediated between their tribe and the colonial administrator. The new 1950-1970 brand of Africa scholars mediated between modern Africa (represented first of all by the nationalist movements) and the Western world in general. But mediation now took the form not of interpreting "traditional African customs and values" but of interpreting "modern African behavior." The Africa scholars sought to interpret this behavior first of all to Western policy-makers at all levels, in order to make them more "sympathetic" to the positions argued by the modern African leaders. And they sought to interpret African behavior to the vast majority of scholars concerned primarily with the West, in order to make them reformulate their generalizations to take into account some of the specificities of the African situation.

Performing this role of mediating interpretation, Africa scholars still were self-congratulatory about the fact that they were thereby overcoming "ethnocentrism." The scholars in the United States assumed this role of "liberal mediation" with even greater enthusiasm than did their European or Soviet colleagues, who however in fact did the same, as did even the African Africa scholars.

But if the Africa scholars continued to be "liberal mediators," did they also continue to be "secular missionaries"? Of course they did. The very same Africa scholars who engaged in the interpretive political tasks turned right around and assigned themselves the role of counselor and advisor to African institutions, overtly and covertly, explicitly and implicitly, invited or uninvited. And they played this role with the best of conscience, pursuing their appointed tasks in the spread of rationality and progress as decreed by the Enlightenment and transmitted via science and scholarship.

The 1969 meeting of the African Studies Association (U.S.) thus came as an earthquake to Africa scholars, first of all in the United States but not only in that country. The meetings were held in the wake of the student and worker rebellions that had been occurring in many parts of the world since 1968. In the United States, a major component of the political turmoil had been the expression of the Black Power movement. The meetings were in Montreal. This meant that, exceptionally, the meetings had a very large non-United States contingent. First of all, the ASA was meeting jointly with our Canadian sister body. Secondly, since it was the first such joint meeting, and since it was taking place in the province of Quebec (itself going through parallel political turmoil), the Canadians had raised money to invite many European and African scholars—from both the Anglophone and Francophone scholarly networks.

We were assembled for the grand opening when a group of Black American Africa scholars seized the platform and put forward a series of demands. These demands had not come out of the blue. There had been signs of discontent for two years previously, including the founding of a Black American grouping of Africa scholars known as the African Heritage Studies Association (AHSA). The political dynamics of the Montreal meeting were complex, and it is not to the point to review them. What is to the point is to see the nature of the demands that were being made.

There were two major complaints, and both revolved around the social role of the Africa scholar. One was the complaint that Africa studies in the United States were built on a foundation of institutional racism, which protected the control of the field by white Establishment scholars located in the major universities. For example, it was argued, there had been virtually no Blacks who were in leadership positions of the ASA, or who were the recipients of major grants by funding agencies. A number of solutions were proposed: opening up ASA membership to non-university persons concerned with Africa, and racial parity on the Executive Council of ASA were among them.

The second complaint concerned what I have called the stance of "liberal mediator." The charge was made that it reflected in some cases hypocrisy and in others inefficacity. This was the period of the unmasking of the CIA's covert involvement in non-governmental organizations, including some associated with Africa studies, such as AMSAC (the American Society of African Culture) and the AAI (African-American Institute). This was also the period when the whole concept of academic non-involvement in overtly political debates was being widely called into question. A number of solutions were proposed: among them were the formal rejection of the legitimacy of links of Africa scholars not only to the CIA but to all other United States governmental agencies as well (State Department, AID, USIA, etc.); and open political support for liberation movements in Africa as well as for progressive governments.

The world of Africa scholarship was deeply split and emotionally wrenched by the confrontation. As an immediate outcome, a great many (perhaps most) Black American Africa scholars withdrew from the ASA, and AHSA transformed itself from being a supplementary structure of United States-based Africa scholars to being a rival organization.

In the following five years, the inter-organizational tension calmed down, but the rift has never been fully healed. Eventually, the ASA responded to the crisis by certain organizational changes: some democratization of membership categories; election of Blacks to leadership positions; the creation of the Committee on Current Issues to permit the regular public airing of Africa-related political issues; adoption of resolutions on political questions. In 1973, the ASA agreed to create a joint delegation with AHSA on a basis of parity to attend the International Congress of Africanists, and agreed to support John Henrik Clarke of AHSA as the sole United States candidate for the Executive Council of the international organization.

That body itself made a symbolic shift of some importance in 1973. It changed its name. It had been known, since its founding in 1962, as the International Congress of Africanists. After deliberation, the group decided that "Africanist" was a label redolent of the outsider looking in (which historically was true, since the term was an emendation of Orientalist), and hence from then on the organization was to be called the International Congress of African Studies.

In the 1970s thus the Africa scholar's social role of "liberal mediator" began to wither away, and there were many individuals who withdrew from the field as a consequence. I would argue this was also one reason for the decline of student interest in Africa studies, though not the only one to be sure.

Meanwhile, much was happening on other fronts besides merely Africa studies. The crisis in developmentalist ideology—of both the liberal and Marxist variety—had led to the reopening of the epistemological and historiographical bases of modern social science. This is not the place to review that subject, but the fact of this happening is central to our story.

In Africa, as a political arena, the "downward sweep of African liberation" which had gone into a long pause in 1965 was resumed dramatically in 1974.

By now African nationalist movements had been superseded by national liberation movements, and this represented more than a mere semantic shift. African Marxisms (my plural is deliberate) emerged on the scene as a major factor for the first time—on the political scene, and on the intellectual scene. And the central locus of Africa studies was shifting from the trinity United States-United Kingdom-France to the African continent.

I have drawn a picture in broad brush strokes. Still I think it is accurate, if not complete. What are its implications for the present? We are in the midst of these changes. It is by no means certain where they will end. The social composition of African scholarship in the 1990s, the ideological premises, and above all the social role of the Africa scholar will be determined by the confluence of transformations in the world-system as a whole (including world scholarship) and the political struggles on the African continent.

The schism of 1969 may, indeed probably will, reappear in an updated and more radicalized form—one in which the veneer will be less race than class. What is sure is that we are being called upon to make renewed fundamental choices in terms of the analytic frameworks we are able and willing to employ, and the values we are able and ready to uphold. In that sense, we are very far from the beginnings of Africa studies, when we rationalized the analysis of exotica. Africa studies is now as central to world scholarship as any other subfield. Indeed, the question is, in what meaningful sense is there today a subfield we can call Africa studies?

PART ONE

Africa and the World-Economy

The Colonial Era in Africa: Changes in the Social Structure[1]

"In any long-term view of African history, European rule becomes just another episode. In relation to wars and conflicts of people, the rise and fall of empires, linguistic, cultural and religious change and the cultivation of new ideas and new ways of life, new economic orientations...in relation to all these, colonialism must be seen not as a complete departure from the African past, but as one episode in the continuous flow of African history.[2]"

The colonial episode, as has been pointed out by many of the contributors to this volume, affected profoundly every aspect of African life. The extent of the influence varied, of course, from colony to colony, depending upon circumstances. One effect, however, appears to have been more or less general. This is the change which colonial rule brought about in the essential frameworks within which social action in Africa occurred. In the process, the relative importance of various social groups shifted considerably. The present essay examines the stresses and strains caused by these changes and the way in which the resulting problems have been resolved.

For our purposes, we shall consider the period of colonial rule in Africa as roughly 1885 to 1960. It is true that a few coastal areas of Africa were under European colonial rule before 1885 (sometimes as early as the sixteenth century), and that about one-quarter of the continent remained under colonial rule after 1960 (or even as late as 1968). Nonetheless, the years between 1885 and 1960 represent the one period during which most of the land area and most of the people of the African continent were under the legal and administrative jurisdiction of one or another of the European powers.

In order to discuss the overall change that occurred between 1885 and 1960, it is useful to make a summary sketch of the general situation in the earlier period, 1500 to 1885. Three features of this period have an important bearing on the subsequent discussion.

First, in various parts of Africa during the sixteenth to the nineteenth centuries, a number of states bearing all the marks of the process we currently call modernization either came into existence or expanded. For instance, we see examples of the consolidation of a reasonably large territory under a centralized, bureaucratic system that encompassed a population far larger than any defined by visible kinship groups. We find specialized production and the production of goods for long-distance trade and for distribution within the state. In addition, this period bore witness to the emergence of a professional trading class, sometimes a distinct branch of the state bureaucracy, sometimes an alien trading class given permission to operate within the boundaries of the state. Important strides were made also in the area of technological development, both by invention and by borrowing.[3]

Secondly, the major relationship between Europe and Africa from 1500 to 1800 revolved around the slave-trade. One consequence of this association was the strengthening of states who served in one way or another as procurers of this export commodity, and the development of a coastal trading class who served as middlemen between the inland procurers and the European purchasers arriving with their boats. A second and perhaps equally important consequence, however, was a delay in the emergence of cash-crop agriculture in slave-trading areas as a result of European interference. Boahen cites the instance in 1751 when the British Board of Trade ordered the Governor of Cape Castle to stop cotton cultivation among the Fante, giving as a reason:

> The introduction of culture and industry among the Negroes is contrary to the known established policy of this country, there is no saying where this might stop, and that it might extend to tobacco, sugar and every other commodity which we now take from our colonies and thereby the Africans, who now support themselves by wars, would become planters and their slaves be employed in the culture of these articles in Africa, which they are employed in in America.[4]

In the third place, during the late eighteenth and the nineteenth centuries, the slave-trade was gradually abolished. Great Britain in particular took it upon herself to try to enforce this abolition on all parties, affirming a doctrine of support for free, "legitimate" trade in Africa. The immediate impact of the drive to end the slave-trade was that trade and profits declined, and many European administrative operations in Africa had to be cut back or abruptly halted. The weaker European powers simply dropped out. Denmark withdrew completely;[5] and the Netherlands, which tried for a time to stay on by maintaining the slave-trade, was eventually forced to transfer her forts to Great Britain.[6] Even the British withdrew from Ouidah (Whydah), and several times contemplated abandoning all their West African forts.[7] That they never actually took this step, however, was due solely to the protests of the merchants, who realized—if some British civil servants did not—that it was Britain, as the dominant world commercial and industrial power, which stood to reap the greatest benefit from the new situation. The abolition of the slave-trade facilitated the reconversion of production to cash-cropping, which occurred notably in West Africa with the rise of the palm-oil and peanut-oil export trade in the nineteenth century. The abolition of the slave-trade released African energies[8] at the same time that the developing European economy now desired the very cash-crops they had previously sought to suppress.[9]

In short, many parts of sub-Saharan Africa, especially West Africa, were engaged in a process of relatively autonomous development, tied to the European world in a limited but important manner through the intermediary of merchants or state trading agents on each side, who were in turn linked, in some cases ambivalently, to political authorities on each side—in the African case, to inland hierarchical chiefs,[10] on the European side, to their respective governments.

Yet, in 1879 this whole structure began to crumble, and by 1900 had ceased to exist. No doubt this was not what Great Britain desired. John E. Flint has stated it succinctly:

> [Before 1879, Britain's] commerce was supremely competitive . . . did not need the protection of colonial tariff preferences, and . . . it seemed that the other powers were in no position to retaliate by establishing colonies of their own as protected areas for their exports. . . . The free traders could dream of the day when Africa would be completely dominated by Britain, but this would not be through colonies, but by gradual penetration, decade by decade, of British trade and British missionaries.[11]

The major difficulty was that while this grand design suited Britain admirably, it suited other European powers such as France and Germany far less well. To challenge effectively the British economic hegemony in the world, the other industrializing powers needed, or felt they needed, larger markets for their industries and access to raw materials. Thus started the scramble for Africa; and once it had been started, Britain had no choice but to join in or be the loser.[12] From the Berlin Conference of 1884 to 1900, Africa was partitioned and "pacified."

The primary objective of this sudden imposition of colonial administration on most of Africa, in contrast with the earlier, long-developing commercial penetration, was to establish political control of the territory, which thereby made it possible to establish primacy in its economic transactions.[13] The ideal was monopolistic rights, although not every colonial power was strong enough to enforce such a policy; and Britain, as we have said, did not need to use extensively the weapon of exclusion. She merely wished to keep from being excluded herself. With these motivations, it became imperative that if possible no area be left in limbo, that European annexation or protection[14] be as extensive as possible.

Colonial conquest, rapidly achieved albeit often with considerable difficulty, involved in its very essence two fundamental changes of the boundaries of social action in Africa, one political, the other economic. Virtually all peoples became subject to a central administration, one of the fifty or so colonies. Each of these colonies absorbed politically a far larger number of entities of varying structures that we have come to call traditional political authorities. Thus, by and large, the scale of political administration became larger, the number of entities in Africa fewer, and above all the boundary lines were altered.

With regard to the second of the fundamental changes—the economic—each colony became part of an international economic network. The basic political decisions that determined the structure of that network were taken centrally and outside of Africa. Economic enterprise within the colony was dependent upon these decisions. The structures were different from those of the earlier, looser networks of which some African states had been a part.

The political boundaries were drawn primarily to include as much territory as could be conquered or negotiated diplomatically. Since the lines were established by each European power essentially out of fear of a claim of sovereignty by another European power, they were frequently arbitrary in terms of the previous lines drawn by the African states now enclosed or divided.[15] The important point, however, is not that pre-colonial political and cultural units were some how divided among European hegemonies but that they were included within, and eventually subordinated to, a new juridical entity, the colonial territory and its administrative and legal systems.

The characteristic link between Africans and Europeans was no longer that between trading partners, each more or less backed up by his separate government. The relationship now was one between European administrators and African subordinates (primarily, as we shall see, chiefs and civil servants). And the trading operation was now carried on within a single political economy rather than between two political economies. If Africans did not play the game according to European rules, they were subject to political sanctions, certainly *de jure* and to a great extent *de facto*. They could be removed from their posts by the Europeans, and removed they were often with great dispatch.

The consequences of the exercise of colonial authority—an authority administered within the framework of a new (and usually, for the African, larger) political unit than before—were several. One was the revamping, often the undermining, of previously existing systems. Whether, as in many hierarchical systems, the "chief" was weakened[16] or, as in some systems, his powers were increased, in all cases the form and operation of the authority system were altered to suit the needs and desires of the colonial power. Moreover, the consequences of these changes were often felt not only in the particular (rural) area where they occurred but throughout the new unit, the colony.[17] In the next place, movements of labor tended to take place within the imperial colonial boundaries, if only because both transportation and currency systems made it the easiest path of the migrant. Where migration patterns crossed international lines, as in the case of Moçambique labor moving to South Africa, such a pattern was often followed with the express encouragement of the colonial authorities. Thirdly, the new political boundaries became in time the logical unit within which associational and political activities took place. Each colony began to acquire a personality, one recognized by its inhabitants. It became, in short, a social reality.

Membership in a specific international economic network led also to major social change in the individual colonies. We have already suggested that the prime objective of establishing colonial administration was the creation of a pre-emptive monopoly.[18] Quite aside from formal political limitations that could now be placed on traders outside the imperial network, the indirect effects of participating in a given currency zone were considerable.

The most immediate effect of colonial rule was its impact on the African traders, whose ability to play their traditional late nineteenth century "monopolistic role as middlemen" was drastically curtailed.[19] The merging of European trading firms into large-scale enterprises capable of mobilizing vast amounts of working capital, commanding superior or exclusive credits with European colonial banks, and having direct access to a European commercial network, put the African traders at a great disadvantage from the outset. These giant firms were in a much better position to take advantage of the expanding economic opportunities brought about by the establishment of colonial rule than were their African counterparts (or Arab traders in East Africa). The change took some thirty or forty years to accomplish completely, but by the end of World War I the radical decline of the relative importance of the African, as well as of the Arab, trading class had become an accomplished fact.[20]

A standard feature of the colonial economy was the development or expansion of an export commodity. Many minerals were extremely profitable, and were developed wherever possible under the aegis of a European firm. Of the total gross output in all of Africa, during the colonial period over two-thirds was produced in South Africa, the Belgian Congo, and Northern Rhodesia. But agricultural products (notably cocoa, coffee, tea, palm products, ground-nuts [peanuts], cotton, tobacco, wine) were in steady expansion throughout the continent. Although in West and North Africa the colonial authorities could partially build on an already established cash economy, the introduction of cash-crops was in most communities the consequence of either colonial administrative pressure on African farmers[21] or of expropriation of the land by white settlers (as in Kenya, Algeria, Southern Rhodesia). Of course, in many instances, despite opposition by the colonial administration or the settlers—who in certain cases preferred to encourage Africans to offer themselves as wage-workers—African farmers proceeded to develop cash-crops because they found them profitable.[22] Whatever the motive for entering the world agricultural market and whatever the social organization of export production, each colonial administration, as the political arm of the metropole, sought to tie a segment of the African population into the larger imperial economy either as independent producers or as wage-workers, and in all cases as consumers. As a consequence, the economic well-being of the African population was continually and increasingly subject to the fluctuations endemic to these systems. Furthermore, once colonial administration had been established, this shift in the basic orientation of the colonial economy often occurred quite early and rapidly.[23]

Both the mines and the cash-crop areas, as well as the commercial-administrative urban centers, needed labor; and they all obtained it largely through circulatory migration, partially forced, partially induced, initially by means of taxation.[24] The need for clerical labor was met through the establishment of Western educational structures. This did not mean, however, that higher administrative posts were open to Africans. On the contrary, at the beginning of this era there were many qualified Africans in the civil service; but soon after the setting up of colonial governments there followed a steady policy of deliberate exclusion, which only ended with the rise of the nationalist movements.[25]

The establishment of firmly-bounded, administered territorial units forming integral elements of a particular imperial economic system, was the main accomplishment of European colonial conquest, one that had been realized by and large throughout most of Africa by the outbreak of World War I. The colonial order was based, as we have said, on a new alliance of Europeans and Africans. On the European side, the key actors were the colonial administrators (joined in some areas in an important secondary role by white settlers). On the African side, the key actors were the chiefs, who were increasingly incorporated into the colonial bureaucracy,[26] and a small urban clerical and professional bourgeoisie, who were largely Christianized. The center of interaction of European and African shifted from the port of trade, at which representatives of two separate societies met, to the administrative offices, in which governors and governed met.[27]

The colonial order was, however, a misnomer. The colonial period was in many ways, as we become ever more aware, an exceedingly disorderly one. There was not only conquest (euphemistically termed at the time "pacification"); there was also the deliberate disruption of existing social organization, a practice the Europeans engaged in in order to reorganize the economy.[28] Both these phenomena, plus the resulting social changes, created a series of underlying strains which led, it now seems inevitably, to the rise of a nationalist movement.

There were three strains of some consequence. The first was the channeling of the African urban middle class, old and new, into administrative positions, primarily within the governmental bureaucracies (both national and local), but to some extent also within the bureaucracies of the export-import firms and the missionary churches. The clerk caught between two worlds has become a common object of literary study. To concentrate on his psychological dilemmas, however, is to miss the key factor, the structural bind in which this class found itself.

The school graduate had virtually no option except to choose a career in one of the three European-controlled bureaucratic structures (government, export-import firms, missions). To rise within these bureaucracies he was obliged to conform not merely to the norms of the organization internally but to a wider code of behavior and manners characteristic of the European (largely middle-class) expatriate in Africa. The more he cut himself off from the customs of his African rural community, the greater was likely to be his reward in the bureaucracy.

At the same time, however, into this same administrative machinery there was introduced another class of people, Europeans who were making their career in the colonies, who not only entered these bureaucracies at a higher level than the African school graduate but who also monopolized the top posts. As the African administrative bourgeoisie grew in numbers, so did the European administrative class, the latter—at least until about the 1950s—at a faster pace than the former. The result of this trend was that the sole career outlet of any significance available to educated Africans not only carried with it an arbitrary (racial) limit of aspiration but a limit that grew tighter and moved *lower* as the years of colonial rule went by. It was inevitable that with every passing year the irritation of this class would increase. However, despite the fact that the proportion of Africans in senior bureaucratic positions declined, their absolute numbers grew because of the steady expansion of the various administrative apparatuses. It thus became more and more plausible to work collectively to change the system, first in various social organizations, later in trade unions and proto-nationalist political groups.

The second source of tension was less universal, its emergence being in part a consequence of the extent of production for the imperial market in a given territory plus the absence of a significant number of white settlers. As the market grew, so did the number of educated urban Africans; and they then became more differentiated as a class. In the tightly stratified system that characterized the colonial period in Africa—and this became ever more marked with the passage of time—pecking orders rapidly emerged, and each stratum perceived an advantage in maintaining a distance between itself and the next lower stratum. The lower stratum in turn sought to blur the distinction, thereby rising. This effort led to conflict over the expansion of educational facilities (advantages to the lower stratum) and the creation of social exclusiveness or reduction of social contact by means of clubs and class endogamy (advantages to the higher stratum.)

In colonial Africa this issue had already arisen in some territories by the end of World War I, and it became acute after World War II. In the higher stratum were the professionals, medium high civil servants and religious personnel, and the more important chiefs in their urban social roles. In the lower stratum were the lower civil servants, the primary school teachers, the health personnel, and the skilled workers, a stratum which showed a significant jump in size during and as a result of each world war. The conflict between these groups, each fighting essentially for the relatively small share of the pie available to urban Africans, was made acute following each world war not merely by the increase in size of the lower stratum, but by the decline in real incomes brought about by the disruption of trade combined with inflationary trends in the imperial mother country.[29] When such conflicts became acute, the "lower middle class" elements expressed their views in the form of more militant and often more radical nationalism, calling for expansion of education, for the suffrage, and for diminution of the legal authority of chiefs.[30]

These lower middle-class elements wanted thus to take on simultaneously both the colonial régime and their principal African interlocutors (the administrative and professional bourgeoisie, plus the higher chiefs).[31] To do this, they needed strength beyond their own numbers and resources. They found immediate support in the African merchant class, such as it was, many of whom were simply graduates who tried to break out of the administrative careers for which the colonial administration had destined them.[32] These aspiring middle-class elements began to seek active support for their struggle in the rural areas, where they hoped to channel the latent and irregularly erupting discontent of the peasantry.[33] This discontent was not new; it was rather a continuing phenomenon of the years of colonial rule.

These unresolved discontents of the rural, monetized populations led to the third source of tension under colonial rule. The colonial system could not meet the demands of the peasantry without altering the basic economic pattern (and this was especially true in settler territories). On the other hand, with time and increasing education, this discontent threatened to become transformed into a conscious radicalism far more dangerous in the long run than simple, albeit destructive, outbreaks of rebellion.

Of course, except in a few relatively egalitarian groups, rural discontent undoubtedly predated the imposition of colonial rule. But colonial rule, once established, exacerbated these sources of irritation in four ways, as a result of which rural discontent was on the rise throughout the colonial era.[34]

In the first place, colonial rule meant conquest. This rule, once imposed, was exercised over chiefs as well as over ordinary men. Chiefs were removed, replaced, strengthened or weakened in power. Whatever the specifics, there was widespread change in personnel and often in structure, and as a result some loss of legitimacy, especially as the chiefs were progressively incorporated into the colonial administrative system as agents performing unpleasant tasks. In addition, Christianity spread largely in the mood of opposition to traditional customs and hence rulers. The combination of these two elements meant a general lessening of the effectiveness of traditional constraints on rebellious behavior.

Secondly, cash-crop production enabled those who controlled administrative decisions of allocation (the chiefs) to determine ownership rights in a system that, in the cash-crop areas, slowly but surely became one of private appropriation. In the course of time, it was largely those with high traditional status who acquired rights to extensive tracts, often at the expense of those who emigrated or were made to emigrate to the towns.[35] From the point of view of the average rural African, the process began to be regarded as chiefly usurpation of the land. Once it was perceived in that light, the ability of the chief to curb rebellious impulses of his subjects (whether directed against him or against the colonial régime) was bound to diminish.

Thirdly, the great geographical mobility, which was the consequence of a labor force with a solid migratory base, led to the spread of ideas, aspirations, frustrations and boldness. Fourthly, there was the discontent that arose in the neglected areas, where the Africans became aware of the growing disparity between their own standards of living and those of the areas favored by the colonial administration. This is what Iliffe has called the "politics of unimprovement."[36]

Thus, broadly speaking, African nationalism represented an alliance against colonial rule of the middle classes (largely urban) as the vocal leadership, and the rural elements (semi-urban) as the not-too-easy-to-control supporters. Two factors seem most likely to have increased the initial militance (violence) of African nationalism. In countries where the middle class was more developed and hence more differentiated, it was more likely to suffer from internal divisions. In that case the lower middle-class element would assume a more militant stance. If the peasantry was more dislocated, more uprooted from traditional social restraints, the spontaneous outbreaks would often be more frequent, more extreme, and their impact on the overall militance of the movement greater. This did depend in part, however, on the extensiveness of the colonial repressive machinery.

The schema thus baldly outlined shows immediately where the conflicting interest within the nationalist movement lay. The leaders and the supporters started out with differing underlying objectives and expectations. Since each segment brought to the nationalist movement a crucial part of the strength needed, each had to suppress its differences momentarily. But the conflicting aims were there from the beginning, available for exploitation by the colonial régime.

The leadership of the nationalist movement was very largely rooted in the administrative-clerical bourgeoisie (whether of the higher or the lower stratum). As we have noted, they found colonial limitations frustrating. They wanted the end of these arbitrary career limits, and it was political sovereignty that appeared to promise fulfillment of this desire. But, if anything, they found the individual limitations in the economic arena even more frustrating. Very few Africans still remained as middle-sized merchants,

The Colonial Era in Africa: Changes in the Social Structure

and their rise within the colonial framework to the rank of large-scale commercial or agricultural entrepreneurs—to say nothing of industrial entrepreneurs—was clearly out of the question. This was perfectly obvious not only to those who, despite everything, persisted as merchants, but also to that larger group of clerks and teachers who cherished such aspirations or who made futile attempts to pursue such inclinations.[37] These middle-class elements wanted control of the state machinery, partly for its own sake to be sure, and certainly for the sake of eliminating career discrimination; but also because they wanted to recapture the role of commercial middleman between Europe and the African hinterland, a role they had played in the nineteenth century and earlier, and of which they had been deprived by colonial rule.

The rural (semi-urban) masses had somewhat more diffuse objectives, less clear in their detail, requiring less obviously a control of the national bureaucratic apparatus. They wanted to be "less oppressed," and saw this being accomplished in one of two ways. One might be designated generically "romantic nativism," which involved shuffling off the overlay of European presence in the rural areas, and hopefully with it the African collaborators, some of the chiefs. Many of the independent neo-Christian cults, many of the messianic movements, some political stirrings were of this nature. They seemed to be heavily "localist" in orientation.

The other path, for the ordinary uneducated man, more modern in appearance and reality, was to aspire to the status of a member of the middle classes through one or both of the two paths of entry: education and cash-earning jobs. The demands of this group for universal education and an expansion of the employment sector were more strident than their demands even for suffrage, though suffrage was seen as a necessary part of the package. These demands were national rather than local in orientation, and nationalist—because the colonial administration was regarded as the first bulwark to be overcome. In an insufficiently expanding economy, these national demands would later take on local, that is "tribalist," qualities, but this is largely a post-independence problem.

Decolonization thus took on the form of a struggle, on the one hand, between a nationalist movement composed of two disparate elements with only some convergent goals; and on the other, the colonial administration allied to a small handful of African collaborators. As time went on, the verbal radicalization of the rural, or semi-urban, groups proceeded or threatened to proceed apace.

The response of the Europeans (outside of southern, settler-dominated, Africa), faced with this array and this perspective, was to come to terms with the middle-class leadership by arranging a rapid transfer of power to them in the expectation of ending their verbal radicalism before it became coherent, ideological and national in organization. From the European point of view, this operation was on the whole successful, since the rapid decolonization did largely accomplish these two objectives.

Decolonization has in one sense meant that the relations between Europe and Africa have returned to their pre-colonial status. The main point of contact is once again at the port of trade. The African entrepreneurial class is once more, just as it was before colonial rule, linked closely to, often part of, the state apparatus. The categories of politician and entrepreneur are heavily overlapping, at least for the present.

This new alliance of economic interests within Africa and the Western world was, however, forged at the expense of many groups, which explains why it met with some resistance. On the European end, the losers included many of the white farmer-settlers (and thus areas like Kenya and Algeria were harder to decolonize than some others), as well as the top European administrators (for whom the loss has been eased by the gradualness of their actual removal and the generous pensions that were arranged). In addition, some big European enterprises have lost out in cases where they were not big enough. (This is true *a fortiori* for Asian economic enterprises.) In the process of carving out an area for African enterprise, the weaker among the Europeans have either been eliminated, or replaced by stronger Europeans. This explains in part why Portuguese economic interests, who fear that the loss of political monopoly would lead to their direct replacement by American, British, French and German firms, have been so resistant to decolonization.[38]

On the African end, the price has been largely paid by two groups: the small handful of chiefs and professionals too compromised in the earlier alliance with the colonial administration; and the mass elements who have been curbed or at least disoriented by the transfer of power. These latter groups were for a while given more educational facilities, to be sure, and some social services. But essentially there has been no shift in the basic economic structure of the various territories, now nations. Job creation has ground almost to a halt, while cash-crop prices continue to decline. Hence the amelioration of the economic lot has been sharply limited. These people are now facing a significant decline in standard of living.

There is no doubt that the "curbing" of these groups cannot continue indefinitely under such circumstances, and one might argue that postcolonial internal disorder—including the ethnic rivalries, the breakdown of parties and the military coups—reflects this fact. But decolonization nonetheless did blunt the impact of the gathering storm and did afford a considerable breathing space for the existing politico-economic system.

The Colonial Era in Africa: Changes in the Social Structure 25

In summary, we have argued that the establishment of colonial rule brought about essentially two types of changes. One occurred in the composition of the groups primarily engaged in the alliance of the Western world and Africa, from merchants with merchants, to administrators with chiefs and clerks. And the second type of change is to be found in the structure of the African social system: the creation of new territorial units and the subsequent involvement of these units in specific imperial economic networks. We have then argued that the process of decolonization and the attainment of independence have reversed the first change while retaining the second. The nationalist revolution thus has been of considerable benefit to the African middle classes, but has had little significance so far as the rural and semi-urban masses are concerned. The new states are being built on the same sands as the old colonial territories, on the sands of mounting social discontent. Ultimately, the present social structures will crumble, but some time may yet elapse before the winds blow and shift sufficiently to bring this about.

NOTES

[1] I am indebted to G. Arrighi, P. Duignan, L.H. Gann, T.K. Hopkins and T.O. Ranger for their critical comments.

[2] 'The continuity of African institutions under colonialism,' in *Emerging theses of African history*, T.O. Ranger, ed. (Nairobi, 1968), p. 191.

[3] Evidence for this can be found in the following volumes, *passim*: Daryll Forde and P.M. Kaberry, eds., *West African kingdoms in the nineteenth century* (London, Oxford University Press, 1967); T.O. Ranger, *Aspects of Central African history* (London, 1968); Jan Vansina, *Kingdoms of the savanna* (Madison, University of Wisconsin Press, 1966); Roland Oliver and Gervase Mathew, eds., *History of East Africa*, Vol. I (Oxford, Clarendon Press, 1963).

[4] Cited in A. Adu Boahen, *Topics in West African history* (London, 1966), p. 113. Boahen adds: 'After the abolition of the slave trade, West Africa was allowed and indeed assisted to produce these very cash-crops but again forbidden, as it were, to produce manufactured goods which she was to continue to receive from Europe.'

[5] 'After the publication of the decree of 1792 prohibiting the slave-trade [the Danish governor was], the first to suggest that, since they were no longer useful as suppliers of slaves to the Danish islands in the West Indies, it might be better to sell the Danish settlements' (Georg Norregaard, *Danish settlements in West Africa*, Boston University Press, 1966, p. 218).

[6] [The government of the Netherlands] 'despairing of the prospects of legitimate trade, wrote off [its West African] settlements as an expensive nuisance and set

about cutting its losses to a minimum' (Douglas Coombs, *The Gold Coast, Britain and the Netherlands, 1850-1874*, London, Oxford University Press, 1963, p. 1). Cf. A.W. Lawrence, *Trade, castles and forts of West Africa* (London, 1963), pp. 168-9. The fort was abandoned in 1807, the very year of the Abolition Act. Cf. Colin W. Newbury, *The western Slave Coast and its rulers* (Oxford, Clarendon Press, 1961).

[7] In 1827 the British government instructed Sir Neil Campbell, the governor of Sierra Leone, that British territory should not be extended...and ordered him to withdraw the British officials and garrisons from the Gold Coast forts' (J.D. Fage, *An introduction to the history of West Africa*, 3rd ed., Cambridge University Press, 1962, p. 126). See also Coombs: 'only the pressures of interested merchants, a determination to keep down the slave trade, and a sense of moral obligation to the natives kept Britain [in West Africa]. In the [eighteen] thirties she came as close as was possible, short of complete withdrawal, to leaving the settlements altogether... In 1853 a Colonial Secretary looked forward to abandoning West Africa once the slave trade was completely suppressed...' (*The Gold Coast, Britain and the Netherlands*, pp. 4-5).

[8] Rodney observes: 'It is obvious that because of the Atlantic slave-trade people could not lead their ordinary lives. The majority of the population of West Africa lived by farming, and agriculture must have suffered during that period. In the first place, the loss of so many people represented a loss of labour in the fields. In the second place, those who were left behind had little reason to plant crops which they might never be around to reap. At the end of the eighteenth century, one of the arguments used by Europeans who wanted to abolish the Atlantic slave-trade was that abolition would allow the Africans to work and produce other commodities which Europeans could not. They pointed out that as long as the Atlantic slave-trade continued people found it extremely difficult to carry on worthwhile activities' (Walter Rodney, *West Africa and the Atlantic slave-trade*, Historical Association of Tanzania Paper No. 2, Nairobi, 1967, p. 16).

[9] Boahen reminds us that the idea of a palm-oil export trade was encouraged by the British Royal African Company in the first two decades of the eighteenth century, but 'this attempt was...abandoned mainly because of the trade in slaves. From the abolition of the inhuman trade, more determined efforts were made and the Africans were now encouraged to obtain oil as well as kernel from the nuts for export' (*Topics in West African history*, p. 123).

[10] A variation on this formula could be seen on the East African coast, where the Sultanate of Zanzibar was a political incarnation of this merchant group, and the merchants were hence in a far stronger position vis-à-vis the inland chiefs. Gray describes the situation thus: 'Sayyid Said's ambition was not to create a territorial, but an economic empire in East Africa. His position was that of a great middleman, controlling the intercourse between East Africa and Europe, Arabia, India, and America' (J.M. Gray, 'Zanzibar and the coastal belt, 1840-1884,' in *History of East Africa*, Oliver and Mathew, eds., 1, 223).

It can be argued that the role of the Khedive of Egypt vis-à-vis the Sudan trade was basically similar. See J.E. Flint's discussion of British hesitation as to whether they would do better using the Sultan or the Khedive in opening up the Lakes region: 'The wider background to partition and colonial occupation,' in *History of East Africa*, Oliver and Mathew, eds., 1, 352-90.

[11] "Chartered companies and the scramble for Africa,' in *Africa in the nineteenth and twentieth centuries*, Joseph C. Anene and Godfrey N. Brown, eds. (Ibadan University Press, 1966), pp. 111-12. This was reinforced by the fact that France, Britain's only serious rival in African trade, was seriously embarrassed by its defeat in the Franco-Prussian War of 1870. Flint analyses the history of this rivalry and the impact of France's defeat in 'The growth of European influence in West Africa in the nineteenth century,' in *A thousand years of West African history*, J.F.A. Ajayi and Ian Espie, eds. (Ibadan University Press, 1965), pp. 359-79. For France's conversion to a protectionist colonial trade policy from 1873 on, see Colin W. Newbury, 'The protectionist revival in French colonial trade: the case of Senegal,' *Economic History Review*, Aug. 1968, 21, no. 2, pp. 337-48.

[12] See Flint: 'The Berlin West African Conference which began in November 1884 thus had its origins in an attempt to destroy British informal influence on the Niger and Congo, the two most important avenues of access to the interior of *Tropical Africa*' ('chartered companies,' p. 121). Similarly, see Hargreaves: 'At last [1884] it seemed agreed that *some* governmental initiative was needed to protect Britain's future commerce in the Niger and the other Oil Rivers—including the Cameroons...' (John D. Hargreaves, *Prelude to the partition of West Africa*, London, 1963, p. 314).

[13] Newbury speaks of the 'fear of exclusion from regional markets as a motive for territorial expansion.' He also demonstrates that the result of colonial occupation was 'some polarization of national trade in the respective colonies of France and Britain' (see Colin W. Newbury, 'The tariff factor in Anglo-French West African partition,' paper presented at Yale University Conference on France and Britain in Africa, Imperial Rivalry and Colonial Rule, 25-29 March 1968 (mimeograph), pp. 29,33.

[14] 'Protection' was simply a formula whereby the British in particular sought to emphasize that their only objective was to keep from being excluded themselves. In theory, a protectorate was limited to control over foreign policy. In practice, it soon became extremely difficult to distinguish a 'colony' from a 'protectorate.'

[15] Arbitrary does not mean deliberately capricious. Hargreaves notes: 'Since European claims were often based upon treaties with African rulers, there were many cases where the new frontiers coincided with traditional ones; other things being equal, the colonial powers preferred to follow chiefdom boundaries, where these were known. But even these boundaries might still divide Africans of the same language and culture, and once they came under effective European occupation they became harder to cross than would have been the case in the past' (*Prelude to partition*, pp. 348-9).

[16] A classic study of how this occurred, even where the colonial authorities intended otherwise, is K.A. Busia, *The position of the chief in the modern political system of the Ashanti* (London, Oxford University Press, 1951).

[17] A careful, detailed study of this process may be found in the article by A.G. Hopkins, 'The Lagos strike of 1897,' *Past and Present*, Dec. 1966, no. 35, pp. 133-

55. Hopkins describes how the intrusion of British authority into the hinterland of what was later the Western Region of Nigeria undermined the control of African farmer-chiefs over slave labor, who transformed themselves into independent cocoa farmers. The rural transformation, combined with a European commitment to low urban wages, led to both an urban labor shortage and to a refusal to raise wages to attract these rural ex-slaves. The result was the Lagos strike, and its suppression.

[18]It is true that Germany, for instance, never seemed quite to establish such a monopoly. But as Henderson has noted, the prevention of counter-monopolies was clearly part of the original intent. 'In the early eighties German expansionists could point to renewed colonial activity by foreign countries. . . . Clearly if Germany did not act promptly the few remaining regions of the world suitable for exploitation would be appropriated by other powers' (W.O. Henderson, *Studies in German colonial history*, London, 1962, p. 4). Similarly, Henry Ashby Turner, Jr.: 'As long as large parts of the non-European world were free of colonial rule, German commerce could get access to the markets and resources of Africa and Asia regardless of the discriminatory policies of the imperialist powers. But if those powers were to carve up all the non-European world, German overseas merchants would be a their mercy' ('Bismarck's imperialist venture: anti-British in origin?' in *Britain and Germany in Africa*, Prosset Gifford and Wm. Roger Louis, eds., New Haven, Yale University Press, 1967, p. 51).

Germany, which started late, and had a poor selection of colonies, thought she would gain more from pressing for free trade than from advocating protectionism as did France. See Louis: 'The Franco-German colonial entente began to collapse during the Berlin Congo Conference of November 1884-February 1885. From Bismarck's point of view, one of the main purposes of the conference was to secure equal commercial opportunities for German traders. Germany's natural ally on this question was free-trading Britain and not protectionist France' (Wm Roger Louis, 'Great Britain and German expansion in Africa, 1884-1919,' in *Britain and Germany in Africa*, p. 9).

Nonetheless, despite a free-trade policy, obligatory in any case for German East Africa under the terms of the Congo Act of 1885, Germany imposed some protectionist tariffs in her colonies, subsidized shipping and sometimes drew material for railway construction exclusively from Germany (cf. Henderson, *Studies in German colonial history*, pp. 37, 61). The effect of more political control on trade patterns was in any case significant. One has but to compare the trade statistics of colonies like Tanganyika or Togo over the period 1890-1960. Up to World War I Germany's role both as importer and exporter rose sharply, and then declined just as sharply as she lost political control.

[19]Peter C. Lloyd, *Africa in social change* (Harmondsworth, Middlesex, 1967), p. 52.

[20]See A.G. Hopkins, 'Economic aspects of political movements in Nigeria and the Gold Coast, 1918-1939,' *Journal of African History*, 1966, 7, no. 1, pp. 133-52 (esp. pp. 134-5). See also Lloyd, *Africa in social change*, pp. 77-8. For East Africa, the pattern is made clear in various articles in *History of East Africa*, Vol. II,

The Colonial Era in Africa: Changes in the Social Structure 29

Vincent Harlow and E.M. Chilver, eds., assisted by Alison Smith (Oxford, Clarendon Press, 1965). The effect of French firms on Senegalese traders in French West Africa was the same. See A. Villard, 'Comment travaille Faidherbe,' *Bulletin d'informations et de renseignements de l'A.O.F.*, Oct. 1938, no. 204, cited in Jean Suret-Canale, *Afrique noire occidentale et centrale*, Vol. II: *L'ère coloniale, 1900-1945* (Paris, 1964), pp. 15-16. Suret-Canale describes the process of formal concessions to European firms in French Equatorial Africa, pp. 29-58.

See also the following account by Vansina of the fate of Ovimbundu traders in Central Africa. [Ovimbundu] 'trade went on uninterrupted throughout the [nineteenth] century...When the [colonial] wars were over [in 1902], the price of rubber had dropped, the colonial governments began to bar access in their territories to traders from Angola, and a great famine in 1911 killed many traders in eastern Angola. In Ovimbundu tradition, this date marked the end of the long-distance trade' (Vansina, *Kingdom of the savanna*, p. 201).

[21] A typical instance was the role of the British administration in fostering cotton production in Uganda. See Cyril Ehrlich, 'The Uganda Economy, 1903 1945,' in *History of East Africa*, pp. 399-402. These pressures were not always rational, as demonstrated in detail for the Gold Coast by R.H. Green and S.H. Hymer, 'Cocoa in the Gold Coast: a study in the relations between African farmers and agricultural experts,' *Journal of Economic History*, Sept. 1966, 26, no. 3, pp. 299-319.

[22] For a discussion of wage-employment versus cash-cropping as alternative options for Africans, and the views of the colonial administration and settlers on these alternatives, see G. Arrighi, 'Labour supplies in historical perspective: the Rhodesian case' (Dar es Salaam, mimeograph, 1967).

[23] R. Szcreszewski argues that the changes in the structure of the Gold Coast economy brought about between 1890 and 1910 determined the pattern of economic production throughout the rest of the colonial period and after independence. See *Structural changes in the economy of Ghana* (London, 1965). A similar argument for Rhodesia has been made by G. Arrighi in *The political economy of Rhodesia*, The Hague, 1967.

[24] How this worked is well described in Lewis H. Gann, *A history of Northern Rhodesia: early days to 1953* (London, 1964), pp. 100-11. Some of the purely economic reasons why migratory labor has continued to be a key element of African economies are expounded in Elliot J. Berg, 'The economics of the migrant labor system' in *Urbanization and migration in West Africa*, Hilda Kuper, ed. (Berkeley, University of California Press, 1965), pp. 160-81.

[25] "In 1883, of the forty-three "higher posts" in the Gold Coast, nine were filled by Africans, including seven District Commissioners' (see David Kimble, *A political history of Ghana: the rise of Gold Coast nationalism, 1850-1928*, Oxford, Clarendon Press, 1963, p. 94). For the exclusion of Africa from the senior civil service about the turn of the century, see pp. 98-105. For resentment of Africans against their formalized subordinacy in the Uganda civil service of 1929, see David E. Apter, *The political kingdom in Uganda: a study in bureaucratic nationalism* (Princeton University Press, 1961), pp. 196-8. Similarly, one must see that the use

of *akida* in German East Africa meant the use of Africans as medium-level civil servants. When this practice was dispensed with by the British, it involved the use of European personnel at lower levels of the civil service than previously.

[26] J.M. Lonsdale calls them the 'political communicators.' He says that: 'In the ideal case, the political communicator, king or chief, whether traditionally legitimate, traditionally recognizable as usurper, or jumped-up mercenary and buccaneer, remained also a social communicator, in close relationship with his tribesmen or peasants' ('Some origins of nationalism in East Africa,' *Journal of African History*, 1968, 9, no. I, p. 121).

[27] This is precisely what Georges Balandier meant by 'the colonial situation' (see 'The colonial situation: a theoretical approach,' in *Social change: the colonial situation*, Immanuel Wallerstein, ed., New York, 1966, pp. 34-61; and also in *Social change*, Max Gluckman, 'Malinowski's "functional" analysis of social change,' pp. 25-33).

[28] The practice is documented for Tanganyika in L. Cliffe, 'Nationalism and the reaction to enforced agricultural improvement in Tanganyika during the colonial period,' Kampala, Uganda, Makerere College, East African Institute of Social Research, *Conference Papers*, Jan. 1965. Cliffe also indicates the direct link between the disruptive regulations of the British and the rise of nationalist sentiment. Compulsory cultivation in the Belgian Congo is described both in Roger Anstey, *King Leopold's legacy: the Congo under Belgian rule, 1908-1960* (London, Oxford University Press, 1966), p. 82; and in Michel Merlier, *Le Congo de la colonisation belge d l'indépendance* (Paris, 1962), pp. 79-87. Merlier says: 'Without the intervention of the State, colonial agriculture could never have been established in the Congo' (p. 84).

[29] This is very well documented for West Africa for the period 1939-49. See Elliot J. Berg, 'Real income trends in West Africa, 1939-1960,' in *Economic transition in Africa*, M.J. Herskovits and M. Harwitz, eds. (Evanston, Northwestern University Press, 1964), pp. 199-238. Berg speaks of the 'universality and severity of the decline' (p. 203). For evidence of a decline in real wages in Northern and Southern Rhodesia 'during the war and early post-war years,' cf. W.J. Barber, *The economy of British Central Africa: a case study of economic development in a dualistic society* (London, Oxford University Press, 1961), pp. 204-8.

[30] To be sure, if for some reason the chiefs, or some chiefs, were at that moment under attack by the colonial administration, the radical nationalists might rally to the support of these chiefs. but in general they were suspicious of the chiefs, even hostile to them, regarding them primarily as agents of the colonial administration.

[31] And sometimes they took on the Asian or Levantine intermediate trading groups as well.

[32] Some of the most unlikely Africans, given the notoriety they later achieved, made such attempts at an early stage in their careers. See, for example, Patrice Lumumba; see also the case of General China (of Mau Mau fame), in his autobiography (Waruhiu Itote, *'Mau Mau' general*, Nairobi, 1967). In the case of 'Field Marshal' John Okello (who played a controversial and noteworthy role in the

Zanzibar revolution), see his *Revolution in Zanzibar* (Nairobi, 1967), pp. 35-83. Oginga Odinga calls himself, in a letter to Jomo Kenyatta in 1952, 'a nationalist businessman' (see his *Not yet uhuru: the autobiography of Oginga Odinga*, London, 1967, p. 101).

[33] The distinction between tribesmen and peasants has been discussed for Africa by Lloyd A. Fallers, 'Are African cultivators to be called "peasants"? in *Current Anthropology*, 1961, 2, no. 2, pp. 108-10. Fallers believes that pre-colonial African cultivators were 'proto-peasants,' ready to be made into peasants by contact with Islamic or Christian culture. Cf. Lonsdale, 'Origins of nationalism,' pp. 123-4.

[34] The literature on peasant rebellions and rural radicalism is expanding at a rapid rate. See, among others: Martin Kilson, *Political change in a West African state: a study of the modernization process in Sierra Leone* (Cambridge, Harvard University Press, 1966), pp. 60-3, 110-12; T.O. Ranger, 'Revolt in Portuguese East Africa: the Makonde rising of 1917,' in *African affairs: Number two*, Kenneth Kirkwood, ed., Oxford University, St. Antony's College, St Antony's papers, No. 15 (Carbondale, Southern Illinois University Press, 1963), pp. 54-80, Robert I. Rotberg, *The rise of nationalism in Central Africa* (Cambridge, Harvard University Press, 1965), pp. 55-92; and Herbert F. Weiss, 'Introduction' in Centre de Recherche et d'Information Socio-politiques, *Congo 1964* (Princeton University Press, 1966), pp. xi-xxii.

[35] Iliffe has described this process for Tanganyika. 'Partly because they had a traditional monopoly, and partly because they were supported by the Germans, the Haya chiefs obtained most of the early profits from coffee-growing... Very much the same happened in Kilimanjaro...Again the chiefs and their courtiers had the best opportunities.' Of course, the chiefs were not always the only ones who obtained land. When, as amongst the Chagga, a group of 'new men' also 'acquired' land rights, rural discontent was fanned by the attacks by these men on the privileges of the rural chiefly planters. See J. Iliffe, 'The age of improvement and differentiation (1907-45),' in *The history of Tanzania*, I. Kimambo, ed. (Nairobi, 1968).

[36] Kimambo, *The history of Tanzania*. The forthcoming work of I. Kimambo on the Pare tax uprisings in Tanganyika will lend support to this argument.

[37] On the difficulties of a business career for Africans under colonial rule, see the vivid description by Odinga in *Not yet uhuru*, pp. 76-94. Iliffe describes two pertinent cases in his article cited above. One is of Klemens Kiiza, a coffee-grower who sought to establish a coffee-curing factory, and after fifteen years of difficulty had to admit defeat in 1946. Iliffe comments: 'This story...shows very clearly the problems which faced an energetic improver in this period: lack of capital, Asian business competition, international economic uncertainty, official suspicion, the necessity and danger of organizing the farmers, and governmental paternalism which restricted enterprise. Even those like Kiiza who gained most during the age of improvement found that they could not gain all they wanted. They were too hemmed in by the structure of colonial rule.'

The second case was that of Erica Fiah, a Ganda shopkeeper in Dar es Salaam before the Second World War. Iliffe says of him: [His] 'business interests as a shopkeeper quickly brought to him the lesson that Klemens Kiiza was learning at the same date in Buhaya. The colonial system was itself an obstacle to improvement beyond a certain point...' Fiah's reaction was to organize an urban radical group in 1934 which drew its membership from African traders and shopkeepers who shared his frustrations.

[38] Even the British, French and Belgian groups have had this fear vis-à-vis American, and, to a lesser extent German, firms (and in the case of the Belgians, French firms).

BIBLIOGRAPHY

Ajayi, J.F.A. 'The continuity of African institutions under colonialism,' in *Emerging themes of African history: proceedings of the International Conference of African Historians held at Dar es Salaam, 1965*, T.O. Ranger, ed., Nairobi, 1968.
Ajayi, J.F.A., and Ian Espic, eds. *A thousand years of West African history*. Ibadan University Press, 1965; reprint 1967.
Anene, Joseph C., and Godfrey N. Brown, eds. *Africa in the nineteenth and twentieth centuries*. Ibadan University Press, 1966; reprint 1967.
Anstey, Roger. *King Leopold's legacy: the Congo under Belgian rule, 1908-1960*. London, Oxford University Press, 1966.
Apter, David E. *The political kingdom in Uganda: a study in bureaucratic nationalism*. Princeton University Press, 1961.
Arrighi, G. *The political economy of Rhodesia*. The Hague, 1967.
Arrighi, G. 'Labor supplies in historical perspective: the Rhodesian case,' Dar es Salaam, mimeograph, 1967.
Balandier, Georges. 'The colonial situation: a theoretical approach,' in *Social change: the colonial situation*, Immanuel Wallerstein, ed. New York, 1966.
Barber, W.J. *The economy of British Central Africa: a case study of economic development in a dualistic society*. Stanford University Press, 1961.
Berg, Elliot J. 'The economics of the migrant labor system,' in *Urbanization and migration in West Africa*, Hilda Kuper, ed. Berkeley, University of California Press, 1965.
Berg, Elliot J. 'Real income trends in West Africa, 1939-1960,' in *Economic transition in Africa*, Melville Herskovits and Mitchell Harwitz, eds. Evanston, Northwestern University Press, 1964.
Boahen, A. Adu. *Topics in West African history*. London, 1966.
Busia, K.A. *The position of the chief in the modern political system of the Ashanti: a study of the influence of contemporary social changes on Ashanti: political institutions*. London, Oxford University Press, 1951.

Cliffe, L. 'Nationalism and the reaction to enforced agricultural improvement in Tanganyika during the colonial period,' in Kampala, Uganda, Makerere College, East African Institute of Social Research, *Conference Papers*, Jan. 1965.
Coombs, Douglas. *The Gold Coast, Britain and the Netherlands, 1850-1874*. London, Oxford University Press, 1963.
Ehrlich, Cyril. 'The Uganda economy, 1903-1945,' in *History of East Africa*, Vol. II, Vincent Harlow and E.M. Chilver, eds., assisted by Alison Smith. Oxford, Clarendon Press, 1965.
Fage, J.D. *An introduction to the history of West Africa*. 3rd ed. Cambridge University Press, 1962.
Fallers, Lloyd A. 'Are African cultivators to be called "peasants"?' *Current Anthropology*, April 1961, 2, no. 2.
Flint, John E. 'Chartered companies and the scramble for Africa,' in *Africa in the nintenth and twentieth centuries*, Joseph C. Anene and Godfrey N. Brown, eds. Ibadan University Press, 1966; reprint 1967.
'The growth of European influence in West Africa in the nineteenth century,' in *A thousand years of West African history*, J.F.A. Ajayi and I. Espic, eds. Ibadan University Press, 1965.
'The wider background to partition and colonial occupation,' in *History of East Africa*, Vol, I, Roland Oliver and Gervase Mathew, eds. Oxford, Clarendon Press, 1963.
Forde, Daryll, and P.M. Kaberry, eds. *West African kingdoms in the nineteenth century*. London, Oxford University Press, 1967.
Gann, Lewis H. *A history of Northern Rhodesia: early days to 1953*. London, 1964.
Gifford, Prosser, and William Roger Louis, eds. *Britain and Germany in Africa: imperial rivalry and colonial rule*. New Haven, Yale University Press, 1967.
Gluckman, Max. 'Malinowski's "functional" analysis of social change,' in *Social change: the colonial situation*, Immanuel Wallerstein, ed. New York, 1966.
Gray, J.M. 'Zanzibar and the coastal belt, 1840-1884,' in *History of East Africa*, Vol, I, Roland Oliver and Gervase Mathew, eds. Oxford, Clarendon Press, 1963.
Green, R.H., and S.H. Hymer. 'Cocoa in the Gold Coast: a study in the relations between African farmers and agricultural experts,' *Journal of Economic History*, Sept. 1966, 26, no. 3.
Hargreaves, John D. *Prelude to the partition of West Africa*. London, 1963.
Harlow, Vincent, and E.M. Chilver, eds., assisted by Alison Smith. *History of East Africa*, Vol. II. Oxford Clarendon Press, 1965.
Henderson, W.O. *Studies in German colonial history*. London, 1962.
Herskovits, Melville, and Mitchell Harwitz, eds. *Economic transition in Africa*. Evanston, Northwestern University Press, 1964.
Hopkins, A.G. 'Economic aspects of political movements in Nigeria and the Gold Coast, 1918-1939,' *Journal of African History*, 1966, 7, no.1.
'The Lagos strike of 1897: an exploration in Nigerian labour history,' *Past and Present*, Dec. 1966, no. 35.

Iliffe, John. 'The age of improvement and differentiation (1907-45),' in *The history of Tanzania*, I. Kimambo, ed. Nairobi, 1968.
Itote, Waruhiu (General China). *'Mau Mau' general*. Nairobi, 1967.
Kilson, Martin. *Political change in a West African state: a study of the modernization process in Sierra Leone*. Cambridge, Harvard University Press, 1966.
Kimambo, I., ed. *The history of Tanzania*. Nairobi, 1968.
Kimble, David. *A political history of Ghana: the rise of Gold Coast nationalism, 1850-1928*. Oxford, Clarendon Press, 1963.
Kirkwood, Kenneth, ed. *African affairs: Number two* (Oxford University, St Antony's College, *St Antony's papers*, No. 15) Carbondale, Southern Illinois University Press, 1961.
Kuper, Hilda, ed. *Urbanization and migration in West Africa*. Berkeley, University of California Press, 1965.
Lawrence, Arnold Walter. *Trade, castles and forts of West Africa*. London, 1963.
Lloyd, Peter C. *Africa in social change*. Harmondsworth, Middlesex, 1967.
Lonsdale, J.M. 'Some origins of nationalism in East Africa,' *Journal of African History*, 1968, 9, no. 1.
Louis, Wm. Roger. 'Great Britain and German expansion in Africa, 1884-1919,' in *Britain and Germany in Africa*, Prosser Gifford and Wm. Roger Louis, eds. New Haven, Yale University Press, 1967.
Merlier, Michel. *Le Congo de la colonisation belge à l'indépendance*. Paris, 1962.
Newbury, Colin W. 'The protectionist revival in French colonial trade: the case of Senegal,' *Economic History Review*, Aug. 1968, 21, no. 2.
'The tariff factor in Anglo-French West African partition,' paper presented at Yale University Conference on France and Britain in Africa: Imperial Rivalry and Colonial Rule, 25-9 March 1968 (mimeograph).
The western Slave Coast and its rulers: European trade and administration among the Yoruba and Adja-speaking peoples of southwestern Nigeria, southern Dahomey and Togo. Oxford, Clarendon Press, 1961.
Norregaard, Georg. *Danish settlements in West Africa, 1658-1850*. Trans. by Sigurd Mammen. Boston University Press, 1966.
Odinga, Oginga. *Not yet uhuru: the autobiography of Oginga Odinga*. London, 1967.
Okello, John. *Revolution in Zanzibar*. Nairobi, 1967.
Oliver, Roland A., and Anthony Atmore. *Africa since 1800*. London, Cambridge University Press, 1967.
Oliver, Roland A., and Gervase Mathew, eds. *History of East Africa*, Vol. 1. Oxford, Clarendon Press, 1963.
Ranger, Terence O. *Aspects of Central African history*. London, 1968.
'Revolt in Portuguese East Africa: the Makonde rising of 1917,' in *African affairs: Number two*, Kenneth Kirkwood, ed. (Oxford University, St Antony's College, *St Antony's papers*, No. 15). Carbondale, Southern Illinois University Press, 1963.
ed. *Emerging themes of African history*. Nairobi, 1968.

Rodney, Walter. *West Africa and the Atlantic slave-trade.* Historical Association of Tanzania Paper No. 2. Nairobi, 1967.
Rotberg, Robert I. *The rise of nationalism in Central Africa: the making of Malawi and Zambia, 1873-1964.* Cambridge, Harvard University Press, 1965.
Suret-Canale, Jean. *Afrique noire occidentale et centrale.* 2 vols. Paris, 1958-64.
Szereszewski, R. *Structural changes in the economy of Ghana.* London, 1965.
Turner, Henry Ashby, Jr. 'Bismarck's imperialist venture: anti-British in origin?' in *Britain and Germany in Africa*, Prosser Gifford and Wm. Roger Louis, eds. New Haven, Yale University Press, 1967.
United Nations Economic Commission for Africa. *Economic survey of Africa since 1950.* New York, 1959.
Vansina, Jan. *Kingdoms of the savanna.* Madison, University of Wisconsin Press, 1966.
Villard, A. "Comment travaille Faidherbe,' *Bulletin d'informations et de renseignements de l'A.O.F.*, Oct. 1938, no. 204.
Wallerstein, Immanuel. 'The Range of Choice: Constraints on the Policies of Governments of Independent African States,' in *The State of the Nations*, Michael F. Lofchie, ed. Berkeley, Univ. of California Press, 1971, pp. 19-33.
Weiss, Herbert F. 'Introduction,' in Centre de Recherche ed d'Information Sociopolitiques, *Congo 1964.* Princeton University Press, 1966.

The Lessons of the PAIGC*

The story of "Portuguese" Guinea is a fascinating one. A national liberation movement in a tiny state, less than a million in population, has been fighting a war with a European country for a decade. It has established control in two-thirds of its country. Had the country been a colony of Britain or France, it would have been independent ten years ago and probably of little more significance than a dozen other small independent African states. Had it been Portugal's only colony in Africa, the Portuguese might have been willing to concede independence to this area of small economic interest.

But the accident of history was that the Portuguese acquired this tiny slice of West Africa and that Portugal's interests in Angola and Mozambique made her unwilling to withdraw from Guinea. However unfortunate for the inhabitants of Guinea and the Cape Verde Islands, this accident has had its fortuitous side. It has produced a remarkable movement, the PAIGC, led by a remarkable man, Amilcar Cabral, and the experience of this movement has added precious knowledge for the benefit of those struggling everywhere.

What can we learn about national liberation movements in general from the experience of the PAIGC? Let us place it in the context of evolving world intellectual history. In the 18th century, the European bourgeoisie

---

*Amilcar Cabral, *Revolution in Guinea* (New York: Monthly Review Press, 1970), 174 pp., $4.95

Gerard Chaliand, *Armed Struggle in Africa* (New York: Monthly Review Press, 1969), 142 pp., $5.50

took heart from the universalist doctrines of the Enlightenment and Kantian philosophy to argue against the constraints of the monarchical state. In the 19th century, the liberal bourgeoisie, however, raised high the banner of *national* independence (particularly in outer Europe—central, eastern, southern Europe) against the oppressive weight of remaining empires. As the bourgeoisie became nationalist, the working classes began to speak of inter-national proletarian solidarity. Nationalism was denounced.

The 1917 Revolution occurred to everyone's surprise, however, in Russia—outside "advanced" Europe. And its echoes were heard in Asia. It was Lenin who first drew the lesson of this unexpected event, and spoke in 1920 of "oppressed and oppressing *nations.*" Stalin later spoke of "socialism in one country." The world socialist movement of various tendencies was from then on never quite sure how to handle the phenomenon of national liberation. But, especially after 1945, it moved towards seeing national liberation as part of the worldwide struggle against imperialism.

The phenomenon of neo-colonialism which has become so visible since 1960 has raised doubts once again about "national liberation." Here is where the PAIGC comes in. And Cabral is willing to face the question head on: "I would even go so far as to ask whether, given the advance of socialism in the world, the national liberation movement is not an imperialist initiative." (p. 71)[1]

Amidst a spate of debunking literature on the left which gives primacy to a fear of co-optation and which inflates the ability of the ruling classes to manipulate everyone including their opponents, Cabral's voice is refreshingly clear. This fear about national liberation movements is a left-wing version of old-style European presumptuousness about Africa, a way of analyzing Africa only in terms of Europe (and America)'s problems, an arrogance more dangerous because it calls itself leftist. Cabral says:

> A rigorous historical approach is similarly needed when examining another problem related to this—how can the underdeveloped countries evolve toward revolution, toward socialism? There is a preconception held by many people, even on the left, that imperialism made us enter history at the moment when it began its adventure in our countries. This preconception must be denounced: for somebody on the left, and for Marxists in particular, history obviously means the class struggle. Our opinion is exactly the contrary. We consider that when imperialism arrived and colonialism arrived, it made us leave our history and enter another history. (p. 65)

This concept of two histories (not historiographies) of oppressed peoples—their own and their oppressors—is extremely helpful and clarifies, *mutatis mutandis*, the situation of oppressed minorities in industrialized countries (e.g., Blacks in the United States) as much as it does that of colonized peoples in Africa. Cabral draws from this concept the appropriate conclusion about the nature of a national liberation movement (and, hence, *mutatis mutandis* again, a Black liberation movement in the United States). Far from being an "imperialist initiative,"

> National liberation is the phenomenon in which a given socio-economic whole rejects the negation of its historical process. In other words, the national liberation of a people is the repairing of the historical personality of that people, its return to history through the destruction of the imperialist domination to which it was subjected. (p. 102).

Of course, liberation, not national independence, is the goal. Hence, "the liberation struggle is a revolution and...does not finish at the moment that the national flag is raised and the national anthem played..." (p. 107) Hence we must distinguish between the strategy at two different historical moments: the colonial situation "in which the nation-class fights the repressive forces of the bourgeoisie of the colonising country" and the neo-colonial situation "in which the working classes and their allies struggle simultaneously against the imperialist bourgeoisie and the native ruling class..." (p. 106)

NATION-CLASS

Let us pause a moment at the concept nation-class. This recalls another hyphenated concept, party-state, invented by the Algerian FLN and taken up recently in a CONCP publication to apply precisely to the PAIGC. (*Guinee et Cap-Vert* Alger: Information CONCP, 1970, 24-25). The hyphenation underlines the argument, the rejection of nineteenth-century theoretical over-simplifications (even those of Marx). While for the nineteenth-century theorists—and many of our contemporaries are still nineteenth-century theorists—classes existed *within* nations, parties existed *within* states, the national liberation movements are forcing into our theoretical consciousness (via *praxis*) the fact that classes and parties exist within a world-system, as do nations and states, and that under certain conditions the parameters of nation and class, state and party so overlap that it is not intellectually useful (*a fortiori* not politically useful) to distinguish them.

But this intellectual classification also brings in its wake an intellectual confusion. In the older analyses, it was quite clear who were the revolutionary forces and who the reactionary. But if we now become even more historically relativist than the older theorists (not merely distinguishing between a feudal and a capitalist era, but between multiple specific aspects of a capitalist era), how shall we determine *objectively* the forces of progress? Cabral does not speak to this question directly but if we look closely at what he says about revolutionary forces, there is an implicit answer.

Cabral describes the beginnings of the PAIGC as a search for the social basis for a movement:

> We had some knowledge of other experiences and we knew that a struggle of the kind we hoped to lead—and win—had to be led by the working class; we looked for the working class in Guinea and did not find it. Other examples showed us that things were begun by some revolutionary intellectuals. What were we then to do? We were just a bunch of petty bourgeois who were driven by the reality of life in Guinea...[We] obviously did not have a proletariat. We quite clearly lacked revolutionary intellectuals, so we had to start searching, given that we—rightly—did not believe in the revolutionary capacity of the peasantry. (pp. 65-66)

What? Not the peasantry? What about Fanon, Mao? "The peasant who fought in Algeria or China is not the peasant of our country." (p. 158) Why so?

> It so happens that in our country the Portuguese colonialists did not expropriate the land; they allowed us to cultivate the land. They did not create agricultural companies of the European type as they did, for instance, in Angola.... This created a special difficulty in our struggle—that of showing the peasant he was being exploited in his own country. (pp. 158-59)

If one cannot count on the three standard classes put forward by one or another theorist of the last 150 years—the proletariat, the revolutionary intellectuals, or the peasantry—to lead the revolution, can one count on that other alternative advocated by socialists from Bakunin to Debray and the Weathermen—the body of committed men, the militants, the fighters, the underground, the military *foco*? Cabral minces no words:

> The political and military leadership of the struggle is one: the political leadership. In our struggle we have avoided the creation of anything military. We are political people, and our Party, a political

organisation, leads the struggle in the civilian political, administrative, technical, and therefore also military spheres. (p. 146)

If Cabral is too polite to spell out whose doctrines he is attacking, Chaliand is less shy: "The experience of the PAIGC contradicts the Cuban *foco* theory...(p. xiv)

THE REVOLUTIONARY PETTY BOURGEOISIE

Does Cabral then have a candidate for the leadership of the national liberation movement? He does, and it is a most extraordinary one, for it is totally unexpected in terms of the history of modern socialist thought. It is a segment of the petty bourgeoisie which he calls the revolutionary petty bourgeoisie. And how can these be identified? Of course by their commitment to the struggle against colonialism. But what about those still uneducated and uncertain? Among what groups will potential recruits be most likely to be found? Again a surprising answer: among the *declassé*. But not just any *declassé*:

> The really declassé people, the permanent layabouts, the prostitutes and so on have been a great help to the Portuguese people in giving them information; this group has been outrightly against our struggle, perhaps unconsciously so, but nonetheless against our struggle. On the other hand, the particular group I mentioned earlier, for which we have not yet found any precise classification (the group of mainly young people recently arrived from the rural areas with contacts in both the urban and rural areas) gradually comes to make a comparison between the standard of living of their own families and that of the Portuguese; they begin to understand the sacrifices being borne by the Africans. They have proved extremely dynamic in the struggle. Many of these people joined the struggle right from the beginning and it is among this group that we found many of the cadres whom we have since trained. (p. 62)

Cabral's honesty in tracing the real social roots of his movement is matched these days by that of one other revolutionary theorist: Huey Newton, who asserts that the social basis of his movement, the Black Panther Party, lies in the revolutionary segment of the *lumpenproletariat*. When we examine closely what Newton means by the *lumpenproletariat* in the American context and Cabral by the *declassés* in the Guinean context, and we make allowances for the differences of the social situations, are they not pointing to the same group: the group that "has nothing to lose but its chains" but is sufficiently oriented to the world-system in its activities and its values to be educable as cadres for a revolutionary movement?

And what shall they be educated to do? Here Cabral is daring once again.

> We must be very clear exactly what we are asking the party bourgeoisie to do. Are we asking it to commit suicide? Because if there is a revolution, then the petty bourgeoisie will have to abandon power to the workers and the peasants and cease to exist *qua* petty bourgeoisie. (p. 70)

Commit class suicide? That is an idea difficult to assimilate. Those that are called upon to do it must be convinced that it is truly essential. And even so, how can you induce men to do it?

It is essential because even though "the neo-colonial situation...offers the petty bourgeoisie the chance of playing a role of major or even decisive importance in the struggle for the elimination of foreign domination," and even if in the process this petty bourgeoisie attains a high "degree of revolutionary consciousness," nonetheless:

> The petty bourgeoisie, as a service class (that is to say a class not directly involved in the process of production) does not possess the economic base to guarantee the taking over of power...[I]n the conditions of colonial and neo-colonial society this capacity is retained by two entities: imperialist capital and the native working classes. (pp. 109-10)

Hence the petty bourgeoisie must in the long run throw in its lot with one base or the other; it must either "betray the revolution or...commit suicide as a class." (p. 110)

And the way you induce men, cadres, to make the right choice is via political education:

> We realised that we needed to have people with a mentality which could transcend the context of the national liberation struggle, and so we prepared a number of cadres from the group I have just mentioned [people in the towns, which we have been unable to classify precisely, who were still closely connected to the rural areas], some of the people employed in commerce and other wage-earners, and even some peasants, so that they could acquire what you might call a working-

class mentality. You may think this is absurd—in any case it is very difficult... (p. 67)

THEORY IN REVOLUTION

This brings us to one of Cabral's principal themes—the centrality of theory:

> The positive balance-sheet of the year 1960 cannot make us forget the reality of a crisis in the African revolution which far from being a mere growing-pain, is a crisis of knowledge. In several cases, the practice of the liberation struggle and its future perspectives not only lack a theoretical basis, but are also to a greater or lesser degree remote from the concrete reality around them. (p. 17)

> ... [I]f it is true that a revolution can fail even though it be based on perfectly conceived theories, nobody has yet made a successful revolution without a revolutionary theory. (p. 93)

It is here that white "progressive democrats," in Portugal and throughout the larger European world, can play their appropriate role. First, of course, they must overcome "their own imperialist mentality, composed of prejudice and ill-founded disdain for the value and real capacity of the African peoples." (p. 18) But Cabral is not making one more "make-the-white-liberals-even-the-white-radicals-feel-guilty" speech. The revolution cannot be built by Africans alone:

> [T]he European left has an intellectual responsibility to study the concrete conditions in our country and help us in this way, as we have very little documentation, very few intellectuals, very little chance to do this kind of work ourselves, and yet it is of key importance: this is a major contribution you can make. (p. 74)

The European "progressive democrats" are thus called upon to work on all fronts: to "study the concrete conditions" in Guinea and elsewhere for that is a "major contribution," to work on their own mentalities, and to organize politically at home "to support the really revolutionary national liberation movements by all possible means." (p. 74) Nor is it hopeless to educate the European working-class movements to their responsibilities, for:

> As we see it, neo-colonialism (which we may call rationalised imperialism) is more a defeat for the international working class than for the colonised peoples. (p. 73)

Cabral is in the direct line of the international socialist tradition of revolutionary optimism: it is possible to educate men within the framework of a theoretically self-conscious movement to pursue their self-interest in the kind of middle-range terms required for revolutionary change, provided one makes realistic assessments of the constraints of social reality at given times and places and provided one never stops reevaluating theory in the light of the new realities constantly being created not only by the structural evolution of the system but by the infusion of new elements by liberation movements themselves.

Cabral's writings are stacatto and uneven, work obviously squeezed in amidst the press of more urgent tasks. It is a measure of his esteem for theory that he has written at all. Chaliand's book is a necessary complement to that of Cabral for two reasons. Cabral gives us a picture of himself as he addresses himself to cadres, educated men, and intellectuals. But Chaliand shows us Cabral as he talks to the ordinary militant, Cabral as the political leader rather than as the theoretician. We need such a portrait to evaluate Cabral's theory, for it gives us the true measure of the man. He comes off well.

But there is a second reason to read Chaliand. Chaliand illustrates the correctness of Cabral's call to "progressive democrats" to study Guinea (and similar situations). For Chaliand is free to reflect in ways that are not open to Cabral, though ultimately most useful to the PAIGC and to other movements. There are two statements Chaliand makes in the theoretical section of his book which are worth pondering:

> After making a tour of capital cities in 1963, Chou En-Lai declared: 'The revolutionary situation in Africa is excellent.' Nothing could be further from the truth. After a few short years, the facade of socialism has collapsed and African realities have begun to appear in their true light. (p. 109)

The second comes in the wake of describing the splits within the Camerounian UPC in the 1960s:

> Thus, the political climate had become one in which the principal enemy was no longer Ahidjo's neo-colonial regime but rather the factions within the UPC itself. Had the Sino-Soviet conflict deepened the rifts between the various groups or had it merely supplied them

with motives for fighting each other under the cover of ideological arguments?

The first point to be made is that the real struggle was not being waged. . . . This inability to solve one's own problems, this incapacity to act according to one's national reality when circumstances are favorable, is the key to the history of all truncated, bloodless party apparatuses that destroy themselves by inventing mad fables to explain away their failures. The problem goes far beyond the specific instance of the UPC: this was the case in Accra, it is now the case in Algeria, and in the future it will be the case elsewhere. (p. 104)

As it is indeed already—in France, in the United States. So we see that the lessons of the PAIGC are not abstract exercises in the study of an exotic small state tucked away in a corner of West Africa. They bear on the problems of Algeria, the United States, and I would add of the USSR. For they bear on the central problematic of the modern world: the conditions under which and the ways in which the majority of the world's population will regain effective and maximal control over their destiny. As Cabral says of the "absurd" idea that one might inculcate a "working-class mentality" in the minds of those who were not bred to it from infancy, "in any case it is very difficult."

NOTES

[1] Cabral is making this particular statement in an interview with *Tricontinental* magazine.

Africa in a
Capitalist World

African studies has gone through three well-known phases as a field of study. Up until 1950 or thereabouts, those studying Africa—they were not yet called Africanists—tended to concentrate almost exclusively on the capturing (or recapturing) of a description of Africa eternal: Launcelot the ethnographer in search of a holy grail of the past that was written in the present tense and was undefiled by contact and uncorrupted by civilization. What was once a myth is now a fairy tale and it would be silly to waste time telling each other the obvious truth that fairy tales are modes of the social control and the education of children.

We then moved collectively into a second phase in which we recognized that there was an African present, and consequently that there was an African past. Thus began the great division of the field of studies which has been so obvious to anyone attending meetings of such organizations as the African Studies Association. There were those who studied what was happening now. They usually called themselves political scientists or economists or sociologists, but some masqueraded under other denominations ranging from architectural planner to urban anthropologist to demograper. There arose a second group who studied what happened before. They usually called themselves historians or archaeologists but they, too, had their aliases: art historian, student of cosmologies, linguist. The two groups maintained a friendly cohabitation under the house of African studies but scarcely could they be said to have had an intimate relationship.

This separation of the present and the past was as artificial and as mythical as the previous collapsing of past and present into one continuing eternity. It was no doubt a great advance in that it permitted some concrete empirical work rooted in concrete historical circumstances to proceed, but it was not satisfying. Those concerned with the present came to realize that much of their scholarship was really a sort of second-hand journalism. And those concerned with the past began to feel that their efforts to prove to non-Africanists that Africa too had splendid kings ultimately proved no more than that naive prejudice was naive. It provided, however, no true answer to the very large questions of Africa's position in the great "rendez-vous de donner et de recevoir"[1] of world cultures. If one wished to say that Africa's economic and technological weakness of today was somehow balanced in a world scale by Africa's glories of yesteryear, there would have to be some clearer, more detailed analysis of the process of evolution from the one to the other.

The logical consequence of this collective discomfort was almost self-evident. Those concerned with the present began looking backwards into the historical past, albeit gingerly. And those concerned with the past began to ask whether the conquest of Africa by Europe in the late nineteenth century marked as sharp an historical discontinuity as they had assumed. So we have J.F. Ade Ajayi addressing the International Congress of African Historians in 1965 on the theme, "The continuity of African institutions under colonialism."[2] Today it is scarcely credible that in 1965 the very title seemed somewhat daring—a measure of how far we have come in the past few years.

Ajayi said then:

> [Historians] should consider the story of how individually or collectively Africans are trying to master the new forces that have descended on them, how and why a man gets himself baptised a Christian, sends his children to school, comes to terms with modern technology by buying a lorry and learning to drive it, and yet insists that the lorry is not just a mechanical device but has a force whose control properly belongs to the god of iron and whose emblems and charms are therefore displayed in the lorry. I find such a man more typical—and more cheering—than the frustrated, paralysed, helpless African portrayed in the theory of disruption.[3]

One historian who was doing what Ajayi called for was Terence Ranger, the organizer of the Congress in Dar es Salaam at which Ajayi spoke. Ranger published soon thereafter a two-part article in the *Journal of African History* entitled "Connexions between 'Primary Resistance' Movements and Modern Mass Nationalism in East and Central Africa."[4]

Ranger asserted that so-called primary resistances, far from being reactionary or backward-looking, looked into the future in the same way as did later nationalist movements. He further argued that the two sets of movements were not merely similar but historically connected.

It was not long before these arguments were attacked by Donald Denoon and Adam Kuper as "ideological history," one that "has adopted the political philosophy of current African nationalism, and has used it to inform the study of African history." What is more, said Denoon and Kuper: "The African historian should be committed to writing the truth, rather than the politic half-truth."[5]

Strong rhetoric, but what is the truth? What is the truth now, and what will it be tomorrow? Who defines it today, and who tomorrow? Who indeed is truly dedicated to the truth, and whose interest does which truth serve? I raise of course the questions of the social bases of knowledge. But I do not wish to stop there. Rather I wish to move on from there to suggesting some conceptual bases for the knowledge of the social reality of Africa.

In 1971, Bernard Magubane published an article in *Current Anthropology* which was an attack on the indices used in studying social change in Africa. In particular, he singled out the work of A.L. Epstein and Clyde Mitchell about Northern Rhodesia as foci for his argument. As is the custom of this journal, the paper was submitted to a large number of scholars for comment, and the article was published simultaneously with the comments and a reply to the comments.[6]

The heart of Magubane's critique was that the categories used by Epstein and Mitchell in their analyses were "extremely superficial and at best ethnocentric," and that they lacked "historical perspective."[7] Magubane's explanation of this was that Epstein and Mitchell reflected their social role:

> As men who basically accepted the "civilizing mission" of imperialism their analyses rationalized and attempted to improve the imperial system. The result was a divided effort at social analysis and propaganda which produced a hodgepodge of eclectic and mechanistic formulations.[8]

The commentators were scarcely gentle with Magubane. Epstein accused Magubane of "dissipating his talents in knocking down the men of straw he himself has set up."[9] Mitchell charged him with the "shoddiest kind of criticism. . .*argumentum ad hominem*. . ." He concluded:

> The pity of it is that all he has to offer is destructive and ill-considered comments on the work of others who, for better or for worse, but

nonetheless in good faith, have faced the challenge and discipline of research of this kind.[10] (Italics added)

While Epstein and Mitchell denounced *ad hominem* arguments, various of the other commentators offered just such arguments in *defense* of Epstein and Mitchell. A.J.F. Köbben suggested that to understand Magubane's attitude, "one would need the concerted efforts of the anthropologist, the historian, and the psychologist, and a lot of empathy, if not compassion."[11] Satish Saberwal observed in milder tones that:

> The chiding that Mitchell and Epstein get at Magubane's hand is, in part, the penalty that pioneers often have to pay.[12]

Simon D. Messing reminded us of the German saying: "Undank ist der Welten Lohn."[13] Van den Berghe accused Magubane of "ideologically inspired innuendo," and called him "not even intellectually honest."[14] Philip Mayer asserted merely:

> [Magubane's] own "existential" situation is...of some relevance, especially as such a single-minded onslaught on "colonial anthropology" seems almost anachronistic in 1970.[15]

In his reply, Magubane observed with sharpness:

> The importance of my critique of "pluralist" writings like Van den Berghe's and of works like that of Epstein, Mayer, Mitchell, etc. derives not from their intrinsic worth, but rather from the near universal acceptance of their conclusions among certain scholars. What we are faced with in the field of African studies is an accumulation of studies that are theoretically false and have congealed into a steadfast intellectual reality. It is revealing but at the same time sad that of those people who replied to my article, only the three "Third World" commentators understood clearly what I was talking about, whereas the rest could only partially agree or were completely impervious to what I was saying. This is a reflection of the fundamental issue of our time: those who stand for a particular order in the world are unwilling to accept challenges to that order. Persuading such people to see that their ideas must be abandoned is like asking those in power to give up their privileges.[16]

Lest we think that such a vitriolic exchange is exceptional, let us return for a moment to Denoon and Kuper's broadside against Ranger and what

Africa in a Capitalist World 51

they termed the "Dar es Salaam school" of historiography. These "nationalist historians," said Denoon and Kuper, might well be regarded "as providing pie in the past rather than an understanding of present problems."[17] In his reply, Ranger had a footnote that reads:

> One day, perhaps, if interest should survive that long, a scholar will be able to investigate what connections there are between the fact that Denoon and Kuper are both young South African exiles recently working in Makerere and the methods and assumptions of their critique of Dar es Salaam historians. I would venture some speculations on this myself were it not for the fact that their own attempt to situate me in my environment serves as a ludicrous warning of the dangers of such an exercise.[18]

No speculation was therefore offered, but Ranger concluded his article with this sentence:

> I am sure that [Denoon and Kuper] will find it easier to serve the goddess of disinterested history when they are not working under the pressure of the profound if obscure forces which impelled their trenchant but totally misleading attack on the historians of Dar es Salaam.[19]

In turn, Denoon and Kuper showed no shyness in their rejoinder:

> Finally, Professor Ranger's mention of our South African backgrounds and his reference to the "profound if obscure forces" which motivated our critique may have puzzled some readers. Is he suggesting a secret subsidy from the Communist Party or the CIA? Or darkly hinting at the emergence of a sinister Pretoria school of African historiography? Our own view is that far from making any such unworthy imputation, this was Professor Ranger's way of saying he could not imagine any good reason for criticizing his school.[20]

The vehemence of feeling is not unfamiliar to those who have followed recent scholarly debates in African studies, although some may feel as did R.H. Tawney when he commented on H.R. Trevor-Roper's criticism of his work: "An erring colleague is not an Amalekite to be smitten hip and thigh."[21] What is to the point, however, is to see if there are underlying themes that would give coherence and unity to a large number of different debates on seemingly different topics. I shall therefore rapidly survey what it is I think Magubane and his critics are arguing about, the nub of the issue between Denoon and Kuper on one side and Ranger on the other, and what is at issue in the somewhat more restrained debate that J.D. Fage and C.C. Wrigley recently engaged in about "slavery and the slave trade." For I think there is a common intellectual issue threaded through these and other debates overlain of course by some strongly felt moral and political issues, and I believe that we can collectively make sense out of the debates only if we bring this underlying issue to the fore.

Note first of all that Magubane's article is about "indices used in the study of social change in *colonial* Africa." One of his opening suggestions was that "a total historical analysis of social change would, as a matter of course, take into account (various) stages in 'acculturation'."[22] He proceeded to outline three, in each of which the response of Africans to the dominant forces in the colonial situation was different. He noted, in terms virtually identical to those of Ajayi:

> In fact the history of the colonial situation, as opposed to its economics, its politics, its sociology, and its psychology, is in large measure a history of the variety of African responses to the new situation, a history of the ways Africans came to terms with a new set of forces, the ways they accommodated, resisted, or escaped.[23]

To the charge of neglect of these considerations, Magubane's critics shouted "foul." I take one response as typical. Clyde Mitchell said: "Epstein's whole book is about the way in which Africans were organizing to change the status quo from 1932 to 1953."[24]

It is worth listening to Magubane's counterattack in his reply at some length:

> Therefore my point in this article was not that Epstein in his book *Politics in an Urban African Community* did not deal with trade unions, but that he gave the wrong kind of explanation as to the source of these movements. To understand African nationalism and give it a correct historical interpretation, one must understand its dual nature. White settlement is a colonialist force in its own right (territorial colonialism) whose ultimate interest is its preservation in the territory it has occupied. The conflict that arose between Africans and white settlers stemmed from the antagonistic confrontation between white colonizing community *qua* community and the African people *qua* people. When the Africans were introduced into mining and secondary industry, the problem was compounded by class factors. Therefore

African nationalism combines the dynamics of national liberation and class struggle. The failure of elite integrationist politics and the beginning of the armed struggle testify to this dual nature. What is the nature of the relation between the two aspects of African nationalism in southern Africa? The comments by Epstein, Mitchell, and Van den Berghe avoid this issue.[25]

Permit me to reformulate this debate into two very fundamental issues: those of time-scope and space-scope. We are not involved in a simplified debate about the relevance of history. Both sides acknowledged this. What they disagreed about was the "correct historical interpretation." They have not even disagreed about the fact that some kind of structural and behavioral change was occurring under colonial rule, although Magubane charged that the others "have tended to take [the colonial situation] for granted, or to assume that its general characteristics are known."[26] But Magubane insisted there are temporal stages within the colonial period—what might be paraphrased as the period of conquest, the period of "acquiescence" (Magubane's phrase), and the period of national liberation. he argued that by neglecting this periodization, Epstein, Mitchell *et al.* were in fact talking exclusively about the middle period. This was of course their privilege, and was a relatively minor peccadillo. What is at issue is the assertion that by this absence of explicit periodization (perhaps in the very innards of their own intellectual processes) they could not interpret meaningfully the data which they collected in a technically impeccable manner.

Nor is this all. The second issue is that of space-scope. Magubane said that the conflict was that of a "white colonizing community *qua* community and the African people *qua* people." He talked of the dual nature of African nationalism: it is, he asserted, both "national liberation and class struggle." But Epstein too spoke of growing national consciousness. He too spoke of the union as uniting workers along class lines. Thus, was not Magubane unfair? To Epstein, he was setting up "straw men."

To make sense of this, we must draw out the *implicit* frameworks of the authors. For Epstein and Mitchell, the geographical frame of analysis was Northern Rhodesia. To the extent that they made use of stratification categories (tribe, class, etc.), these were for them categories of this territorial unit. For Magubane, although he did not say so explicitly, the use of these boundaries distorted the data and made no operational sense. How can a movement be simultaneously one of "national liberation" and one of "class struggle," if the unit of analysis is not larger than the colonial territory—at the very minimum that of the imperial political framework, and more reasonably, as I shall soon argue, that of the world-economy.

Let us now turn to the debate about the so-called Dar es Salaam school of historiography. Here Denoon and Kuper were quite explicit about the issue of time-scope and space-scope. They made it the heart of the debate. Although in many ways I would assimilate[27] their position on the essential underlying issue with that of Epstein and Mitchell, they took the initiative in this debate, seeming to invert the sides by accusing Ranger (whose position I would assimilate to that of Magubane) of provinciality of time and scope.

Denoon and Kuper started their analysis by citing Ranger as depicting in 1965 the likely intellectual debate of the future in these terms: "The Africanist historian...will increasingly find his main adversaries not in the discredited colonial school but in the radical pessimist,"[28] that is, men who employ what Ranger called "Fanonesque analysis." Denoon and Kuper said of this categorization by Ranger:

> In this confrontation Professor Ranger takes the side of the Africanist by which is meant the historian whose concerns include the study of nationalism. In practice, the frequent use of the term *African* is likely to mislead, since the recommended focus for historians is not the whole continent but African activity within national boundaries and generally for a national purpose. The analysis repudiates not only a Fanonesque view, but also any view involving generalization on a scale larger than that of nation—whether a world view, an imperial view or a continental approach. The recommended approach, then, is African nationalist.[29]

Thus, the issue of space-scope is at the forefront of the critique.

Ranger, however, flatly denied the correctness of this preception of his position:

> I do not believe...that a historian should concentrate on African activity within national boundaries. To extract such a view from my work cannot be achieved without a dexterity which comes close to manipulation.[30]

Rather, Ranger asserted his position to be quite different:

> The historian "must insist that nationalism is a live subject"—not the *only* subject, not the *most important* subject, but a live subject. So far from being concerned to argue that *all* African historical studies should in some sense be nationalist I was concerned to urge that nationalism should *still* be studied.[31]

So is there then no argument? Is it all a misunderstanding? Not quite. It turns out on closer analysis that the debate over space-scope is a bit of a front for a more real debate about time-scope. Much of the debate centers around the contents of two books of essays about Tanzania, one edited by I.M. Kimambo and A.J. Temu and the other by A.D. Roberts.[32] Denoon and Kuper took these volumes as the quintessential products of the group they were attacking. Denoon and Kuper cited the Introduction to *A History of Tanzania* in which Professors Kimambo and Temu wrote:

> There has been no attempt to deal with colonial administrative structures. This is because our main interest has been on the African himself.[33]

To which Denoon and Kuper responded:

> Historians of political development within colonial dependencies, in any part of the world, would be rightly appalled at such a self-imposed limitation.[34]

Denoon and Kuper pointed out that Ranger had challenged previous writers for having regarded certain new African institutions—specifically African independent churches—as "an abnormality, almost a disease."[35] This was, they said, "a straw-man's thesis"[36]—shades of Epstein attacking Magubane. To pursue the parallelism of the two debates, Denoon and Kuper taxed their opponents with disparaging the ethnographers:

> Finally, the members of the school show a certain shyness about using the works of the anthropologists who worked in Tanganyika during the colonial period. The social anthropologists were the main group of scholars active in colonial Africa; they worked in the vernaculars; and they published accounts of East African societies and social movements over many years. Not only are their ethnographies invaluable historical documents, but their interpretations would often be suggestive for the historian. The reason for this neglect appears to be the association of anthropology with colonialism.[37]

But how is all this a debate about time-scope? This surfaces clearly in the debate about pre-colonial East Africa. Denoon and Kuper asserted that the authors writing various local histories in the Roberts volume had failed to prove their generalizations, that in the editor's own chapter, "there is a sense of straining to find...'roots of nationalism.'"[38] They cited J.E.G.

Sutton's chapter in the Kimambo-Temu volume in which he began with the banality that the Tanzanian nation "is the product of a long historical process stretching back hundreds, even thousands of years"[39] and snidely commented that Sutton "does not in practice attempt to Tanzanianize the australopithecines."[40]

What was all of this leading up to? Two statements: one of shock, and one of assertion. The one of shock reads:

> Perhaps this [previous quote] may be regarded as a recognition that a full continuity of large-scale anti-colonial sentiment is not always to be found. At all events, [Lonsdale's] Dar es Salaam colleagues—Gwassa, Iliffe and Temu—appear still to be convinced of the existence of a "missing link" between early resistance and TANU nationalism in Tanzania, while Roberts would like to push back the roots of resistance on a national scale well into the nineteenth century.[41]

And the assertion:

> Scholars who regard the outside world's interventions in Africa as having achieved more than nationalism, and who consider that colonialism has been replaced very frequently by neo-colonialism, are not likely to be convinced by the implication that colonial policy was of scant significance even during the colonial years.[42]

But was this the implication these writers wanted to have drawn? Ranger said it missed the point:

> What most of the contributions to *A History of Tanzania* do stress is African initiative, African choice and African adaptation...But there are two things which it is very important to make plain. The first is that to stress African *agency* is by no means to stress African heroism or efficiency; the second is that a common concern with what Africans did and how they affected their history can lead to a most un-common and varied set of conclusions. The inquiry into African *agency* is not the resting point which defines a *school*, but the beginning point out of which all sorts of major differences will arise.[43]

What distinguishes in the end Denoon and Kuper's analysis from the ones they criticize is the emphasis placed on the analysis of the colonial era. Denoon and Kuper argued that because of a "nationalist" political

Africa in a Capitalist World 57

perspective, Ranger *et al.* ignored some concrete and specific features of colonial administration in favor of mythological "connexions." Ranger argued rather that to understand African behavior in that period required situating it in a longer time-scale of historical development, the exact bounds of which Ranger did not pursue in this debate.

To demonstrate that this debate is not merely one about how to interpret the colonial period, let us turn to the argument about slavery and the slave trade. John Fage entitled his article "Slavery and the Slave Trade in the Context of West African History."[44] The title itself suggests the spacescope. As for the time-scope his summary depicted it as covering "especially...the period from the fifteenth to the nineteenth century." We shall see however that this was not in fact his time-scope, since his analysis involved going further back in time.

Fage started by rejecting both the thesis that slavery was a flourishing institution in West Africa prior to European intrusion and the thesis that it was purely exogenously imposed. And basing himself largely on Philip Curtin,[45] he also rejected the idea that slave-trading in West Africa had "a disastrous effect on its population."[46] Rather, he put forward a different interpretation which he summarized as follows:

> [E]conomic and commercial slavery and slave-trading were not natural features of West African society, but...developed, along with the growth of states, as a form of labour mobilization to meet the needs of a growing system of foreign trade in which, initially, the demand for slaves as trade goods was relatively insignificant. What might be termed a "slave economy" was generally established in the Western and Central Sudan by about the fourteenth century at least, and had certainly spread to the coasts around the Senegal and in Lower Guinea by the fifteenth century. The European demand for slaves in the Americas, which reached its peak from about 1650 to about 1850, accentuated and expanded the internal growth of both slavery and the slave trade. But this was essentially only one aspect of a very wide process of economic and political development and social change, in West Africa.[47]

To argue this position, Fage had to start by undermining the attack on Fage's previous statement by Walter Rodney, whose evidence Fage acknowledged to be crucially relevant.[48] Fage discounted Rodney's finding of the absence of a slave work-force in West Africa prior to the arrival of European slave-traders as true perhaps for the Upper Guinea Coast but not for either the Lower Guinea Coast or the interior. Fage's essential explanation was that the area that Rodney studied was atypical, essentially because it "was an economically little developed and backward region."[49]

For the other areas, Fage contended the picture was very different:

> In general, we can be confident that what the Portuguese sought to do in Lower Guinea from about 1480 was to profit by imposing themselves (as later they would do in East Africa and Asia) on already existing patterns of trade, and that they from there organized kingdoms in which the idea of foreign trade, carried on under royal control and in accordance with state policy by established merchant classes or guilds, was already well established. Such a system involved the use of slaves—and an appreciation of their economic value—in a number of ways: as cultivators of crops for market on the estates of kings or nobles; as miners, or as artisans in craft workshops, as carriers on the trade routes; and even as traders themselves; as soldiers, retainers, servants, officials even, in the employ of kings or principal men in the kingdom.[50]

Did nothing then change for Fage in West Africa when the Europeans came in the fifteenth century? It's not entirely clear. Fage said that:

> [The] slave trade...in West Africa...was part of a sustained process of economic and social development. Probably because, by and large, in West Africa land was always more abundant than labour, the institution of slavery played an essential role in its development; without it there were really few effective means of mobilizing labour for the economic and political needs of the state...
> On the whole it is probably true to say that the operation of the slave trade may have tended to integrate, strengthen and develop unitary, territorial political authority, but to weaken or destroy more segmentary societies. Whether this was good or evil may be a nice point; historically it may be seen as purposive and perhaps as more or less inevitable.[51]

The picture thus that we have from Fage is that there existed some long historical process which began at some unspecified point prior to the fifteenth century in which the European intrusion was merely one of a series of factors which contributed to this "inevitable" and "purposive" evolution. When the Europeans finally conquered West Africa, this was merely one more step in this process:

Africa in a Capitalist World

The steps taken by Europeans against the slave trade and slavery therefore hastened the day when, in their own economic interest they thought it necessary first to conquer the West African kingdoms, and then to continue the process, initiated by African kings and entrepreneurs, of conquering the segmentary societies and absorbing them into unitary political structures.[52]

We see then clearly that for Fage a meaningful unit of analysis is West Africa from prior to the fifteenth century to the present in which the principle dynamic of social organization and transformation is "state-building."

How different had been Rodney's article. First notice the title: "African slavery and other forms of social oppression on the Upper Guinea Coast in the context of the Atlantic slave-trade." The context (that is, the space-scope) was not "West Africa" but the "Atlantic slave-trade" which was in fact shorthand for the European world-economy. Rodney saw this period as one in which "African society became geared to serve the capitalist system,"[53]—that is, the *world* capitalist system. He stated:

> Historically, the initiative came from Europe. It was the European commercial system which expanded to embrace various levels of African barter economy, and to assign to them specific roles in global production. This meant the accumulation of capital from trading in Africa, and above all the purchase of slaves and their employment in the New World.[54]

Thus, the period 1600-1800 is far from being a middle period in a continuing West African historical pattern as Fage envisaged it; for Rodney it was "the first stage of the colonial domination of Africa by Europeans,"[55] a "protocolonial" period[56]—hence part of a world-historical pattern.

C.C. Wrigley entered into this debate, saying very correctly:

> [Fage's radical reassessment of the Atlantic slave-trade] brings near to the surface certain theoretical assumptions which I believe to be imbedded in a large part of recent African historiography...[57]

And the assumption that Wrigley was most concerned about bringing to the fore is that slavery and the slave-trade are a necessary condition of the "political development" of West Africa, an inevitable aspect of state-formation.[58] As Wrigley noted, this stands Rodney on his head:

Hitherto, a historian who was at pains to establish that Africans were enslaving one another before the first caravels dropped anchor off their coasts would have been immediately identifiable as a "colonialist"; he would be manifestly seeking to denigrate the African people and to saddle them with part of the blame for the ensuing calamity of the Atlantic trade. Fage, however, is unmistakeably congratulating West Africans on having *achieved* the institution of slavery without European help.[59]

This, continued Wrigley, was "historicism," taking "classificatory types, formulated in the first place for their heuristic value" and translating them into "developmental stages, conceived as having real existence and arranged in a hierarchy which is both chronological and qualitative."[60] Such historicism is ethnocentric and condemns Africans "to limp painfully in the footsteps of Europe."[61] Note here an interesting paradox. It is suggested that the consequence of using a West African space-scope, as did Fage, can lead to conclusions that are Europo-centric. It is equally implied that using a European space-scope (taking Europe in the 17th and 18th centuries to include at least parts of West Africa), as did Rodney, can lead to conclusions that place in appropriate perspective what Ranger calls "African agency."

How then do we proceed? In his most recent book, *How Europe Underveloped Africa*, Rodney devoted Chapter Two to "how Africa developed before the coming of the Europeans up to the fifteenth century." He gave an explanation that is in the tradition of a recent French literature about the "African mode of production." I myself do not find this part of Rodney's exposition very satisfying. Nor as a matter of fact do I get the impression that Rodney himself does. For he concluded the chapter with a reflection which I endorse entirely:

> One of the paradoxes in studying this early period of African history is that it cannot be fully comprehended without first deepening our knowledge of the world at large, and yet the true picture of the complexities of the development of man and society can only be drawn after intensive study of the long-neglected African continent.[62]

This then is how I think we must proceed. To understand Africa, we must reconceptualize world history. And for the scholarly world to effectuate such a reconceptualization, we as Africans must do our share by doing our work within such a perspective. I am not calling for intellectual supermen. I am merely asking that we concentrate on grinding a new pair of glasses, and that we wear these new glasses in the very process of grinding them. This is a hard task, but not a new one, since this is the only way in which man has ever invented the new truths that caught up his new realities and yet simultaneously criticized these new realities in the light of human potentialities.

One key aspect to the process of reconceptualization is to bring to the fore our implicit theories. And this means specifying time-scope and space-scope and justifying our choices. At the same conference in Dar es Salaam at which Ajayi made his appeal to study the continuities of African institutions under colonialism, Ivan Hrbek gave an unfortunately neglected paper entitled "Towards a periodisation of African history."[63]

Hrbek attacked the relevance of conventional Europo-centric periodizations for Africa, including those of Marxist dogmatists like Endre Sik.[64] He suggested various landmarks or watersheds, working backwards. The most recent was that of the 1960s—the achievement of independence by many states. The second however was not 1884-1885 but rather the moment of "the integration of African societies into the sphere of world economy and later world politics."[65] He dated this, with some reservations, as the first decade of the twentieth century. Farther back, he hesitated to give a continent-wide date. Although he would have liked to distinguish what he called "contact zones" and "isolated zones" at that point in time, he pointed out that during the period 1805-1820 there were a large number of major happenings in both zones. He listed the jihad of Osman dan Fodio; the rise of the Zulu under Chaka; the eclipse of Bunyoro and the rise of Buganda; the foundation of modern Egypt under Muhammed Ali; the unification of the Imerina on Madagascar under Radama I; the rise of Omani hegemony on the East African coast under Sayyid Said. According to Hrbek what makes these six instances parallel is that they all "pointed in one single direction: the growth of a unified and highly centralized state with an absolute monarch unrestricted in his power by any freely elected council."[66] This was also the moment of the abolition of the slave trade, and although Hrbek dismissed any connection, I am not so sure that he was correct in doing so.

Going further back, Hrbek indicated some skepticism about the conventional belief that the fifteenth or sixteenth century marked a turning point.

> [S]ometimes exaggerated assertions as to the far-reaching consequences of the slave trade are pronounced. In fact the coming of the Europeans and the start of the slave-trade were of direct influence only in coastal regions and their immediate hinterlands...In the "isolated" zones African societies continued their independent development without any extracontinental influence...[67]

Finally, Hrbek argued a still earlier turning-point—somewhere between the first and fifth centuries A.D.

> ...when iron working was already known in large parts of Africa and when the introduction of new food-plants [from Southeast Asia] enabled the Bantu and also the West African ethnic groups to occupy the forested areas...[68]

I outline Hrbek's dates not to defend them but to indicate how different they are from more conventional dating, as suggested not only by many standard texts but by such a critic of these texts as Rodney: that is, pre-1500, 1500-1885, 1885-1960.

A second analyst who came up with dates with some similarities to those of Hrbek is Samir Amin who suggested the following: a *pre-mercantillist* period going far back into history and going up to 1600; a *mercantillist* period going from 1600-1800; *completed integration into the capitalist system* (the nineteenth century to the present).[69]

But, you will say, is it so important whether we date a shift at 1500 or 1600, at 1885 or the first decade of the twentieth century? Do we have any tools of historical measurement that are so fine? And what practical consequence can such a seemingly esoteric debate have? The answer is of course that our measures are gross and we should not pretend otherwise. But the debate is not esoteric because behind it lies the issue not of the years, but of the conceptual apparatus we have used to come up with one set of dates or another. And this is not merely important; it is all-determining.

To make sense of African history, we must have a theory of human society. If we go back to the year 1000 or thereabouts, our knowledge of what was going on in Africa is far more sparse than any of us would like. We know there were great migrations. We know that in various places there were state-apparatuses. We know that in some places there was long-distance trade. But we do not know too much—in part because we have not really looked for the answers—about the geographical bounds of the various divisions of labor in Africa. No doubt there were many mini-systems, largely or entirely self-sufficient. But how many *worlds* were there—that is, arenas in which there were systematic sustained exchanges of essential goods? And even more difficult, how many of these took the form of a world-empire—that is, a single division of labor with multiple political systems? We know that historically the first world-economy to overcome the basic instability of this systemic form and therefore survive over a long period of time is the world capitalist world-economy which originated as a European world-economy in the sixteenth century. But we also know that the course of human history has seen the passing existence of many world-economies, some of which disintegrated and others of which became transformed into world-empires.

Take for example Mali. At its height was it a world-empire or part of a larger world-economy that included parts of the Maghreb as well as areas in the forest zone to the south, within which the state of Mali was only one of many political systems? I suspect the latter is true for at least part of the time, but the hard research remains to be done. Instead of writing epicycles around an evolutionary theory of a "feudal" stage of social development by talking first of an "Asiatic mode of production" and then of an "African mode of production," don't we have to undertake a fundamental reassessment of all the varieties of redistributive modes of production, all of which seem to require some kind of political channel of redistribution and all of which seem to inhibit progress in technological productivity because of the absence of a market towards which production is oriented?

What we learn about Mali may enable us to explain intelligently for the first time Carolingian Europe. I am not calling for a systematic comparison. We are not yet at that stage. For we do not even yet have a systematic categorization of the parameters of each, using terms that are at least translatable one to the other. For almost all our work has started from political definitions of space-scope which has prevented us from systematically analyzing social systems—divisions of labor (that is, economic entities)—which *may or may not* have a single political framework.

If now we turn to a slightly later point in time, something did change in the sixteenth century—not in Africa, but in the world. In the sixteenth century there emerged a European world-economy centered on a combination of Atlantic and Baltic trade which included geographically within its division of labor an area including northwestern Europe, the Christian Mediterranean, northeastern Europe (but not Russia) and Hispanic America. The mode of production was capitalist. Though the genesis of this structure can be dated about 1450, it is only with the Treaty of Cateau-Cambrésis in 1559 that the possibility that this world-economy would go the way of all previous ones—transformation into a world-empire or disintegration—was definitely eliminated. And thus it was at this point that the capitalist mode of production (which can exist only within that structure known as a world-economy) could be said to have become the mode of production of this system, therefore determining of the social relations of *all* sectors of this world-economy.

Why such a capitalist world-economy should have arisen in Europe and not elsewhere (say, China) is an interesting question. Why it should have arisen at this point of historical time is too. I have tried to speak to these questions elsewhere and it is not to the point of this discussion to dwell on them. We must look rather to the consequences.[70]

A capitalist world-economy is based on a division of labor between its core, its semiperiphery, and its periphery in such a way that there is unequal exchange between the sectors but dependence of all the sectors, both economically and politically, on the continuance of this unequal exchange. One of the many consequences of this system is found in state-structure, the peripheral states being weakened and the core states strengthened by the ongoing process of exchange. A second of the consequences is that each sector develops different modes of labor control, consonant with the principle that highest relative wages are paid in the core sectors and lowest relative wages in the periphery. This is why at this moment in time there emerged in eastern Europe the so-called (and misnamed) "second serfdom" and the *ecomienda* system in Hispanic America. Both are forms of coerced cash-crop labor on estates producing for a capitalist world-market.[71]

In addition, in the Americas plantation slavery was developed. Plantation slavery is a form of capitalist wage-labor (labor offered for sale as a commodity on a market) in which the state intervenes to guarantee a low current wage (the cost of subsistence). However there is an additional cost: that of the purchase of the slave. If the slave is "produced" within the world-economy, his real cost is not merely the sales price but the opportunity cost (of failing to use his labor under other wage conditions at presumably a higher level of productivity). As Marc Bloch suggested a long time ago, under these conditions slaves are too expensive[72]—that is, they do not produce enough surplus to compensate for their real cost.

The *only* way to render plantation slavery economically feasible in a capitalist system is to eliminate the opportunity cost, which means that the slaves must be recruited outside the world-economy. In that case, the opportunity cost is borne by some other system and is a matter of indifference to the purchasers. This would change of course if one totally exhausted the supplier and there were no replacement on similar terms. But historically this had not yet occurred at the moment the slave-trade ended.

Trade with an external arena of a world-economy is fundamentally different from trade within the world-economy between the core and peripheral sectors. We can see this if we compare trade in the sixteenth century between western Europe and Poland on the one hand and between western Europe and Russia on the other, or during the same period of time trade between Spain and Hispanic America on the one hand and Portugal and the Indian Ocean area on the other.[73]

There are three visible differences. One, trade within the world-economy is trade in essentials, without which the world-economy could not continue to survive. It involves a significant transfer of surplus, given that a world-economy is based on a capitalist mode of production. It is trade that responds to the world-market of the world-economy. Trade of two world-systems, each external to the other, involves what was called in the sixteenth century the "rich trades." In more precise terms, we can say such trade involves the exchange of products that both sellers define as of very low value but that both buyers define as of high value. This is not capitalist exchange, and is in fact dispensable exchange. There is profit to be made by long-distance traders but this is precisely the kind of profit made by such traders over thousands of years of such trade—a profit based on high price discrepancies due to rarity of the product at the place of consumption and oversupply of the product at the place of production.

Second, trade within a capitalist world-economy weakens the state-structure of a peripheral country involved in it. The steady decline of the power of the Polish king from about 1500 to 1800 is a clear case in point. Trade in external arenas does not weaken and probably strengthens the state structures of the trading partners. One can point to the increase of the strength of sultans in Malaysia at this same period.

Third, trade within a capitalist world-economy weakens the role of the indigenous commercial bourgeoisie in the periphery. Trade with an external arena strengthens the role of the indigenous bourgeoisie.

Thus far, as you will see, I have assiduously avoided discussing where European trade with West Africa in what Amin called the *mercantillist period* (1600-1800) fits into this picture. The reason is that the answer is not as clear-cut as we would like it. It is evident that this trade between Europe and West Africa meets the description of trade in the external arena on the last two grounds. It strengthened various state-structures in West Africa, and it strengthened the role of the indigenous commercial bourgeoisie. But can it be said to have been luxury trade, and even more can it be said to have been trade that did not involve a substantial transfer of surplus?

One piece of evidence that it could be so described is deductive in nature. Were it not so, were West Africa part of the periphery of the European world-economy, then the cost of slaves in the Western Hemisphere would have had to bear the opportunity cost of their physical loss to West Africa, and that presumably would have made them too expensive *in the economics of the total economy* to be used. And used they were, extensively, as we know. The loss of course to West Africa was very real.[74]

But this could be taken to be circular reasoning. Let me therefore speak directly to the two descriptive features: was the slave-trade trade of items each seller valued low? And was there no significant transfer of surplus?

The answer is, I believe, that the situation evolved. Victorino Magalhães Godinho gave some detailed accounts of the nature of the trade between Portuguese and Africans at a whole series of points along the West African coast down to Angola *in the sixteenth century*. It seems clear that the main items traded at that time for slaves were brass and copper bracelets ('Manillas'), various size trays, barrels of conches, kerchiefs, skullcaps, and some uncut cloth.[75] I do not believe it would be inaccurate to say that this was an exchange of items each seller valued low for what they each valued high. Nor do I think it inaccurate to say that at this point in time it was a trade in non-essential goods, in that a cessation for any reason would not have upset the respective economies fundamentally, and consequently would have had few implications for the social organization of the respective social systems despite the fact that for Europeans the trade was most profitable,[76] as long distance trade usually is.

This seems to be less the case as we go forward in time. But how much less? Christopher Fyfe's textbook account seems ambivalent. On the one hand he noted that as of the seventeenth century, firearms became a major import. And firearms might be said to be an essential product. Indeed, he said that *by the end of the eighteenth century*, "there were factories in England [in Birmingham] turning out special arms for the African trade...."[77] And thus he implied that such trade was a regular part of the European division of labor. On the other hand, he called the remaining imports (other than firearms) "luxuries rather than necessities; they merely supplemented local manufactures with imports of superior quality."[78] Still, he observed further: "As manufactured goods were imported increasingly, local industry tended to suffer,"[79]—a feature we would associate with a process of peripheralization. We thus have an ambiguous set of characteristics describing this trade. Fyfe's own summary points to the argument of evolution over time:

> So, though foreign imports tended to be luxury goods, and the country still remained self-supporting in essentials, as the demands for imports grew steadily, the area was increasingly tied to the economies of countries overseas.[80]

I believe some of this ambiguity dissipates if one goes carefully through Rodney's detailed analysis of "The Nature of Afro-European Commerce."[81] Rodney divided European exports to West Africa into five categories: metal, cloth, alcoholic beverages, weapons, and "a miscellany of baubles, bangles, and beads."[82]

Of the last category, he said: "For both Europeans and Africans, the numerous items of trumpery were placed at the bottom of the scale of values."[83] This would indicate that the trade was not then trade in items

Africa in a Capitalist World 67

disparately valued. He cited *Purchas his Pilgrimes* as saying that such items could buy nothing but foodstuff. There are two things to say about this analysis. First, it is contradicted by the evidence of Godinho which I cited just above. Second, even insofar as trumpery were traded for foodstuffs only, Europeans thought they were getting a wild bargain. Rodney himself cited John Ogilby's statement in his 1670 work that the Africans "do not set a high rate upon the best of their commodities"[84]—in which case the Europeans *were* buying items they valued high but the seller valued low.

On firearms, the one item that might be deemed "essential" trade, Rodney cautioned against giving them too much significance. First of all, he noted that it was a phenomenon that particularly grew in importance in "the later part of the eighteenth century."[85] Second, he suggested that the import of firearms had marginal social consequences:

> It would be attractive to set this category of goods apart as the main stimulus to slaving, on the grounds that guns were used to capture slaves to buy more guns to capture more slaves. If they added a new dimension to military techniques, then they would also have been decisive in relations among the Africans themselves, but in reality their importance was narrowly circumscribed in the period under discussion. European firearms made an impact at a very late date; the first period of Hispano-Portuguese slave trading, for example, had little or nothing to do with the import of firearms. Furthermore, while it is true that coastal residents had by the end of the eighteenth century re-armed themselves with European weapons, the same did not apply to the inhabitants of the interior; and nevertheless it was the Mande-Fula combination in the hinterland which extended domination over coastal tribes, demonstrating clearly that European firearms did not automatically influence the African balance of power.[86]

Rodney was similarly skeptical about the importance of alcoholic beverages. He then reminded us that ordinarily Europeans were required to offer assortments of items for sale, and that European traders often practiced "rooming"—that is, replacement of more expensive items by cheaper ones.

"Rooming" was possible "because the Africans themselves were neither knowledgeable about the price of each European product nor concerned about that factor,"[87] which is another way of saying that the price of the exchange was not determined by the world-market. Rodney used as part of his explanation of how this could be so Polanyi's argument that while the

Europeans were working within the framework of a capitalist conception of the economic process, the Africans were operating on a system of "gainless barter." Rodney observed:

> In Polanyi's opinion. . ., it was the European system which adjusted to the African. Evidence taken from Upper Guinea helps to substantiate as well as to modify this interpretation.[88]

The modifications Rodney seemed to suggest were that adjustment was in fact "mutual"; that "historically, the initiative came from Europe"; and that over time "African society became geared to serve the capitalist system."[89]

Where are we then? I would summarize the situation as follows. From 1450 to circa 1750, West Africa was in the external arena of the European world-economy and not part of its periphery; that up to 1750 the bulk of the trade could be considered as "rich trades"; and thus that up to that point the two social systems were separate.

However, 1750-1760 or thereabouts marked a major turning point in the European world-economy. It marked the end of the century-long depression which had so exacerbated the mercantilist conflicts between the Netherlands, England, and France. It marked the inception of England's "industrial revolution" which would have contradictory impacts on West Africa.

In the first place, the industrial revolution expanded enormously the demand for sugar and cotton production in the Western Hemisphere, which in turn expanded the demand for slaves. This accelerated demand had to be paid for at a higher price, including the sale of firearms. This in turn led to an atmosphere propitious to the creation of large state-structures—in West Africa, and elsewhere in Africa and the world external to the European world-economy. Thus we see the great spurt that Hrbek observed in Africa in state-building from 1805-1820.

Meanwhile in Europe, England finally definitely eliminated France as a rival for economic hegemony in the Napoleonic Wars—the culmination of two centuries of relative French decline. This then opened the European world-economy as of 1815 to global expansion, for the new scale of European production required a world-wide market of purchase and sale. It was at this point in time that Africa, the Middle East, Asia, and Oceania began to be systematically incorporated into the now single global capitalist system, in almost all cases as parts of the periphery.

Once West Africa was part of the periphery and not the external arena, however, slavery was too costly. For slave-trading meant paying an ever higher purchase cost plus now a real diminution in the system's economic productivity (by removal of manpower from a region). Of all countries, Britain had the most to gain from a proper functioning of the capitalist world-economy, so it took the lead in abolishing the slave-trade and substituting "legitimate trade,"—that is, encouring the production by Africans of cash-crops (for example, palm oil) for the world market.

But once incorporated into the periphery, the African state-structures became a threat to the easy flow of unequal exchange. As long as England had world hegemony, it seemed less costly to keep them in check and/or deal with them than to conquer them. However, Britain's hegemony came to be threatened in the world capitalist system—a phenomenon we can date as beginning approximately in 1873, the moment when the constraints of worldwide effective demand created a system-wide depression which in many ways lasted into the beginning of the twentieth century. Among other consequences, this threat to hegemony took the neo-mercantilist form of "preemptive" colonization[90]—to wit, the scramble for Africa, which had the additional advantage of eliminating all strong state-structures in the African periphery.

We are arguing, then, that as of 1750 began a process of steady incorporation of Africa into the capitalist world-economy whose first stage was that of *informal empire* and whose second stage was that of *colonial rule*. We must now turn to stage three—*decolonization*, which can be seen as the completion of this historic process.

As long as the demands made on Africa by the other parts of the world-economy were limited—Africa as producer or Africa as consumer—a colonial system was adequate to the political overseeing of these demands. A small investment in bureaucratic super-structure (including armies) was sufficient to ensure that the most lucrative mines were mined, and that enough cash-crop production was arranged to bear the administrative overhead of colonialism. It was not entire fiction (though it was stated in pious self-exculpating terminology) that colonies were not necessarily profitable exercises, and that a major problem was to make sure that they were "self-financing" and not a drain on the metropolitan treasury.

That is to say, they may not have been profitable—or at least *very* profitable—from the perspective of the metropolitan country as an entity. Colonies of course could be very profitable to individual entrepreneurs or firms, including and even especially to the white settlers. But to make them really profitable, money had to be invested that would have the effect of greatly expanding the rate of productivity and the size of the salaried workforce (the latter being crucial in their capacity as consumers).

For increased investment to result in higher productivity and sufficient distribution to create a minimal local market, indirect rule was the most efficient mode. For only Africans could easily get Africans truly to increase their productivity, and for that these new managers would have to be rewarded. Furthermore, the rewards themselves had the effect of creating the new local markets. And thus by the simple principle that higher quantity at lower rates of profit can equal greater overall profit, the economic expansion of the post-Second World War period in Africa has magnified the economic transfer of surplus from the African periphery to the center far beyond anything that occurred in colonial rule.

To be sure, the fact that first the United States, then West Germany, and latterly the Soviet Union wanted access to these peripheral areas was a consideration that speeded up decolonization—but I now believe this factor was less important than I and many others previously thought. Even without that pressure, decolonization made sense, for the independent governments of Africa are far more efficacious "indirect rulers" than the *obas* and *mwamis* of the colonial era.

And the progress towards industrialization in Africa, far from countering this trend, has been part of the same picture. I agree entirely with Samir Amin's summary of this situation:

> With industrialization it is the internal market which begins to provide the primary impetus for growth, even though this market is a distorted one. However in this...phase the export trade retains its earlier structure (export of primary goods). It is on the import side that a structural modification is noticeable. Imported industrial goods and food products replace manufactured consumption goods (the appearance of food imports in countries which are still primarily agricultural reflects the distortion in the allocation of resources)...From this moment on, the aggravation of the contradictions inherent in [this phase is] characterized by a new, but still unequal, international division of labor in which the periphery becomes the exporter of "classical" industrial products (thereby leaving to the center the benefits of specialization within the more modern industries), and the importer of food surpluses from advanced capitalist agriculture. The establishment of runaway industries in the Far East is indicative of this new tendency of the system. It is by no means impossible that Africa will rapidly begin taking part in this new international division of labor....[91]

With this in mind, one can be somewhat pessimistic about the ability of a so-called radical African regime to buck the system, as I have been in one recent paper.[92] One can be stern about the validity of any of these regimes calling itself a socialist regime, as I have been in another.[93] I would not want anyone to conclude therefore that I think that Africans or the rest of us are helpless before a juggernaut of economic givens. For by processes that have often been elucidated, economic givens make possible certain political thrusts. And seen as political thrusts, many efforts can be justified even if they fall far short of their ostensible objectives. For example, Amin concluded his analysis by an unusual defense of *ujamma*. He did not say it would transform either Tanzania or the African continent. He argued rather that there was a *de facto* convergence of interests in contemporary Africa between the "marginalized masses, the urban proletariat, and impoverished and half-proletarianized poor peasantry." The key political problem for those who seek change is to maintain this alliance. He deduced consequently:

> [Any] development of production based on profit [that is, individual profit—I.W.] (particularly agrarian capitalism) which puts this alliance into question will prove negative in the long run, even if in the short run it facilitates the rapid growth of production.[94]

Any further discussion of the linkage not only between a policy of *ujamaa* but between the future role of the national liberation movements in southern Africa and the modes of world political confrontation within the framework of the capitalist world-economy would be long to develop, and I shall not do it here.

Let me return instead to the fundamental thrust of our argument. Africa is today part of a single world-system, the capitalist world-system, and its present structures and processes cannot be understood unless they are situated within the social framework that is governing them. Furthermore, this capitalist world-system has not emerged full bloom out of nowhere but rather has been the framework of African life—albeit in a perhaps thinner way than today—for about two centuries. Prior to that, African world-systems were non-capitalist systems. They related as external arenas to specific other world-systems, including in one case the European capitalist world-economy.

To understand this earlier period is in many ways far more difficult than to understand the present, for we shall have to sharpen our understanding of social systems to do it. We shall have to rework our knowledge of world historical data (as well as expand it) in order to analyze coherently how pre-capitalist economies functioned, which will—I believe—open many doors for us. Africans have proudly asserted in recent years that they have as much to offer as anyone in the *rendez-vous de donner et de recevoir* of world cultures. Equally, we as Africanists—and Africans first among the Africanists—must be ready to participate in the *rendez-vous de donner et de recevoir* of collective knowledge about a social world whose coherence and cohesion is ever more evident as the praxis of world transformation forces us to see it, to face up to it, and to make our moral choices within it.

NOTES

[1] I believe the phrase is that of Leopold-Sedar Senghor, but I cannot locate it. In any case, the sentiment is elaborated in the essay by Cheikh Hamidou Kane, "Comme si nous nous etions donne rendezvous," *Esprit*, n.s., 29, No. 299 (Oct. 1961): 375-387

[2] J.F. Ajayi, "The Continuity of African Institutions under Colonialism," in T.O. Ranger, ed., *Emerging Themes of African History* (Nairobi: East African Publishing House, 1968), pp. 189-200.

[3] Ajayi, "Continuity," p. 200.

[4] T.O. Ranger, "Connexions between Primary Resistance Movements and Modern Mass Nationalism in East and Central Africa," in *Journal of African History*, IX, 3:437-453; IX, 4:631-641.

[5] Donald Denoon and Adam Kuper, "Nationalist Historians in Search of a Nation: The New Historiography in Dar es Salaam," *African Affairs*, 69, 277 (Oct. 1970):348 (hereafter cited as "Nationalist Historians").

[6] Bernard Magubane, "A Critical Look at Indices Used in the Study of Social Change in Colonial Africa," *Current Anthropology*, XII, 4-5 (Oct.-Dec. 1971): 419-431. It is followed by "Comments" (pp. 431-439) and a "Reply" (pp. 439-445).

[7] Magubane, "A Critical Look," pp. 430-442.

[8] Magubane, "A Critical Look," p. 430.

[9] Epstein, "Comments on Magubane, 'A Critical Look'," p. 432.

[10] Mitchell, "Comments on Magubane, 'A Critical Look'," p. 436.

[11] Köbben, "Comments on Magubane, 'A Critical Look'," p. 433.

[12] Saberwal, "Comments on Magubane, 'A Critical Look'," p. 438.

[13] Messing, "Comments on Magubane, 'A Critical Look'," p. 434.

[14] Van den Berghe, "Comments on Magubane, 'A Critical Look'," p. 438.

[15] Mayer, "Comments on Magubane, 'A Critical Look'," p. 433.

[16] Magubane, "Reply," p. 439.

[17] Denoon and Kuper, "Nationalist Historians," p. 347.

[18] Terence Ranger, "The 'New Historiography' in Dar es Salaam: An Answer," *African Affairs*, 70, 278, Jan. 1971, p. 55 (hereafter cited as "An Answer").

[19] Ranger, "An Answer," p. 61.

[20] Donald Denoon and Adam Kuper "The 'New Historiography' in Dar es Salaam: A Rejoinder," *African Affairs*, 70, 280, July 1971, p. 288 (hereafter cited as "A Rejoinder").
[21] R.H. Tawney, "Postscript to the Rise of the Gentry," in E.N. Karus-Wilson, ed., *Essays in Economic History*, Volume I (London: Edw. Arnold, 1954), p. 214.
[22] Magubane, "A Critical Look," p. 419.
[23] Magubane, "A Critical Look," p. 420.
[24] Mitchell, "Comments on Magubane, 'A Critical Look'," p. 436.
[25] Magubane, "Reply," p. 441.
[26] Magubane, "A Critical Look" p. 419.
[27] When I say I "assimilate" one man's position to another, I do not mean that either endorses the arguments of the other in their respective articles but simply that in treating three debates successively, I see the same underlying issue recurring and wish to identify sides A and B in each.
[28] Terence Ranger, "Introduction" to Ranger, ed., *Emerging Themes of African History*, p. xxi, and cited in Denoon and Kuper, "Nationalist Historians," p. 331.
[29] Denoon and Kuper, "Nationalist Historians," p. 331.
[30] Ranger, "An Answer," p. 51.
[31] Ranger, "An Answer," p. 52.
[32] N. Kimambo and A.J. Temu, eds., *A History of Tanzania* (Nairobi: East African Publishing House, 1969); A.D. Roberts, ed., *Tanzania Before 1900* (Nairobi: East African Publishing House, 1968).
[33] Cited in Denoon and Kuper, "Nationalist Historians," p. 335.
[34] Cited in Denoon and Kuper, "Nationalist Historians," p. 335.
[35] T. Ranger, *The African Churches of Tanzania*, Historical Association of Tanzania Paper No. 5 (Nairobi: East African Publishing House, n.d.), p. 4. Cited in Denoon and Kuper, "Nationalist Historians," p. 336.
[36] Denoon and Kuper, "Nationalist Historians," p. 336.
[37] Denoon and Kuper, "Nationalist Historians," p. 337. Ranger responded by talking of "Denoon and Kuper's fantasies about our lack of interest in mission sources and our contempt for anthropology..." "An Answer," p. 54.
[38] Denoon and Kuper, "Nationalist Historians," p. 341.
[39] J.E.G. Sutton, "The Peopling of Tanzania," in Kimambo and Temu, p. 1, cited in Denoon and Kuper, "Nationalist Historians," p. 342.
[40] Denoon and Kuper, "Nationalist Historians," p. 342.
[41] Denoon and Kuper, "Nationalist Historians," p. 346.
[42] Denoon and Kuper, "Nationalist Historians," p. 347.
[43] Ranger, "An Answer," p. 59.
[44] J.D. Fage, "Slavery and the Slave Trade in West African History," *Journal of African History*, X, 3, (1969): 393-404 (hereafter cited as "Slavery").
[45] Philip D. Curtin, *The Dimensions of the Atlantic Slave Trade* (Madison, Wisconsin: University of Wisconsin Press, 1969), cited in Fage, "Slavery," p. 398.
[46] Fage, "Slavery," p. 403.
[47] Fage, "Slavery," p. 404.

[48]"In default of evidence of the relation between the existence of an external demand for slaves and of slavery and an internal trade in slaves for the West African Sudan, we must turn to the Guinea area, where commonly the first truly external traders were the European sea-traders, who first arrived on the coasts in the fifteenth century. The evidence for Upper Guinea, from the Gambia to modern Liberia, has been analysed by Dr. Walter Rodney." Fage, "Slavery," p. 395. Fage's footnote reference is to Walter Rodney, "African Slavery and Other Forms of Social Oppression on the Upper Guinea Coast in the Context of the Atlantic Slave-Trade," *Journal of African History*, VII, 3 (1966): 431-443. Since Fage's article appeared, Rodney's monograph has come out: Walter Rodney, *A History of the Upper Guinea Coast, 1545-1800* (Oxford: Clarendon, 1970).

[49]Fage, "Slavery," p. 397.

[50]Fage, "Slavery," p. 397.

[51]Fage, "Slavery," pp. 400, 402.

[52]Fage, "Slavery," p. 403.

[53]Rodney, *History of the Upper Guinea Coast*, p. 199

[54]Rodney, *History of the Upper Guinea Coast*, p. 199.

[55]Walter Rodney, *West Africa and the Atlantic Slave-Trade*, Historical Association of Tanzania Paper No. 2 (Nairobi: East African Publishing House, 1967), p. 21.

[56]Rodney, *History of the Upper Guinea Coast*, p. 118.

[57]C.C. Wrigley, "Historicism in Africa: Slavery and State Formation," *African Affairs*, 70, 279 (April 1971): 113 (hereafter cited as "Historicism").

[58]Wrigley, "Historicism," p. 117.

[59]Wrigley, "Historicism," p. 116.

[60]Wrigley, "Historicism," p. 121.

[61]Wrigley, "Historicism," p. 124.

[62]Walter Rodney, *How Europe Underdeveloped Africa* (London: Bogle-L'Ouverture Publications, 1972), p. 80.

[63]Ivan Hrbek, "Towards a Periodisation of African History," in Ranger, ed., *Emerging Themes of African History*, pp. 37-52 (hereafter cited as "Periodisation").

[64]See Hrbek, "Periodisation," pp. 38-42.

[65]Hrbek, "Periodisation," p. 45.

[66]Hrbek, "Periodisation," p. 48.

[67]Hrbek, "Periodisation," p. 49.

[68]Hrbek, "Periodisation," p. 51.

[69]See Smir Amin, "Sous-développement et dépendance en Afrique noire contemporaine," *Partisans*, No. 64, (mars-avril 1972): 3-34.

[70]All the statements in this paragraph are dealt with in great detail in my *The Modern World-System I: Capitalist Agriculture and the Origins of the European World-Economy in the Sixteenth Century* (New York: Academic Press, 1974).

[71]I elaborate this argument in "The Rise and Future Demise of the World Capitalist System: Concepts for Comparative Analysis," *Comparative Studies in Society and History* XVI, 4, Oct. 1974, 389-415.

Africa in a Capitalist World

⁷²"Experience has proved it: of all forms of breeding, that of human cattle is one of the hardest. If slavery is to pay when applied to large-scale enterprises, there must be plenty of cheap human flesh on the market. You can only get it by war or slave-raiding. So a society can hardly base much of its economy on domesticated human beings unless it has at hand feebler societies to defeat or raid." Marc Bloch, "The Rise of Dependent Cultivation and Seignorial Institutions," in *Cambridge Economic History of Europe*, I, M.M. Postan, ed., *The Agrarian Life of the Middle Ages*, 2nd ed., (Cambridge: at the University Press, 1966), p. 247.

⁷³See my *The Modern World-System I*, ch. VI.

⁷⁴See Rodney: "It is obvious that because of the Atlantic slave-trade people could not lead their ordinary lives. The majority of the population of West Africa lived by farming, and agriculture must have suffered during that period. In the first place, the loss of so many people represented a loss of labour in the fields. In the second place, those who were left behind had little reason to plant crops which they might never be around to reap. At the end of the eighteenth century, one of the arguments used by Europeans who wanted to abolish the Atlantic slave-trade was that abolition would allow the Africans to work and produce other commodities which Europeans could buy. They pointed out that as long as the Atlantic slave-trade continued people found it extremely difficult to carry on worthwhile activities." *West Africa and the Atlantic Slave-Trade*, p. 16.

⁷⁵Vitorino Magalhães Godinho, *Os Descrubrimentos e a Economia Mundial*, Volume 2 (Lisboa: Ed. Arcadia, 1965), esp. pp. 528, 532.

⁷⁶"The Venetian Cadamasto was told in 1455 that voyages to Guinea yielded a return of between six and ten times the outlay...Elsewhere [in West Africa] the Portuguese gathered less dazzling but still substantial riches." A.F.C. Ryder, "Portuguese and Dutch in West Africa before 1800," in J.F. Ade Ajayi and Ian Espie, eds., *A Thousand Years of West African History* (Ibadan, Nigeria: Ibadan University Press, 1965), pp. 220, 222.

⁷⁷Christopher Fyfe, "West African Trade, A.D. 1000-1800," in Ajayi and Espie, *A Thousand Years of West African Trade*, p. 248 (hereafter cited as "West African Trade").

⁷⁸Fyfe, "West African Trade," p. 249.
⁷⁹Fyfe, "West African Trade," p. 249.
⁸⁰Fyfe, "West African Trade," p. 252.
⁸¹Rodney, *History of the Upper Guinea Coast*, ch. VII.
⁸²Rodney, *History of the Upper Guinea Coast*, p. 172.
⁸³Rodney, *History of the Upper Guinea Coast*, p. 172.
⁸⁴Rodney, *History of the Upper Guinea Coast*, p. 172.
⁸⁵Rodney, *History of the Upper Guinea Coast*, p. 176.
⁸⁶Rodney, *History of the Upper Guinea Coast*, p. 177.
⁸⁷Rodney, *History of the Upper Guinea Coast*, p. 188-189.
⁸⁸Rodney, *History of the Upper Guinea Coast*, p. 192.
⁸⁹Rodney, *History of the Upper Guinea Coast*, p. 199.
⁹⁰See my "The Colonial Era in Africa: Changes in the Social Structure," in L.H.

Gann and Peter Duignan, eds., *Colonialism in Africa, 1870-1960,* Vol. II: *The History and Politics of Colonialism, 1914-1960* (Cambridge: at the University Press, 1970), pp. 399-421.

[91] Samir Amin, "Transitional Phases in Sub-Saharan Africa," *Monthly Review,* 25, 5 (Oct. 1973): 54-55 (hereafter cited as "Transitional Phases").

[92] See "The Range of Choice: Constraints on the Policies of Governments of Contemporary African Independent States," in Michael F. Lofchie, ed., *The State of the Nations* (University of California Press, 1971), pp. 19-33.

[93] See "Dependence in an Interdependent World: The Limited Possibilities of Transformation Within the Capitalist World-Economy," *African Studies Review,* XVII, 1 April 1974, pp. 1-26.

[94] Amin, "Transitional Phases," p. 56.

Africa, the United States, and the World-Economy: The Historical Bases of American Policy

We normally define the "foreign policy" of a "state" as that set of short- and middle-run objectives vis-à-vis the world polity that are seen as serving the "interests" of the "state." However, there are hidden in such an innocuous definition all sorts of assumptions and debatable points.

One such assumption is that state policy (decisions taken by political leaders and bureaucrats) can have an impact on some institutions (primarily, but certainly not exclusively, other governments) that will significantly affect the allocation of power and hence the distribution of reward in the world-system. This is no doubt true to some extent, but clearly it is infinitely more true of core-states of the world-economy (such as the United States) than it is of states considered in the economic periphery (as for example probably all African independent states are today).

A second assumption is that "states" have "interests"; this is more debatable. Lenin spoke of the state as the "executive committee of the ruling class," and this is perfectly acceptable as a rough approximation, provided several points are noted: "executive committees" are not absolute monarchs but operate within constraints; groups with differing interests located within the framework of the state have some access to political power, albeit considerably unequal access; groups outside the state often have access to power within that state's political machinery; and the extent to which a "ruling class" is homogeneous and united varies over time and space.

A third assumption is that since a state's interests are relatively continuous, the foreign policy of a state will survive minor (and perhaps even major) perturbations of regime.

A fourth assumption is that one can locate these interests somewhere. Their usual location is internal to the state. But insofar as interests refer to shares in the distribution of profit, they must relate to the economic framework within which profit is distributed. And this framework in the modern world-system is not a national one but that of the world-economy, which therefore means that the primary interest of a state is to obtain or retain an optional position within this world-economy—to be in its core rather than its periphery or semiperiphery. Since, however, this study is concerned with relational concepts—core, periphery, etc.—by definition it is not possible for all states to have an optional position.

Since in addition the history of the system shows that it is possible to shift position,[1] all states must be in a situation of perpetual insecurity, from which it follows that foreign policies are never benign, always assertive (or aggressive if one wants to be pejorative), and never ultimately bound by formalities. This viewpoint, essentially espoused by such different personalities as Machiavelli, Henry John Palmerston, Lenin, and Hans Morgenthau, is occasionally deprecated as "cynical"; but such deprecation is ideological rhetoric. The view is rather a simple description of one of the primary mechanisms of a capitalist world-economy—the use of state machineries not to facilitate but to distort the law of supply and demand in the world market as the primary determinant of prices, and hence of profits; the rest is commentary.

The point of this is that if one wants to understand the bases of American foreign policy toward Africa, one has to place both America and Africa in their historical relationship to the evolving world-economy.

HISTORICAL DEVELOPMENTS

The historical development of America's role in the world-economy is well known, certainly in its gross outlines. From the American Revolution to the Civil War there were two somewhat contradictory trends in American economic growth. On the one hand there was an industrial sector that sought to use the federal government in classic mercantilist ways— increasing barriers to external trade, both by investment in infrastructure and removal of domestic barriers, and protecting American industry against the then world hegemonic power, Great Britain, by means of a tariff. And on the other hand there was an expanding cash-crop exporting sector that developed ever-increasing ties of dependence to Britain.[2] For whatever reasons adduced,[3] this internal conflict of interest led to the North's victory in the Civil War and to the enactment of the series of measures (from railway construction to the Homestead Act, to high tariffs) that permitted the remarkable industrial surge in America during the late nineteenth century.

As British economic hegemony became increasingly precarious, in a virtually steady decline from 1873 to the First World War,[4] the United States emerged as a more effective challenger to Britain than Germany or France; the United States closed off its own market to Britain and then began to compete as an exporter, primarily to Latin America, the Far East, and Europe. This situation was climaxed by the acute differentials in U.S. and British growth patterns brought about by the First World War. The United States replaced Britain as the world's leading economic power as of that time, but held unquestioned hegemony only in the period from 1945 to 1965, during which time the United States came to be faced with the same kind of challenges from Western Europe and Japan that Great Britain had faced from the United States and Germany as of 1873.

The history of Africa's involvement in the world-economy was quite different from that of the United States. One can date Africa's incorporation into the capitalist world-economy at about 1750,[5] the time of the upturn of the European world-economy from its century-long relative contraction. Africa subsequently went through three stages of development—informal empire, colonial rule, and decolonization—that mark three points on a curve of ever-deepening involvement in the world-economy.

Africa's informal empire, which ran roughly from 1750 to 1885, marks the early phase of limited cash-crop exports, including in the first 75 years or so the transformation of slave export from the "luxury" trade it had once been to the bulk staple it then became. Slavery as a staple coming from a peripheral area of the world-economy is ultimately uneconomic[6] and was replaced in West Africa by "legitimate commerce," as in the case of the famous palm oil for soap. Essentially, however, during this period Africa was a minor producer for the world-economy and a minor importer.

It was the world-economic contraction beginning in 1873 that ultimately got the "scramble for Africa" going in the sense that it led France and Germany to push toward "pre-emptive colonization" of Africa and Britain to react defensively by emulation.[7] European conquest of Africa was a process in which it took 20 years to achieve even the primary "pacification." But this was just in time for the world-economic upturn at the beginning of the twentieth century; the expanded world market created a demand for the launching of the cultivation of the series of African cash crops that colonial agricultural and tax policies now enforced, as well as for the exploitation of African mineral resources.

The initial African expansion soon reached a relatively stable plateau,[8] in part because of the limitations of production given the mode of social organization, and in part because the world saw another agricultural depression from 1921 to the Second World War. The post-World War II rise in world demand for African primary resources coincided with both the rise of African nationalist movements and the conversion of European powers to decolonization—with the exception of course of Portugal, which was too weak to neocolonize.[9]

What decolonization did was to create in Africa the social framework in which it would be possible to convert the totality of agricultural land to cash-cropping (which would represent a considerable increase in land area used to this end), expand to a maximum the exploitation of mineral resources, and encourage the development of a limited sector of primary transformation industries (thereby reinforcing world demand for the machinery exports of core countries). Widespread expropriation of underproductive food-growing regions would politically have been extremely expensive in a colonial structure but it was perfectly feasible for independent African states to take such action, whether by decree or by the free play of the market, especially in the wake of what have been ever more frequent droughts.

Thus far in this discussion the U.S. role in the world-economy has been described without mentioning Africa and Africa's role without mentioning the United States. This is no accident because thus far the economic histories of the two regions have had virtually no direct linkage, although of course both histories are the consequence of the workings of the same world economic system and hence each presupposed what was happening in the other region.

Without direct linkage between two regions there would normally be very little place for the overt appearance of diplomacy. Normally an absence of diplomatic initiatives by a core nation vis-a-vis a peripheral area of the world-economy would be designated as a foreign policy of "indifference." And it would not be grievously off-base to so characterize U.S. foreign policy toward Africa from 1789 to 1960, and quite possibly to today.[10]

But "indifference" is far too neutral a term. In fact in general it is the case that from her perspective the United States was perfectly content with what was happening in Africa and therefore seldom felt any need to intervene in a significant way. However, a review of U.S. attitudes toward the main political issues of Africa since 1945 may reveal the possible pattern for the future. For we may expect that the U.S. foreign policy of "indifference," or perhaps it should be called "relative satisfaction," is now coming to an end.

The primary political issue in Africa since the Second World War has been the struggle for national independence, led by nationalist movements in the various units of colonial administration. This struggle has had two phases. The first was the so-called downward sweep of African liberation, which involved proclamations of independence beginning in 1956, climaxing in the cascade of independences won in 1960, and more or less petering out in 1964 when Zambia became the last major country to achieve independence in this wave. The wave included virtually all colonies that had belonged to Britain, France, Belgium, and Italy.

The second phase—now at an end—was the struggle for national liberation in Portuguese and southern Africa. In this phase African nationalists have faced a far stronger opposition to decolonization (or its equivalent, majority rule) from Portugal and the white African settlers (in Angola, Mozambique, and Rhodesia).

The demands of the nationalist movements in both phases have been essentially identical in each territory. The movements have utilized virtually the same moral and pragmatic arguments to win adherence to their cause, both from their own populations and from the outside world. In every instance the movements initially engaged in political activities to obtain their objectives, and in virtually every instance there have been moments of disorder and rioting. In all cases except Portuguese and southern Africa, the colonial power responded by first deprecating the strength and legitimacy of the nationalist movement but later negotiating a transfer of power, usually to the very same nationalist movement. In those cases where the willingness to negotiate came relatively late—for example in Kenya or Algeria, where the presence of settler communities retarded this development—the movement for independence took the form of armed struggle, as it is doing today in Portuguese and southern Africa.

Throughout this whole development U.S. foreign policy has been remarkably consistent; John Foster Dulles set the tone for it on June 1, 1953, and there has been no substantial deviation from his proclaimed policy in the subsequent years. In a speech to the American nation following a trip to the Near East and Southern Asia, Dulles made the following remarks regarding the issue of colonialism:

> Most of the peoples of the Near East and Southern Asia are deeply concerned about political independence for themselves and others. They are suspicious of the colonial powers. The United States too is suspect because, it is reasoned, our NATO alliances with France and Britain require us to try to preserve or restore the old colonial interests of our allies.
>
> I am convinced that United States policy has been unnecessarily ambiguous in this matter. The leaders of the countries I visited fully recognize that it would be a disaster if there were any break between the United States and Great Britain and France. They don't want this

to happen. However, without breaking from the framework of Western unity, we can pursue our traditional dedication to political liberty. In reality, the Western powers can gain, rather than lose, from an orderly development of self-government.

I emphasize, however, the word "orderly." Let none forget that the Kremlin uses extreme nationalism to bait the trap by which it seeks to capture the dependent peoples.[11]

U.S. POLICY IN THE COLONIAL PERIOD

The essential elements of U.S. policy in the colonial period are (1) the priority of world political alliances for the United States, (2) the urging of the wisdom of decolonization on Europe, and (3) the opposing of any political "radicalism" in Africa. Within the framework of these premises there has been some disagreement about pace; the conservative viewpoint has differed from the liberal viewpoint in the assessment of how strongly and how publicly one might "urge the wisdom" of decolonization, and how seriously to take the radical rhetoric of particular African leaders or movements.

Thus for example in 1955 Dulles said that Goa was a "province" of Portugal and not a "colony,"[12] while the then U.S. representative to the United Nations, Henry Cabot Lodge, said that Algeria was "administratively an integral part of the French Republic," and that it would be a "grave danger to the future of the United Nations [if it took up] questions whose consideration would conflict with the provisions of Article 2, paragraph 7 [of the U.N. Charter]."[13]

A different viewpoint was expressed by the then Senator John F. Kennedy, at that time chairman of the Subcommittee on Africa of the Senate Foreign Relations Committee. Kennedy introduced Senate Resolution 153 (85th Congress) on July 2, 1957, which urged the U.S. government to

> place the influence of the United States behind efforts. . .to achieve a solution that will recognize the independent personality of Algeria and establish the basis for a settlement interdependent with the French neighboring states. [The Resolution further provided that if no progress were shown by the following General Assembly of the United Nations, the United States should] support an international effort to derive for Algeria the basis for an orderly achievement of independence.[14]

Dulles commented the same day that the "problem of Algeria is one of exceptional difficulty," noting that "if anyone is interested in going after colonialism, there are a lot better places to go after it than in the case of France"; he cited Latvia, East Germany, and Hungary.[15]

No doubt under President Kennedy the United States was willing to be slightly more open in its position, occasionally voting in the United Nations in favor of resolutions critical of Portuguese colonialism. On the occasion of a resolution on the situation in Angola, Adlai Stevenson, the U.S. representative to the United Nations, on March 15, 1961, told the Security Council:

> The United States would be remiss in its duties as a friend of Portugal if it failed to express honestly its conviction that step-by-step planning within Portuguese territories and its acceleration is now imperative for the successful political and economic and social advancement of all inhabitants under Portuguese administration—advancement, in brief, toward full self-determination.[16]

Stevenson's principal argument was the danger that if Portugal did not engage in "step-by-step planning," the result would be similar to the situation in the Congo, then in turmoil:

> I do not think it would be straining the truth to conclude that much of the Congo's problems result from the fact that the pressure of nationalism rapidly overtook the preparation of the necessary foundation essential to the peaceful and effective exercise of sovereign self-government. The important thing for us, then, is to insure that similar conditions do not exist for the Angola of tomorrow.[17]

But except for the minor nuance of voting for a few U.N. resolutions on Portugal and on South Africa, U.S. attitudes toward nationalism in as yet nonindependent African states were substantially the same under Presidents Kennedy and Johnson as under President Eisenhower; the United States still argued that primary initiative lay and should lie with Europe. Thus it never supported any U.N. resolution on Southern Rhodesia that was opposed by the United Kingdom. And on March 18, 1965, then Assistant Secretary of State for African Affairs G. Mennen Williams included in his "five pillars" of U.S. policy one that urged "encouragement of other countries of the world, particularly the former European metropoles, to recognize their continuing responsibilities toward Africa."[18]

Thus it was only in the continuing logic of these basic premises that under President Nixon, Assistant Secretary of State for African Affairs David Newsom stated U.S. Policy toward southern Africa in this fashion on September 21, 1971:

> Our differences with the African independent nations are essentially over how change in southern Africa will be achieved... not whether.... We believe change will come in southern Africa. Economic and demographic pressures make this inevitable...We can understand the impatience which leads to demands for the use of force. Nevertheless, we see little prospect for its effective use in bringing change in southern Africa, and we cannot favor its use.[19]

Thus basically on the political issue that for Africans has taken priority ever since the Second World War— decolonization—U.S. policy has been quite consistent. It has adhered to a position that was characterized by M'hamed Yazid, when he was the Algerian National Liberation Front's (FLN) representative at the United Nations during Algeria's War of Independence, as "anti-colonialism de dimanche."

This however did not preclude behind-the-scenes U.S. pressure on slow-moving colonial authorities, as is said to have occurred vis-à-vis Belgium in 1960 and vis-à-vis Portugal during the Kennedy era. But neither at the other end of the continuum did it preclude backing up the efforts of a colonial power to contain an overly radical nationalist movement by the tactic of ceding power to a friendlier group, as in the U.S. support for France's manipulation in Cameroun just prior to Cameroun's independence in 1960. This U.S. support for France took the form of opposition within the United Nations to a U.N.-supervised preindependence election in Cameroun that would have tested the true strength of the nationalist movement in question, the Union Populaire du Cameroun (UPC).

However, on the whole the United States relied on the steady workings of the various forces present on the African scene to bring about results that in general were in the U.S. interest. For the United States operated in the confident expectation that direct U.S. involvement was not necessary to bring about the dual U.S. objective: an expansion of African involvement in the world-economy, and a relative open door for U.S. investment and trade. Both the continuation of direct colonial rule and the coming to power of revolutionary regimes might threaten this, but the "wind of change" was both strong enough and gentle enough to make both unlikely (except possibly in southern Africa).

U.S. POLICY IN THE ERA OF INDEPENDENCE

Once independence began to be achieved the United States moved quickly to increase its direct diplomatic links with the various African states. The then Vice President Nixon, heading the U.S. delegation for the celebration of the independence of Ghana on March 6, 1957, proceeded to make a tour of the various independent states (few in number at the time); and in his report of April 7, 1957, to President Eisenhower he recommended the creation within the U.S. Department of State of a Bureau of African Affairs.[20] Such a bureau was in fact created on August 20, 1958. When a whole series of African states became independent in 1960, the Eisenhower administration hesitated to name separate ambassadors to each state, especially in the former French territories. This was partly out of deference to French sensibilities. One of the first measures of the Kennedy administration was to decide that each African state would have its own ambassador. This symbolic move was followed by a further gesture: President Kennedy sought to arrange meetings with as many African heads of state as possible. He named presumably "sympathetic" ambassadors to Guinea[21] and to the United Arab Republic (UAR),[22] two African countries with whom U.S. relations had been somewhat strained.

The concrete meaning of these symbols has to be measured in two arenas: forms and degree of U.S. economic transfers to African governments; and reactions to, and involvement in, internal upheavals in African independent states.

If one looks at U.S. economic involvement in Africa, whether via private enterprise or government assistance, the overall figures are small. Taking 1965 as an optimal year (after most African states had achieved independence and before the recent perturbations in the world market had set in), one finds in the following figures that Africa represents a total of about 4 percent of both U.S. exports and imports, of which South Africa represents about a third (the figures are in $ million): in fact the pattern, going back to the period beginning after the Second World War and continuing to now, has remained fairly steady.

Exports		Imports	
Worldwide	$27,346.2	Worldwide	$21,366.4
Africa, total	1,224.1	Africa, total	875.1
South Africa	437.8	South Africa	225.1

Source: *Survey of Current Business* 46, no. 12 (December 1966).

Looking at the book value of U.S. investment abroad, it is notable that despite a fairly continuous worldwide increase, South Africa has continuously represented about 1 percent of the total (see Table 1). The rest of Africa represented another 1 percent up to about 1960, when it jumped to about 3 percent.

TABLE 1. Book Value of U.S. Investment Abroad ($ million).

	All Regions	Africa	South Africa	Rest of Africa
1929	7,527	130	77	53
1936	6,690	120	55	65
1943	7,861	131	50	81
1950	11,788	287	140	147
1957	25,262	664	301	363
1965	49,328	1,918	529	1,390
1971	86,000	3,833	964	2,869

Note: Figures for "Rest of Africa" in 1929 and 1936 include French Oceania, Indochina, and Thailand.

Source: Figures are drawn from the following issues of *Survey of Current Business*: vol. 32, no. 2, December 1952, Table 1, p. 8; vol. 40, no. 9, September 1960, Table 1, p. 20; vol. 47, no. 9, September 1967, Table 3, p. 42; vol. 52, no. 11, November 1972, Table 7a, pp. 28-29.

A look at U.S. trade relations with African countries other than South Africa reveals that for 1965 only four of these countries exported more than $50 million worth of goods to the United States (Ethiopia, Ghana, Liberia, and Nigeria) and only six imported more than $50 million from the United States (Egypt, Liberia, Libya, Morocco, Nigeria, and Zaire). This represents the absolute importance of these countries as U.S. trading partners. However, it can also be discerned how relatively important the United States was to each of them by seeing how the United States ranked as a trading partner compared to other countries: the United States was the main recipient of exports for only four of these African countries—Ethiopia (which sent the United States about three-quarters of its total exports), and Guinea, Liberia, and Uganda (each of which sent the United States less than half but more than a third of its exports). The United States was the main country from which goods were imported only in the case of Guinea (about half) and that of Liberia (about two-thirds).

Figures for total U.S. aid (all forms) to African nations for the period from 1946 to 1967 are shown in Table 2; since U.S. aid has been drastically reduced in the years since 1967 these figures can be taken as a reasonable base from which to draw various inferences.

Those African countries for whom overall U.S. aid figures are relatively high (defining "high" generously), either in absolute terms (over $100 million) or on a per capita basis (over $10) or in both cases, fall into five categories, as shown in Table 3.

Each of these categories merits brief attention. In the first category, Liberia of course is the historic "semicolony" of the United States, and a country with significant U.S. investments; Libya and Morocco were the sites of two major U.S. air bases, both now discontinued. The nations in the second category—Algeria, Guinea, Tunisia, and Zaire—show fluctuating figures over the years, almost directly correlated with the relations these countries had with France (and in the case of Zaire with Belgium). For example over half of all U.S. aid to Algeria was given in the two years immediately following Algerian independence when relations with France were at a nadir. The nations in the third category are all in northeast Africa, strategically overlapping with the Arab world. Three of these countries— Egypt, Somalia, and Sudan—are Moslem and notoriously "neutralist" in their foreign policy, receiving considerable aid over time from Russia as well as from the United States; the fourth, Ethiopia, has come to be in many ways a second (after Liberia) U.S. "historic" interest, with key U.S. military communications installations and the largest single amount of U.S. military aid ($124.1 million).

These three categories suggest that the United States has paid primary attention to those countries in which it had direct military interests and those countries in which it could not rely on its European allies to oversee the political and economic "needs" of the regimes in power.

From this point of view both the fourth and fifth categories may seem to be anomalies, but they are anomalies easily explained. The fourth category—Ghana, Nigeria, and Sierra Leone, which comprise ex-British West Africa—received extra U.S. attention for several reasons: (1) the British objected to U.S. ties less than the French did because of the so-called special relationship Britain developed with the United States in the period after 1945; (2) insofar as Blacks in the United States served as an interested pressure group, the primary historical orientation had been to only a few countries—Liberia, Ethiopia, South Africa, and British West Africa; (3) the former British territories offered no linguistic barrier; and (4) Ghana was the "first" Black African state to obtain independence, and Nigeria was the largest in population. As for Gabon and Zambia, which comprise the fifth category of major U.S. aid recipients in Africa, they are both countries with rich natural resources and relatively small population.

TABLE 2. U.S. Aid to African Nations, 1946-67.

Nation	Total Aid ($ million, including—in parentheses—military aid)	1967 Population (in millions)	Per Capita (rounded)
Algeria	193.2	12.4	16
Botswana	5.1	0.6	1
Burundi	6.8	3.3	2
Cameroun	28.3 (0.2)	5.5	6
Central African Republic	4.4	1.4	3
Chad	7.4	3.4	2
Congo (Brazzaville)	2.1	0.9	2
Dahomey	10.5 (0.1)	2.5	4
Ethiopia	222.3 (124.11)	23.4	10
Egypt	1,038.9	30.9	34
Gabon	7.0	0.5	18
Gambia	1.0	0.3	3
Ghana	209.9	8.4	25
Guinea	71.4 (1.0)	3.7	19
Ivory Coast	32.8 (1.1)	4.0	8
Kenya	59.7	9.9	6
Lesotho	2.1	0.9	2
Liberia	243.2 (6.9)	1.1	221
Libya	208.5 (16.5)	1.7	123
Malagasy Republic	12.5	6.9	2
Malawi	14.0	4.1	3
Mali	18.6 (2.8)	4.8	4
Mauritania	3.4	1.1	3
Mauritius	0.5	0.8	1
Morocco	586.7 (54.0)	14.2	41
Niger	12.9 (0.1)	3.5	4
Nigeria	207.2 (1.5)	44.5	5
Rwanda	6.1	3.3	2
Senegal	27.8 (2.8)	3.7	8
Sierra Leone	36.2	2.4	16
Somali Republic	68.5	2.7	25
Southern Rhodesia	7.0	4.5	2
Sudan	127.4 (2.2)	14.3	9
Swaziland	0.1	0.4	*
Tanzania	56.4	10.9	5
Togo	13.2	1.7	8
Tunisia	521.1 (24.9)	4.5	116
Uganda	27.9	7.9	3
Upper Volta	9.6 (0.1)	5.1	2
Zaire	372.8 (20.9)	16.7	22
Zambia	49.2	4.0	12

*Less than half a dollar.
Source: Compiled by author from figures of U.S. Agency for International Development, in *AID Economic Data Book—Africa* (PB 180-910) and *AID Economic Book—Near East and South Asia* (PB 180-909).

Hence even a standard percentage of U.S. aid, if given in relation to the overall level of U.S. contribution to the world market, appears as high in the per capita calculations.

Thus the aid figures tend to confirm the analysis that the U.S. "interest" in Africa was expressed primarily and preferably through the agency of western European intermediaries. It was only when this was not possible, either because of some direct pressures originating within the United States or because of and absence or a breakdown (even temporary) of western European political capabilities, that the United States moved in directly. And even then on the whole it was scarcely massive intervention, although massive intervention generally was not necessary.

TABLE 3. Major U.S. Aid Recipients among African Nations, 1946-67.

Category of African Nations	Total Aid (in $ millions)	Per Capita Aid (rounded)
Direct U.S. interests		
Liberia	243.2	221
Libya	208.5	123
Morocco	586.7	41
Quarreled with European ex-metropole		
Algeria	193.2	16
Guinea	71.4	19
Tunisia	521.1	116
Zaire	372.8	22
No obvious metropole		
Egypt	1,038.9	34
Ethiopia	222.3	10
Somalia	68.5	25
Sudan	127.4	9
Ex-British West Africa		
Ghana	209.9	25
Nigeria	207.2	5
Sierra Leone	36.2	16
Other		
Gabon	7.0	18
Zambia	49.2	12

Source: Compiled by author from figures of Agency for International Development, in *AID Economic Data Book—Africa* (PB 180-910).

U.S. INTERVENTION

This then raises the question of whether there have in fact been situations in Africa in which massive intervention might have been seen by the United States as "necessary." There was clearly no African situation similar to that in Vietnam, where the nationalist movement was led by a Communist party in a country bordering a state governed by a Communist party. Nor was there a situation similar to that either in the Dominican Republic or in Cuba, which were both geographically close to the United States and where the United States had long since renounced the idea of using European intermediaries for its own imperial interests. The situation in most of Africa was not even comparable to that in the Middle East, which involved not only a strategic commodity (oil) but geographical proximity to the USSR, and a U.S. commitment to Israel based in part on domestic political considerations.

Still for a world hegemonic power, which the United States certainly has been since 1945 (and probably since 1918), all natural resources are important, all political upheavals potentially dangerous, and all unfriendly regimes at least minor thorns. Considering the number of coups d'etat, attempted coups, and civil wars in Africa since 1960, it is noteworthy that only one country, Zaire, has been the scene of massive direct U.S. involvement; in all others the U.S. involvement has been indirect and/or discreet. Three questions should therefore be discussed: what accounted for U.S. involvement in Zaire; what accounted for U.S. "indirection" and/or "discretion" elsewhere; and whether the historical conditions that explain both of these phenomena are likely to continue?

Zaire (formerly the Congo) became an independent state on January 30, 1960: within ten days the army had rebelled, the government of the richest province in Zaire had proclaimed its secession, Belgian troops had invaded the country, and the central government had appealed for military and economic assistance from the United Nations. Subsequently there was a civil war in Zaire in 1963-64, and a rebellion/invasion in 1967; since that time, however, internal turmoil has been minimal.

Politically Zaire has gone through a number of regimes. It was first governed by a parliamentary coalition led by a radical nationalist, Prime Minister Patrice Lumumba, in 1960. There followed a period of almost a year in which there were two regimes—one headed by Lumumba and the other by President Joseph Kasavubu—both claiming to be the country's legitimate central government. A secession movement in Katanga province, led by Moise Tshombe, was finally overcome by U.N. forces in December 1962. In 1965 Kasavubu suspended parliament; and in December of that year there was a military coup d'etat led by General Joseph Mobutu, who has since ruled the country as president. American massive intervention can be seen at various points in this history. The United States gave full support not merely to U.N. assistance in the 1960-65 period but also to the arrogation by U.N. personnel of a degree of direct intervention in the Congo's internal affairs that was contested by many Congolese, in particular by Lumumba; several of the key U.N. Secretariat officials involved were U.S. citizens. The United States also lent its support (certainly after the event and quite probably before it) to the ouster of Lumumba by Kasavubu in 1961. It was this ouster (of dubious legality) that led to the crisis of legitimacy mentioned above. Following this the United States took the lead within the U.N. General Assembly for a credentials vote that ultimately favored Kasavubu over Lumumba.

Once the crisis of legitimacy was momentarily resolved, the United States gave active political and economic support to the new prime minister, Cyrille Adoula, who was considered by most observers to be the Congolese political leader most favorable to close political cooperation with the United States. After much hesitation the United States threw its weight behind the abovementioned U.N. military intervention that ended the secession in Katanga. During the civil war in 1964 the United States gave direct logistical support to the use of Belgian paratroopers to give crucial military edge to the central government (by then headed by Tshombe) against the forces of the Congolese National Liberation Council. When Mobutu overthrew the Kasavubu government in 1965 the United States responded to this action with active sympathy and perhaps covert assistance. When the Mobutu government was faced with a mercenary rebellion in 1967, crucial military assistance was given to the central government by the United States, both directly and through the intermediary of the Ethiopian government. Throughout this period and afterward the U.S. ambassador was generally considered to be the most influential diplomat in Kinshasa, Zaire.

What was it about Zaire that occasioned such massive activity on the part of the United States, unparalleled elsewhere on the African continent? There are certain obvious and elementary facts. Zaire is a large country centrally located. Its former metropole, Belgium, was by and large unable to maintain a steady patronage relationship with Zaire, partly because of the collapse of good relations at the time of independence and partly because Belgium was ultimately too weak herself, both militarily and economically. In addition Zaire is a wealthy country in terms of natural resources and industrial potential. The breakdown of internal order immediately after independence seemed intolerably great, and Zaire was also plagued by an acute shortage of personnel trained for higher bureaucratic positions as a result of Belgium's policies during the colonial era.

But all of this seems insufficient to account for both the degree and persistence of U.S. intervention in Zaire. Therefore was there anything else that made the Congo crisis seem to call for such a massive response by the United States? This observer thinks there was, but to uncover this one has to place the Congo crisis in the larger context of the evolving U.S. and African roles in the world-economy. U.S. intervention in the Congo was the opening salvo of more general U.S. involvement in southern Africa and it was brought on by an emerging world economic crisis whose early signs began appearing precisely around 1960.

It is still a bit early to sketch with any definitiveness what has been happening in the world-economy since 1945, but one can see the broad outlines of this situation: there has been a fairly steady inflation of prices and a fairly steady expansion of total world production; and there has of course been a fairly steady population rise. But the crucial problem is the relation of total production to effective demand. The world has been moving into a crisis in effective demand, presaging a downturn in total production and hence an acute competition for markets for manufactured goods and an acute concern for "export" unemployment.

The problem is that effective demand can only really be measured inferentially. In 1945 U.S. production was unrivaled because of the destruction of European plants by wartime devastation. The imbalance, however, was so great that although the socially expressed demand for goods was higher than world production, financial liquidity was low (the so-called dollar crisis) and hence credit had to be drastically expanded. The Marshall Plan served to restore European financial liquidity and the Korean War created a sharp rise in demand for imports from the economic periphery, including Africa. This rise in demand for peripheral primary production led to a rapid rise in net government income but also to a decline in real wages that fed the fires of anticolonial nationalism.[23] This accounted for an initial thrust toward decolonization that was reinforced by cold war competiton and a desire to expand total productivity in the periphery; thus the so-called downward thrust of African liberation, which found its first major stumbling block and ultimate brake in the Congo crisis.[24]

The "reconstruction" of western Europe (as well as of Japan) was fairly well completed by 1955 or 1960 at the latest, and the United States began to feel real competition in the world export market about this time. This accounts for two major developments: (1) the first steps toward detente, initiated by Eisenhower and Nikolai Bulganin in 1955, confirmed by the test ban agreement reached by Kennedy and Nikita Khrushchev in 1963, and made more concrete by the meetings of Nixon and Leonid Brezhnev in 1973; and (2) the beginning of a political disengagement of western Europe from the United States, launched and still principally sponsored by France, furthered by Willy Brandt's Ostpolitik, and yet to reach its apogee.

One of the critical factors in this overall situation has been the prospective patterns of world trade. The USSR wanted technological support to become a competitive exporter of manufactured goods, while both the United States and western Europe wanted ultimate access to the vast and potentially very lucrative Soviet internal market. And all three groups began to worry about peripheral areas both as prospective markets and as sources of the ever-expanding world demand for primary resources.

After the spiraling inflation launched by the credit expansion during the Vietnam War and the consequent U.S. balance-of-payments dilemmas; after the continuing infighting on the world currency scene; after the abandonment by the United States (in 1971) of its free-trade stance and the political truce with China; and after the so-called energy crisis and its effective reallocation of world income primarily at the expense of western Europe and Japan, to talk of a current crisis in effective demand may not seem very daring. But the turning points on the various curves all began somewhere between 1955 and 1960.

In this kind of competitive squeeze there are the competitors (the United States, western Europe, the USSR, and Japan); the areas that are relatively insignificant economically; and the areas that are arenas of competition because they are not only strong enough in resources, developed enough in infrastructure, and large enough in size to be significant suppliers and markets but also large enough to make a difference during a long-term world cyclical downturn. There are a number of these latter areas: China, Southeast Asia (especially Indonesia), the Indian subcontinent, the Arab world, southern Africa, Brazil, and probably Canada. Each of these areas may be seen as an arena of world politico-economic struggle in which of course one major element are the forces indigenous to the area.

In regard to Africa it is quite clear that it is no longer a viable policy for the United States to pursue its interests in so crucial an arena as southern Africa via European intermediaries since it is far from clear that U.S. and western European interests are identical, and since it is clear that internal political struggles will crucially affect the economic ties of southern Africa with the rest of the world in the coming 25 years.

U.S. involvement in Zaire was the launching pad of this new U.S. attitude toward southern Africa; Zaire was the first part of southern Africa to flirt with the idea of drastic political realignments, and 1960 was the point where

U.S. policy first became actively aware that there was a need to be concerned with southern Africa in view of long-term economic trends.

EXPLOSIVENESS OF THE CONGO CRISIS

There were two extremely explosive aspects to the Congo crisis. One was the political volatility of the Congo itself, which was the result of a combination of factors: a thinness of the layer of trained cadres (who elsewhere in Africa had tended to play a conservatizing role after independence); a lack of time for the Movement National Congolais (MNC), the potential movement of national control, to establish real dominance before independence (which meant the risk that it would use appeals to radical mobilizing techniques after independence to achieve this dominance); the populist style of Lumumba, the leading Congolese politician; and the relative wealth of the Congo, which put great resources at the disposal of the political leadership. Many of these were transitory phenomena, as time indeed has shown, but they meant that as of 1960 there was a clear possibility that a radical nationalist regime could in fact consolidate power.

While that in itself was quite probably enough for many to cast anathema upon it, the Congo situation was aggravated by the beginnings of the nationalist revolution in Angola. It is rather clear that a Lumumba government securely in power would have given extensive support to an Angolan national liberation movement (indeed such support was already in evidence immediately in the wake of Congolese independence). The potential of such support to Angola is analogous to what Tanzania later gave to the Mozambique Liberation Front (FRELIMO), with two differences: it would have come much earlier on, when the Portuguese were far less prepared for it, and the western world less certain of its immediate stance; and it would have come from a country—the Congo—with far more resources to throw into the fray. It could have made a considerable difference to the whole history of liberation movements in southern Africa. Portugal might have crumbled, Rhodesia might never have been able to proclaim a Unilateral Declaration of Independence (UDI), and South Africa might have found itself without buffers. The Congo crisis gave the white forces of southern Africa crucial time in which to consolidate their defensive structure.

It is not that all outside forces wanted to preserve a political status quo in Zaire; it is that various forces each wanted certain kinds of very "contained" change. The United States wanted what it eventually got: a politically stable, economically conservative regime in Zaire whose only true interest in Angola is to help establish there a regime of exactly the same variety. Translated into the terms of the Angolan liberation movements, this has meant obstruction of the Popular Movement for the Liberation of Angola (MPLA), considered a "dangerous" movement.

Britain was basically interested in the same outcome in Zaire as the United States sought. The British would probably have had a slight preference for a "Kenya" solution in Southern Rhodesia, but ultimately UDI represented only a minor annoyance. France would have preferred a regime in Zaire less tied to the United States but the French have been aware all along that by themselves they can only be marginally competitive; they have kept their options open in Zaire without investing much in the arena.

The same can ultimately be said of the USSR, which has played a continually passive role, responding to demands for aid—from Lumumba and from national liberation movements—by granting it but never excessively. For the USSR knew all along that the possibilities of detente and hence of technological assistance from the West were dependent on Soviet willingness to take part in the various areas of competition as a member of the "club" of the rich (which had its rules) rather than as an ally of indigenous radical forces. This is made very clear in a recent semi-official statement by Herbert J. Spiro, a member of the Planning and Coordination Staff of the U.S. Department of State. In a study of the implications for Africa of U.S.-Soviet detente, Spiro noted:

> The first—and the last—threat of a major Soviet-American confrontation in Africa occurred shortly after the Belgian Congo received its independence, and no real confrontation took place. . . . This is not to say that issues of substance have evaporated, either between the U.S. and the USSR, or among other states. . . .
> However, both sides evidently recognize that neither the nuclear nor the ideological issues can be resolved at present, so that everyone— and especially those to whom enormous power has given special global responsibilities—will have to learn to live with the postponment (in the Hegelian sense, *Aufhebung*) of their resolution.[25]

Finally the African white settlers wanted time, and that they got. They also wanted an active ally in Zaire, which probably would have made possible the overthrow of both Kenneth Kaunda in Zambia and Julius Nyerere in Tanzania, but that they did not get—thanks to the United States.

This points up the difference of interests between the United States and the white settlers, at least as it has thus far been demonstrated. The white settlers basically hope to construct a new industrial nexus in the world-economy and thereby use the current world economic contraction to bargain for far better trade terms than they presently have by profiting from the competition among the core states (including eventually even the USSR). Had their maneuvers in Zaire in the 1960s succeeded they might have been able to proceed to establish an economic common market that would have included both Zaire and Zambia as well as Angola, Mozambique, and Rhodesia—a group that would have been a truly powerful political instrument. This clearly ran counter to long-term U.S. interests, which is no doubt why France has flirted with assisting in the construction of the common market in southern Africa (both by its policy in Zaire and by its policy vis-à-vis South Africa).

Therefore apart from Zaire why did the United States not intervene on a massive scale elsewhere in Africa? The simple answer, already indicated, is that she did not need to; indeed such intervention would have been counterproductive.

From an economic point of view access to trade in areas other than southern Africa seemed and still seems marginally important to the United States. In any case the major obstacle to such trade, if there has been one, has been the resistance at various times and places to U.S. intrusion by the French government. And in the larger context of differences between the United States and France this issue has been a very minor one. On the affirmative side the most significant U.S. assistance was support for Ghana's Volta Dam project and for Guinea's FRIA aluminum development operations. In both cases U.S. firms were directly interested and in both cases it was hoped to gain political mileage out of such assistance. In the case of Ghana, Great Britain offered no objection. And in the case of Guinea, France's attitude was precisely the motive for the assistance. In both cases failure to assist would have been regarded as greater "interference" than the assistance, and might have led ultimately to Soviet aid, as in the 1960 Aswan Dam project.

From a political point of view U.S. intervention might have been occasioned by the existence of persistently unfriendly or unstable governments, either of which could possibly have resulted in consequences that the United States would have been unhappy about. But was this actually the case? Of the so-called radical governments almost all were very careful not to offend the United States on crucial matters; for example both Algeria (under Ahmed Ben Bella) and Guinea refused refueling rights to Soviet military transport during the Cuban confrontation of 1962. The only exceptions to this rule were the aforementioned Congo government of Lumumba and possibly Kwame Nkrumah's Ghana in the last years of his regime. There is no doubt that the United States assisted in world economic sanctions against Ghana in 1964-65 by being most unsympathetic to Ghana's balance-of-payments dilemmas, and that this international freeze contributed directly to Nkrumah's inability to satisfy internal complaints against the regime. The United States certainly treated Nkrumah's successor, General Ankrah, in a more sympathetic manner (just as it did with General Suharto after President Sukarno in Indonesia or with Augusto Pinochet after Salvador Allende in Chile).

Did Nkrumah therefore do anything to warrant an extra ingredient of U.S. hostility, as compared to Sekou Toure, Nyerere, Modibo Keita, or Ben Bella? No doubt yes; it was Nkrumah's combination of very active involvement in southern African internal affairs plus his active "subversion" of neighboring conservative regimes that ultimately seemed an intolerable perturbation of a relatively delicate status quo. It was probably the unpredictability and volatility of Nkrumah's intervention mechanisms combined with their persistence that aroused wrath and fear. When all is said and done, however, it is quite possible that even had the United States been studiously neutral in Ghanaian politics, Nkrumah might have had difficulty surviving. He had burned many internal bridges and stirred enmity among other governments in the region, so that the African forces arrayed against his regime were impressively strong.

As for the question of unstable governments in Africa there have been only a few instances of continued internal disorder. In the cases of the Sudan, Rwanda, and Burundi the issues remained local and never acquired an international dimension. In the cases of Cameroun and Chad there were French troops to aid the governments in putting down rebellions of groups with leftist orientations. And in the major civil war of Nigeria, there was the strange alignment of Britain and the USSR in support of the federal government and France and Portugal in support of Biafra. Thus in all these cases it was easy for the United States to take the stance of mild and passive support for the reigning government; the situations were all in hand.

CONCLUSION

Historically, given Africa's role in the world-economy and given a fundamentally expanding world-economy in the twentieth century, the United States has had little reason to have more than the mildest interest in

Africa. It has been content to leave Africa as a *chasse-gardee* of western Europe, occasionally prodding the Europeans to extend some timely political concessions to African elites and occasionally stepping in to fill gaps left by the European powers.

The only significant exception has been the U.S. policy toward Zaire in the years since Congolese independence in 1960. As noted above, this active concern for Zaire stems primarily from Zaire's key role in the emerging politics of southern Africa; moreover the United States is now in the process of becoming actively involved in the internal politics of southern Africa because of the long-term cyclical downturn of the world economy. As a result of this downturn southern Africa has become a key arena of economic competition among the core powers of the world economy.

This downturn was presaged around 1960, became widely visible in 1971, and as of this writing has not halted. It is clear that in view of this one can expect a massive political intervention by the United States in southern Africa in the coming years, even with the drastically changed conditions following the coup d'etat in Portugal.

But with whom will the United States ally itself politically? Clearly not with the African governments that are emerging in the area, whose policies are yet to be defined. And quite possibly not always with the white settler governments, with whom the relationship is bound to be ambiguous, given the contradictory nature of some of the interests involved. No doubt the optimal objective for U.S. interests to pursue is the erection of politically stable, economically friendly African-controlled regimes, of which Mobutu's Zaire stands as a model. Can this be achieved? Such a question goes beyond the frame-work of this study. However, among the possible scenarios that are within the realm of the conceivable for Africa over the next 10 to 20 years, one might consist of American pressure on South Africa to concede the independence of Namibia, with the establishment in Namibia of a government having the political complexion of Botswana; the restoration of Zimbabwe to the path of decolonization à la Kenya, as the British originally envisaged it; a split in the Nationalist Party in South Africa and a U.S. encouraged regime of the *verligtes* and the United Party combined with some of the Bantustans moving forward to independence; and a southern African common market going south from Zaire and Zambia and linked in various ways economically to the United States. None of this is beyond Henry Kissinger's fertile imagination.

Of course alternative scenarios are possible. For example the Rhodesian settlers might refuse to be sacrificed to the larger interests of the United States and the South African whites. The French and the Russians might combine forces to forestall various U.S. maneuvers. Revolutionary nationalist upheaval might be strong enough and simultaneous enough throughout the world so that the capacity of the United States to intervene in southern Africa would be seriously circumscribed. The possible regeneration of an African revolutionary movement inside South Africa might suddenly produce a militarily relevant internal opposition to the regime. In that case after years or so one might emerge with a southern African "common market" that would resemble in tone and outlook the China of today; in which case some worthy successor to Kissinger may also fly to Johannesburg.

Of the two scenarios which better serves the interests of the people of southern Africa? And which better serves the interests of the United States? The answer is obvious for both southern Africans and Americans; it depends on how you define those interests, in terms of which groups within both areas; it is for each of them to choose.

NOTES

[1]Immanuel Wallerstein, "Dependence and an Interdependent World: The Limited Possibilities of Transformation Within the Capitalist World-Economy," *African Studies Review*, (April 1974).

[2]See Stuart Bruchey, *The Roots of American Economic Growth, 1607-1861* (New York: Harper and Row, 1968).

[3]These conflicting trends are explained by Barrington Moore, Jr. in *The Social Origins of Democracy and Dictatorship* (Boston: Beacon Press, 1966), chap. 3.

[4]Whether this decline dates from the 1870s or the 1890s is a debatable subject; see E.H. Phelps-Brown and S.J. Handfield-Jones, "The Climacteric of the 1890's," *Oxford Economic Papers* n.s., vol. 4, no. 3 (October 1952): 279-89, and D.J. Coppock, "The Climacteric of the 1870's," *Manchester School of Economic and Social Science* 24, no. 1 (January 1956): 21-31.

[5]"Africa in a Capitalist World," *Issues* 2, no. 3 (Fall 1973): 1-11.

[6]Wallerstein, "The Rise and Future Demise of the World Capitalist System: Concepts for Comparative Analysis," *Comparative Studies in Society and History* XVI, 4, Oct. 1974, pp. 389-415.

[7]See "The Colonial Era in Africa: Changes in the Social Structure," in *Colonialism in Africa, 1870-1960*, vol, 2, *The History and Politics of Colonialism, 1914-1960*, ed. L.H. Gann and Peter Duignan (Cambridge: Cambridge University Press, 1970), pp. 399-421.

[8] Evidence of this in the Gold Coast is given in R. Szereszewski, *Structural Changes in the Economy of Ghana, 1891-1911* (London: Weidenfeld and Nicolson, 1965).

[9] Address delivered by the late Amilcar Cabral, October 20, 1971, Finland, published in *M. Amilcar Cabral a Visite la Finlande les 19-22 octobre 1971.*

[10] For example if one looks at the collection of basic documents of American foreign policy in the 1940s one finds not a single reference to Africa; see U.S. Congress, 81st Cong., 1st sess., Senate doc. no. 23, *A Decade of American Foreign Policy: Basic Documents, 1941-1949* (Washington: U.S. Government Printing Office, 1950). A similar collection for 1950-55 shows a reference only to Libya, with whom the United States signed an agreement for the use of defense facilities on September 9, 1954; see U.S. Department of State, *American Foreign Policy: Basic Documents, 1950-1955* (New York: Arno Press, 1971), vol. 2, pp. 2207-23.

[11] U.S. Department of State, *American Foreign Policy: Basic Documents, 1950-1955*, op. cit., pp. 2173-74.

[12] Ibid., pp. 2294-95.

[13] Ibid., p. 2301.

[14] U.S. Department of State, *American Foreign Policy: Current Documents, 1957* (New York: Arno Press, 1971), p. 1071 n.

[15] Ibid., pp. 1071-72.

[16] U.S. Department of State, *American Foreign Policy: Current Documents, 1961* (New York: Arno Press, 1971), p. 884.

[17] Ibid.

[18] U.S. Department of State, *American Foreign Policy: Current Documents, 1965*, Publication 8372 (Washington: U.S. Government Printing Office, 1968), p. 628.

[19] *Department of State Bulletin*, October 11, 1971, pp. 6-7.

[20] See U.S. Department of State, *American Foreign Policy: Current Documents, 1957*, op. cit., p. 1066.

[21] See William Attwood, *The Reds and the Blacks* (New York: Harper and Row, 1967).

[22] See John S. Badeau, "U.S.A. and U.A.R.: A Crisis in Confidence," *Foreign Affairs* 43, no. 2 (January 1965): 281-96.

[23] Elliot J. Berg, "Real Income Trends in West Africa, 1939-1960," in *Economic Transition in Africa*, ed. Melville J. Herskovits and Mitchell Harwitz (Evanston: Northwestern University Press, 1964), pp. 199-238.

[24] For further discussion see *Africa: The Politics of Unity* (New York: Random House, 1967).

[25] Herbert J. Spiro, "United States-Soviet Detente: Implications for Africa," paper delivered at Third International Congress of Africanists, Addis Ababa, December 9-19, 1973, pp. 3, 11.

The Three Stages of African Involvement in the World-Economy

The historiography of modern Africa has been a battleground of so-called Eurocentric versus so-called Afrocentric interpretations, and we have passed from early crude versions of each to a state of sophisticated and subtle arguments about analytical primacy. This intellectual battle of course reflects a wider social battle. But in the end both versions seem to me to be wrong. At a certain point in time, both Europe and Africa (or at least large zones of each) came to be incorporated into a single social system, a capitalist world-economy, whose fundamental dynamic largely controlled the actors located in both sectors of one united arena. It is in the reciprocal linkages of the various regions of the capitalist world-economy that we find the underlying determinants of social actions at a more local level.

It will be said that this ignores the relative autonomy of the acting groups. It does indeed in the sense that all systemic analysis denies the real autonomy of parts of a whole. It is not that there are no particularities of each acting group. Quite the contrary. It is that the alternatives available for each unit are constrained by the framework of the whole, even while each actor opting for a given alternative in fact alters the framework of the whole.

An analysis then must start from how the whole operates, and of course one must determine what is the whole in a given instance. Only then may we be able to draw an interpretative sketch of the historical outlines of the political economy of contemporary Africa, which is in my view an outline of the various stages (and modes) of its involvement in this capitalist world-economy.

The essential elements of a capitalist world-economy include the creation of a single world division of labor, production for profit in this world market, capital accumulation for expanded reproduction as a key mode of maximizing profit in the long run, emergence of three zones of economic activity (core, semiperiphery, and periphery) with not merely unequal exchange between them[1] but also persistent merchandise trade imbalances,[2] a multiplicity of state-structures (strongest in the core, weakest in the periphery), and the development over time of two principal world class-formations (a bourgeoisie and a proletariat) whose concrete manifestations are however complicated by the constant formation and reformation of a host of ethno-national groupings (Wallerstein, 1972, 1974a, 1975b). This historically unique combination of elements first crystallized in Europe in the sixteenth century (Wallerstein, 1974b), and the boundaries slowly expanded to include the entire world. This is why it could be thought of, quite misleadingly, as the "expansion of Europe" (when it was really the "expansion of the capitalist mode of production") and why it could lead to both Eurocentric and, by reaction, Afrocentric versions of modern African history.

Because the capitalist world-economy originated in one part of the globe and then expanded to include all parts, areas (such as Africa) not within the original boundaries were at one point in time outside the world-economy and at a later point in time incorporated into it. At the earlier point in time, to the extent that various African systems and the European world-economy were in trade contact one with the other, they were in each other's "external arena," and the trade was of a nature quite different from that which would subsequently occur between the African periphery and the European core of the capitalist world-economy. It is to this early period that we must first turn in order to clarify later developments.

Trade between external arenas is trade in "luxuries" (Wallerstein, 1974b). If it is not, if the trade becomes trade in essentials, the two arenas have become one, a single division of labor. "Luxury" may be defined in terms of consumption, as does Samir Amin: "In the strictest sense of the term, luxury goods are those for which the demand originates from the part of profit which is consumed" as opposed to demand coming from wages (1974).[3] Or it may be defined in terms of whether the products are themselves means of production, as does Piero Sraffa, luxury products being those *not* used in the production of others:

> Luxury products have no part in the determination of the system. Their role is purely passive. If an invention were to reduce by half the quantity of each of the means of production which are required to

> produce a unit of a "luxury" commodity of this type, the commodity itself would be halved in price, but there would be no further consequences....
> What has just been said of the passive role of luxury goods can readily be extended to such "luxuries" as are merely used in their own reproduction either directly (e.g., race horses) or indirectly (e.g., ostriches and ostrich eggs) or merely for the production of other luxuries (e.g., raw silk).
> The criterion is whether a commodity enters (no matter whether directly or indirectly) into the production of *all* commodities. [1972:6-7]

In terms of either of these definitions, the trade of various parts of Africa with various European traders prior to about 1750 falls in this category, especially if we bear in mind Amin's stricture about "the historically relative nature of the distinction between mass consumption goods and luxury goods" (1974).

Indeed the point that should be borne in mind is that the kind of trade the Portuguese launched in West Africa, in the Congo region, and in East Africa in the fifteenth and sixteenth centuries (and in which subsequently other European powers engaged) at first was essentially of the same nature, and involved essentially the same products, as the trans-Saharan trade that dates at least to the tenth century A.D. and the Indian Ocean trade that goes back further still (Alpers, 1973:111-113).

All of this trade prior to 1750 which involved African states with partners outside of themselves was "long-distance trade" whose quantity varied on a market determined less by demand than by effective supply, that is, of products successfully transported from the point of production to the mart. As a consequence, production was not determined by variations in this demand but by the politico-technological ability of the long-distance traders to transport the material. The resulting trade involved no transfer of surplus, but could in fact be considered a mutual windfall.

Because this was so, this trade had very limited consequences for the social organization of the trading societies, except to strengthen somewhat the political machineries that guaranteed it. A stoppage in the trade, which occurred frequently over the centuries, had relatively few repercussions other than on the lives of the state officials and merchants directly living off the trade. The data on the nature of the trade between Europe and Africa from 1450 to 1750 has not yet been collected in a sufficiently systematic manner to verify this argument definitely, but I have presented previously some evidence that would support this interpretation (Wallerstein, 1973:7-

9). What is important here is to suggest what may have happened around 1750 to have changed the situation.

In fact, as with all such situations, the change was not abrupt. It was the case that since about 1700, the export in slaves from West Africa began to increase in importance in response to a growing demand in the Caribbean area[4] and a relative diminution of interference with movement on the seas. In a recent calculation, Richard Bean located the shift in curve quite precisely:

> Both the price of slaves in Africa and the number of slaves doubled after the Peace of Ryswick in 1697. From then until the reductions in the trade following 1807, slaves were clearly the most important export of Africa. [1974:354-355]

Looked at more closely, decade by decade, we see that the export of slaves from Africa to the Western Hemisphere rises quantitatively until 1750, after which it remains at a high level until 1810.[5]

PHASE I: 1750-1900

Slave exports from Africa had certainly now ceased to be a "luxury" item from the point of view of the capitalist world-economy. They were, in Sraffa's terms, "entering into the production of all commodities." And the quantitative expansion of the trade was in turn having its effect on the social structures of the exporting regions. As has long been noted, the growth of the slave trade led to the expansion of such states as Dahomey and Oyo. Although, as Hopkins (1973:106) cautions us, "it would be mistaken to imply that the slave trade was a necessary condition for the formation of large, centralised states in West Africa,"[6] the point is that the initial impact of increased trade was by and large to strengthen the state structures in the exporting arena, a consequence typical of trade in the external arena.

But matters could not stop there precisely because Africa, or at least the coastal regions, were now being in fact "incorporated" into the world-economy and thereby becoming peripheralized.

It was about 1750 that the capitalist world-economy was emerging from the long-term relative contraction which it had been suffering since about 1620. This contraction had led to acute competition among those states that were in the core of the world-economy in 1620—the United Provinces, England, and France. This competiton took the form of mercantilist closure for both England and France in order to strengthen their position against the United Provinces, which, as of 1620, was more efficient economically. One aspect of this mercantilism was the creation of closed imperial trade networks between the European metropoles, the Caribbean, and North America. The slow increase in economic activity that resulted accounted for the steady increase in importation of slaves after 1700.

But by 1750, the whole world-economy was in an upswing once again, and England and France were in the last stages of their struggle for economic (and political) hegemony in the world-economy. This world-economy could now sustain a considerably increased production of manufactures, provided one could rapidly augment primary production. There was thus a rush to expand. One obvious place was in the Caribbean. As a result:

> In the second half of the eighteenth century the French government offered bounties to slave ships leaving France for Africa, and made an additional payment for every slave they landed in the French West Indies. This concern is understandable when it is realised that...sugar was the largest single item imported into England in the eighteenth century [Hopkins, 1973:91]

Nor did Britain's growing military success vis-à-vis France in fact lessen French economic activity, at least at first:

> England's supremacy was the result of the relatively quick pace of her commercial expansion and was not brought about by an absolute decline in French commerce with West Africa...Indeed, the tempo of French activity in West Africa actually increased after 1763, following Choueul's efforts to develop Africa to compensate for the loss of Canada, and to free the French West Indies from dependence on British ships for supplies of slaves. [Hopkins, 1973:92][7]

The pressure to expand the geographic bounds of the capitalist world-economy began to be felt from 1750 on. One of the easiest ways to expand total primary production to feed the industries that were being established was to expand extensively, to include new areas of primary production, because this involves the windfall profits of labor and land priced below world market rates. Of course, in addition, primary producers already in existence sought to maintain and expand their production.

This double effort to expand led to a labor shortage within the world-economy and hence accounts for the need for more slaves. Thus there came to be a growing demand in Africa for slaves at the same time as there was a growing demand for the use of African land—and African labor on African land—for primary crop production.

At first, the prior demand took priority. It accorded with the existing mores and trade channels. And neither Britain nor France could take the chance that the other would surge ahead in such areas as sugar production in the West Indies. Furthermore, it was precisely the acuteness of their rivalry that strengthened the hand of slave-raiding states in West Africa like Ashanti.[8] The crucial aspect to note of such states is that they were engaged less in wars than in "raids," as Daaku insists, which were "made possible mainly by the introduction of firearms" (1968:136). Ashanti (and its analogues) thus became part of the periphery[9] of the capitalist world-economy not by *producing* slaves but by raiding them from areas outside this world-economy.

This kind of involvement of coastal West Africa made it impossible, however, to use these same areas as cash-crop producing areas. Daaku speaks of the failure of the Dutch attempt to create sugar, cotton, and indigo plantations in West Africa, explaining it thus:

> It can be said that between the 17th and 18th centuries, West African interest was permanently subordinated to that of the West Indies and the Americas. This more than anything else must be the explanation for why the Europeans did not interest themselves in both the political and economic well being of West Africa, rather than the popularly accepted view that the African system of land tenure, their numerical superiority and the inhospitable climate debarred the Europeans from taking other interests apart from the commercial in affairs of Africa. [1968:138-139]

But it did not necessarily have to remain eternally true that both trade partners would be primarily served by the primacy of the slave trade. The situation did in fact change. As the British moved into clear hegemony in the world-economy, their priorities shifted, and their ability to make these priorities prevail increased. Furthermore, it now became profitable for some Africans to produce agricultural crops for this world-economy, as we shall see.

Thus the slave trade served as the cutting edge of the peripheralization of Africa in the period 1750-1900, but it was also incompatible with it, because the production of slaves is less profitable than cash-crop production, forcing slaves to be continuously drawn from outside the world-economy. Hence, we see a clear pattern of geographic dislocation. As the nineteenth century proceeded, the slave trade died out in West Africa and to a lesser extent in Angola, to be replaced by a slave trade based on the East African mainland, whose incorporation into the world-economy would not come about until the very end of the nineteenth century.

Let us trace the steps of this shift of locus. The abolition of the slave trade by Great Britain, the prospectively hegemonic world power, as Boahen points out:

> rendered illegal as much as nine-tenths of European trade with the coast of West Africa. A huge economic vacuum was thus created and the British hoped that it might be filled by the encouragement of the cultivation of exportable commodities such as white rice, indigo, cotton, coffee and palm oil. [1974:179][10]

What served British interest, however, did not necessarily serve the interest of other actors in the world-economy. The slave-trading African states saw their principal source of wealth attacked and, in Boahen's words, "found abolition incomprehensible." He goes on to point out the *short-term* economic dilemmas of the African traders:

> Like other powerful rulers, the Asantehene now had the problem of the disposal of war captives. Though he strongly denied going to war simply to acquire slaves, he pointed out that one of the readiest ways of disposing of war captives who could not be absorbed locally was to sell them. At the time of aboliton [1807] he had twenty thousand captives on his hands whom, he frankly confessed, he could not feed, adding that unless I kill or sell them, they will grow strong and kill my people. [1974:179]

Similarly, some European groups equally were dismayed by abolition. It was the weakness of Portugal's export position in the world-economy that explains why she "was clinging to the Atlantic slave-trade and to the institution of slavery in Brazil" (Rodney, 1968:62).

Neither slavery nor the slave-trade was abolished from one day to the next in the capitalist world-economy. Rather, there was a century-long disengagement from the use of slave labor, during which not only did many sectors of the world-economy resist this process, but its leading proponent, Great Britain, sacrificed logical consistency to the complex and contradictory economic needs of powerful internal forces. Eric Williams succinctly summarized the dilemma:

The British West Indian planters pleaded that theirs was a free labour economy which deserved protection from slave grown products in Brazil and Cuba. Britain's textile industry was, however, completely dependent on the slave grown cotton of the Southern States of the United States of America. [1964:15][11]

Nonetheless, the major thrust was toward abolition—in West Africa, in Angola, and in the Cape Colony, leaving East Africa relatively untouched until much later. And those hurt by this shift moved to minimize or recoup their losses.

In Angola, the Portuguese sought to replace revenue from the slave trade with increased taxation on the African population, increased customs duties, and the expansion of the area under Portuguese sovereignty, which then precisely ran into British opposition because both expansion and customs dues "would inevitably curtail the freedom of trade then enjoyed by British merchants" (Wheeler, 1971:54).

In the Cape, where, since 1716, slaves had been imported (Omer-Cooper, 1966b:347-348) from West Africa, Madagascar, and Mozambique, as well as from the East Indies (those who would come to be called the Cape Malays), the British administration undermined not merely the ethos but the economic basis of the Boer farm units:

> The price of slaves [in the Cape], driven up by the limitation of supply which resulted from the stopping of the slave trade in 1807, had risen too high for slaves to be used very extensively by frontier farmers operating on small capital. [Omer-Cooper, 1966a:369]

Eventually, this economic (and hence cultural and political) pressure on the Boers would culminate in the Great Trek of 1837 (Patterson, 1957, chap. 1; Davenport, 1969:287-297).

East Africa, by contrast, began to play in the nineteenth century the role that West Africa had played in the eighteenth. It remained largely outside the capitalist world-economy, the slave trade expanding steadily[12] and strengthening thereby slave-trading state structures on the mainland.[13] While the mainland areas came to be the external arenas of slave recruitment, the Indian Ocean islands (particularly Zanzibar, but also Madagascar, Reunion, and Mauritius) became peripheral areas of the world-economy, producing export crops for exchange with Europe and obtaining slaves from the mainland as workers.[14]

The abolition of the slave trade by Great Britain was most efficacious and had the greatest consequences in West Africa. Economic "substitutes"

The Three Stages of African Involvement in the World-Economy 109

grew up: timber trade in coastal Sierra Leone, palm oil in the Niger Delta and Dahomey, groundnut oil in Gambia and Senegal. Thus, as Fyfe notes:

> The colonial economic relationship...was intensified. The volume of manufactured imports from the expanding factories of Europe increased steadily, pushing the frontier of import-export trading inland and bringing more peoples within the European trading sphere. [1974:47][15]

The growth of this trade began to affect the structure of production in West Africa. Some previous economic activities—blacksmithing, iron smelting, even the mining of iron—declined, "ruined by the competition of cheaper and purer iron bars imported from Europe," as well as by

> increasing quantities of cheap European imports of iron basins, matchets, knives, hoes, wire and other metal goods turned out by the expanding mass production techniques of the industrial revolution. [Flint, 1974:387]

Nor was African textile production better able to maintain its local market untouched. In the seventeenth and eighteenth centuries, the African producers had effectively resisted European intrusion because of product differentiation, but this began to change once the English mills began to mass produce cheap cotton cloth after the mid-eighteenth century (Flint, 1974:388-389). Nor, as Fyfe notes, were Africans able to establish new industries:

> Produce was exported in a raw state. No processing industries grew up; a few factories which were opened in Freetown in the 1840s for pressing groundnut oil soon closed. The French prohibited oil-processing in Senegal. [1974:47]

In short, West Africa was being peripheralized or, in the splendidly arrogant phraseology of the Sierra Leone Company, made to conform to "the true principles of Commerce," that is, "the export of British manufactures in return for African produce."[16]

Peripheralization is a corrosive process. Trade with an external arena requires strong partners—to guarantee its continuity (since presumably the internal economic needs of the systems that are trading are not dependent or less dependent on the continuity of the trade) and to minimize transaction costs when the intermittent trade occurs. But trade within a capitalist world-economy must be able to respond rapidly and accurately to the demands of the market, capitalist producers seeking to control the vagaries of the market by expanding vertical and horizontal integration to the degree the technology and political systems permit.

From the point of view of the dominant economic forces—that is, those with most capital, who were now located largely in Europe—the "strong" states of West Africa were potential competitors.[17] As peripheralization proceeded, the local bourgeoisies might come to utilize the local state structures to erect mercantilist barriers. Ideally what the core countries wanted was a direct channel to primary producers, an unencumbered economic alliance.

The political response of Africans in the first three-quarters of the nineteenth century was mixed. As already noted, slave-trading rulers were unhappy about abolition, but they sought to compensate in several ways: warfare with neighbors, which was in the end mutually destructive and contributed to the decline of these states; creation of export-crop estates using slave labor, which was often undermined by competition from peasant farmers producing for the export market more efficiently; creation of alliances between the state and small producers, which was difficult and did not succeed because of all the forces opposing such an alliance. A.G. Hopkins underlines the limits of the contradictions involved in these attempts to conserve the relatively strong state structures as peripheralization proceeded:

> The difficulties of the progressive rulers arose first from an internal conflict of interest stemming from a basic change in the structure of export-producing firms, and second from the fact that they were unable or unwilling to make the necessary adjustments in the time allowed by impatient and often unsympathetic foreigners. For a while it seemed that there was a chance of stabilizing the existing frontier between Europeans and Africans on the West Coast, but in the last quarter of the century the indigenous rulers were called upon to make concessions upon such matters as railways, internal tolls and slavery, which they judged, quite rightly, would undermine their independence. [1973:145]

One may view as essentially similar the source of the continuing latent tensions between the British and the strong states established by the Boers in southern Africa[18] and by the Omani Arabs in eastern Africa (John Flint, 1963).

Indeed, not only were the European countries faced with strong states with whom their interests increasingly diverged but some of the now flourishing African merchant classes were thinking of inspiring new ones, such as the Fanti Confederation.[19] Presented by James Africanus Horton to Lord Granville as a mode of relieving the imperial exchequer,[20] the proposal received an ambivalent and ultimately negative British response.[21] Furthermore, as the quantity of total export trade from Africa continued to expand steadily, if slowly,[22] there was growing competition in the coastal trading markets

> between European and African jurisdiction over the traders. In the mutually antagonistic methods of bringing sanctions to bear against thieves and debtors, in the struggle between the rough justice of the "palm oil ruffians" and the attempt to extend the power of colonial courts, in the sanctions of African boycott and European naval blockade lay a search for authority which transcended the search for trade. [Newbury, 1969:84][23]

As long as the capitalist world-economy lived under the smug and clear hegemonic control of Great Britain, roughly 1815-1873, the peripheralization of African coastal regions advanced slowly, like lava curling down a mountainside. But when the capitalist world-economy erupted into a major crisis of accumulation, whose onset was signaled by the market crash of 1873, the rules of the game suddenly changed. For one thing, Great Britain's hegemony was now openly challenged anew by France, her perennial rival; by Germany, sharply rising as Europe's new great political and economic power; and by her erstwhile junior partner, the United States.

What this meant for Africa was that the process of political decline would be suddenly accelerated as the European powers, first tentatively and then in a sudden onrush, undertook the "scramble for Africa," dividing up the continent (somewhat unevenly) and "pacifying" those who dared to resist.

Prior to partition, Britain dominated trade in Africa throughout the nineteenth century. But already in mid-century, the percentage was declining, even though it was still the leading commercial power. Newbury summarizes the situation on the west coast as follows:

> Expressed as a percentage, the United Kingdom share with British possessions on the Coast declined between the fifties and sixties to about half of their total trade, as German, French and American agents took advantage of the lack of restrictions at Bathurst, Freetown,

Cape Coast and Lagos...British trade with other parts of the coast (though still much greater than Britain's stake in her own West African colonies) also declined. [1969:79]

Furthermore, the value of the particular export products was declining. The boom in palm oil ended in 1861, caused by the expansion of worldwide commodity production, as competitive products from the U.S., Australia, and India come on the world market (Hopkins, 1973:133).

This is not the place to argue once more the immediate causes of partition. I will merely assert my view that in a contracting world market, France and Germany sought to seal off areas of this market from Britain by colonization, to which the only sensible response by Britain was to join the scramble (and indeed largely win it). Thus, one does not have to argue the economic importance of particular areas to explain colonization, for it was above all "preemptive colonization" (Wallerstein, 1970). G.N. Uzoigwe wrote:

> Evidently those in Britain who cried for new markets had every reason to be alarmed. It can, of course, be argued that since the cry for new markets only became loud in the 1890's when Africa had practically been partitioned, it was a mere rationalization after the event. It must be pointed out however that those in authority were not unaware of Britain's economic difficulties in the 1880's. That this consideration may have driven them to participate in the greatest international share-out in world history cannot be ruled out. Rosebery's summary of the partition as pegging out claims for futurity explains a great deal about this...Indeed Africa may have been partitioned in the 1880's but this was only on paper. The real partition took place in the 1890's with effective occupation. [1974:34]

Whatever the immediate explanation, there was indeed effective occupation. The slave trade finally ended throughout Africa.[24]

Phase I was the phase of "informal empire,"[25] that is, those areas of Africa, mainly on the coast, that came to be incorporated into the capitalist world-economy as peripheral zones retained their local sovereign political institutions for the most part. It is not that sovereignty was never alienated by a core state. It is that the expense of direct political domination was avoided to the extent possible because it was seldom required to maintain the flow of commerce. Gallagher and Robinson seize the situation precisely when they say, "By informal means if possible or by formal annexations when necessary, British paramountcy was steadily upheld" (1970:145). By the end of the nineteenth century, however, all African sovereignty disappeared (except that of Liberia and Ethiopia). The way was open now for a second integration of Africa into the capitalist world-economy, which would occur in the twentieth century, one that would not only be more extensive but more intensive, as it would begin to reorganize the class structure.

PHASE II: 1900-1975

We have seen that the combination of the growing competition of British (and other European) merchants versus indigenous Africans and the growing challenge of German, French, and American industry to British world market hegemony together led to the dislocation of the balance that sustained "informal empire" and hence to the scramble for Africa.

The period 1873-1897 was a period of contraction in the capitalist world-economy (Schumpeter, 1939:321-325, 335-341, 356-366). When the phase of expansion occurred, notably during the period 1900-1913, there was an alteration in the world terms of trade in favor of agricultural exports (Lewis, 1952). In effect, there was a felt shortage in the supply of world raw materials, and hence it was eminently profitable to initiate new (or expanded) production of export crops in Africa. However, since these areas were now under direct European political control, the largest part of the profits of this expansion could be diverted into European hands either by direct ownership of the agricultural domains, by monopsonistic control of the purchasing of the product for export, by monopolistic control of transportation facilities, or by direct taxation. The direct benefits of colonization for Great Britain, presumably the reluctant dragon, have been argued by Richard Wolff:

> In terms of supplying food and raw materials imports, colonial administration meant for Britain ultimate control and hence a greater measure of security than would have obtained if France or Germany or another power had annexed the territories. Also, whatever the final destination of food and raw materials export from any colony, British political control almost always meant British predominance in the financing, insurance, and freight for the colony's exports, and hence British balance of payments advantages. Foreign political control could and frequently did deny Britain such predominance, regardless of the relative prices of the services provided by Britain and other

countries. Finally,...colonial control enabled the British authorities to determine to a large extent the choice of foods and raw materials developed and exported from any colonial territory. Thus, it is reasonable to conclude that, in the absence of Britain's new empire, her security, her gains from invisible exports, and both the general mix and quantities of food and raw materials supplied to world markets would have been less favorable to her. [1974:23]

And nothing is said here of the advantage to individual settlers.

One of the reasons why, given a felt shortage in the world-economy of certain commodities, it is so eminently profitable to open up *new* areas for peripheral inclusion in the world-economy (as opposed to intensifying production in old areas) is the low cost of labor in terms of world market prices at a given era. There is a school of thought that sees these low wages as the marginal sales value of previously unutilized labor. Thus Szereszewski argues of the new cocoa industry in the Gold Coast in the period 1891-1911:

> [T]he first forest belt of the Gold Coast had a built-in capacity to increase its real output under certain stimuli which disturbed the equilibrium position of individual economic units. This resulted from the existence of unutilised labour potential and from the fact that labour services were the limiting factor over a wide range of activities: the economic units could react to the introduction of new commodities, to new price situations and to changes in transport conditions with increased flow of exportable output. . . . This was basically an *under-employment situation* in the sense that the resources of the economy—land and labour—were at the low level of *physical utilisation* determined by the preferences of the population for income and leisure and the available conversion rates between the two. [1965:84-85][26]

In this theory, economically virgin land and labor await the plucking by world capitalism. In fact, this was not historically true for West Africa, which by the 1880s had "an internal exchange economy of some magnitude," as Marion Johnson points out in specific response to this explanation (1974:180). Still it might be argued that it was true for some of the land areas brought into cash-crop cultivation at that time. We would then retain the explanation of the profitability but look for *institutional* in addition to *market* factors to explain the emergence of this agricultural production for the world market.

The Three Stages of African Involvement in the World-Economy

One of the vital mechanisms involved in the utilization of this "surplus" labor force was the development of a transportation network which would keep the total cost of the product on the world market competitive,[27] and such "external economies" depended in turn on an active role of the colonial governments. Fieldhouse recognized this when he warned us against seeing colonial rule and informal empire as "merely points along the same spectrum, differing in degree rather than kind."

> The distinctive feature of an imperial economic system was that the metropolis could, within limits, create the formal framework for economic activity and in some degree determine the character of development. [1971:600]

To appreciate, then, the dynamics of the evolution, we must take into account that the colonial governments operated in a double context: they reflected the economic needs of the various metropolitan economic actors, as mediated through political pressures on the government (both in the metropole and directly on the colonial administrations), but as a substructure they had their own immediate needs to fulfill. What is striking in this early period of colonial rule is that the larger needs of metropolitan economic institutions for expanded cash-crop production in Africa coincided with the administrative needs of the colonial officials. Export production was needed to provide a tax base sufficient to cover the costs of administration. And export production provided an ideological reinforcement. It was seen as part of the "civilizing" process, as well as an alternative to the slave trade. Finally, as Barber notes:

> Mixed with these factors was a consideration of prudence. The *pax* in Africa, it was widely believed, depended on the provision of opportunities for Africans to earn money incomes. Otherwise, idleness among African men might well breed mischief and thereby expensive threats to the new order. [1964:301]

Moreover, the point is that in terms of income to those African producers who had already been related to the world market during the late nineteenth century, a period of slump, there was a rise in income from the improvement in world terms of trade. Hence, Hopkins is probably right when he says that "it helped to reconcile Africans to colonial rule, and so made the task of the new administrations much easier than it would otherwise have been" (1973:183).

Thus opportunities were created by the favorable world market, and both metropolitan economic interests and colonial administrators were interested in seizing the opportunities offered. The modes of possible response to these opportunities, in terms of the formal organization of the new agricultural enterprises, were varied. In fact, empirically Africa knew three such modes: African peasant farming, European concessions, and white settler farming.[28] Within limits, these modes corresponded to geographical areas: peasant farming in West Africa, concessions in Equatorial Africa, white settlers in the East, South, and North (although there were some pockets of peasant farming in these latter areas—most notably in Uganda).

Why were different modes employed? From the point of view of colonial administrators, the preferred mode was the one that was easiest in terms of its consequence for administration. Presumably African peasant farming usually fit this bill best. First of all, it required least disruption and dislocation of Africans and hence the least administrative machinery to enforce. Secondly, it represented a dispersal of economic power and hence minimized the growth of economic entities *within* the colony that could put forward political demands upon the administration. It was a path of least resistance.

Obviously, however, it required a situation where Africans could be tempted into cash-crop production with perhaps some technical assistance and a little judicious coercion. Thus, the more involved some local Africans had been previously in market-oriented activities, the more likely it was that there would be speedy response to market opportunities. This explains why the coastal and forest regions of West Africa were likely candidates for this mode.

The other factor, however, was the political strength of persons interested in an alternative mode of development. Thus, the question should be posed as follows: given that there might be said to be an initial administrative bias in favor of African peasant production, under what conditions do concessionary companies or white settlers displace the peasantry as the mode of development?

How do we explain, for example, that of the two major arenas of French colonization in Black Africa—West Africa and Equatorial Africa—the latter developed a concessionary regime and the former did not?[29] Basically, it represented a competition between two French interest groups—those involved in large import-export firms and those seeking monopolistic concessions. The former were well established in West Africa as a result of the long commerce of the nineteenth century but were not similarly established in Equatorial Africa. This seemed to make the difference in who won out (Suret-Canale, 1964:37-39). In terms of securing production for the world-economy, the two systems both "worked." As Jean Suret-Canale put it:

> [I]n French West Africa, colonial trade *(la traite)* reigned under the auspices of "free trade"—and of the *de facto* monopoly of merchant houses. The exploitation of the "independent" African peasant occurred through the mediation of the market...
> In French Equatorial Africa, colonial trade reigned via the channel of large colonial [chartered] companies, holding legal monopolies. On the surface, investments in agriculture, forestry, and mining were more significant if one believes the titles of the companies and the activities projected in their statutes.
> Actually, it was import and export that constituted their real activity, with this difference that the facade of free trade was more often replaced by pure and simple brutal plundering, the companies considering the men and the product of their labor as their property. [1964:39, 41]

A second important arena of concessionary development was the Congo Free State, which from 1885 to 1908 constituted a juridically "independent state" owned and personally governed by King Leopold II of Belgium. This bizarre political structure created a situation in which it was in the personal financial interest of the head of the colonial administration to invite in concessionary companies. Under the *régime domanial* the state appropriated all so-called "vacant land," which it then sold to willing buyers (Stengers, 1969:265-271). The concessionary companies that bought much of this land felt they had the right to exploit the African's labor for their own private profit, thereby reaping "unheard of profits" and creating "veritable hells-on-earth," wherein "the lot of the Africans was tragic" (Stengers, 1969: 270-271).

As it turned out, the generic administrator's instinct against concessions as a mode of development was right, for concessions turned out to be a less profitable mode from the point of view of the world-economy as a whole. Between 1900 and 1920, "French West Africa appeared relatively prosperous, while French Equatorial Africa suffered bitter distress" (Coquery-Vidrovitch, 1969:193).[30] As for the Congo Free State, Merlier points out the other side of Leopold's financial advantage:

> These Leopoldian expropriations retained their speculative character. Thanks to the concessions, the companies speculated on the stock

exchange but seldom exploited the land. Each expropriation enriched Leopold II and those close to him, the crooks who hung around the royal family and the offices of the companies: they rushed to divide up the concessions into smaller lots and resell them to less important companies or to settlers. Often the land consisted of vast swamps that could not be cultivated...Except for some operations that involved simple gathering *(la cueillette)* undertaken in accessible areas, the granting of concessions did not often result in effective occupation of lands and forests. [1962:58]

It was thus as much because of their inefficiency as because of the cruelties associated with them that the Belgian government after 1908 sought to liquidate the Leopoldian concessions.[31]

If we now take the second alternative to peasant farming, the installation of white settlers, we discover that settlers came usually because they pressed to come, and frequently against the will or at least to the discomfort of the administrators. There were three main areas of white settlement: southern Africa, North Africa, and East Africa. Each deserves a brief word.

The origins of white farming in South Africa center on the fact that the Cape was a strategic way station on the world's sea routes, first for the Dutch, then for the British. When in the late nineteenth century, diamonds and gold were discovered, this led to still further white immigration and confirmed the role of South Africa as an area of white settlement, both in farming and in mining. It was in a sense, however, the white farming that protected politically the role of whites as the skilled personnel of the mining operations, as the later history of Zambia and Katanga was to prove.

It was the presence of white settlers in the Cape that explains why the British South Africa Company turned to white settlers to recoup its losses in its Rhodesian "concession" when the hopes of mineral wealth turned out to be fruitless and the African revolts posed a political threat.[32] This was ultimately to be enshrined in the self-government act of 1923, the critical political base for the unilateral declaration of independence of 1965.

In the German areas, settlers came because they pushed to come, and they encountered ambivalent responses from the administrators. In Southwest Africa, it was quite possibly only the transfer of power from Germany to South Africa after World War I that enabled the settlers to survive the growing hostility of the government.[33] As for German East Africa, its history involved a constant strain between the settlers and the Africans and an open. hostility toward the settlers on the part of the most successful governor, Albrecht Rechenberg.[34] The oscillation of colonial administrative attitudes was to continue under the British Mandate and result in an inability of the settlers to consolidate political power.[35]

If we turn to North Africa, we find that the French administration in Algeria did not start out in clear support of settlers. The so-called founder of French Algeria, General Bugeaud, was, in Charles-André Julien's phrase, "profoundly anti-settler." He was converted to "official and systematic colonization" only to counter the "private and anarchic colonization which has led to the massacre of Mitidja" (1964:231). Under the Second Empire, the administrators still were cool to settlers:

> This is because the Emperor preferred capitalist colonization, which did not require the intervention of the State, to family colonization and settlement which required administrative overseeing. The government, by favoring primarily large concessionaries, indicated disinterest in the fate [of the settlers] and refused to offer them assistance in case of difficulty. [Julien, 1964:403]

It is only in 1871 with the simultaneous defeat by Germany (and the impulses it created for compensatory outlets), the repression of the Paris Commune, and the putting down of the Kabyle uprising that white settlement politically won out in Algeria (and thus consequently in the latter part of the century in Tunisia and Morocco):

> The end of the war [of 1870-71] marked the opening, in effect, of the era of colonization triumphant. Reassured by the repression, proud of its vitality and spirit of its correctness and of its republican and civilizing vocation, the European population felt itself at last free to impose, on the country and the indigenous masses, a political, economic and social dominance that nothing could shake. [Julien, 1964:500]

In fact, it is only in Kenya that the colonial authorities seemed to have been committed from the outset to white settlers as a solution to the need for cash-crop production. It seems that the most likely source of this relative unusual position on the part of administrators, in striking contrast to British attitudes in neighboring Uganda, may have been the sense of British officials that the earlier disruption by slave trading combined with the absence of hierarchical states had created a situation in which Africans would not respond to cash-crop market opportunities.[36] Furthermore, the building of the railroad had established a high cost load for the administration, which required urgent measures to secure immediate income (Low, 1965:21-22).

Thus we have argued that the essential objective of the second phase of African incorporation into the capitalist world-economy was to create sufficient cash crops to meet world needs as defined at this stage and to sustain the political administrative costs that European powers had forced on each other. Where possible, this was done by using Africans as the farm managers (as well as the farm laborers), either in the form of small peasant holdings or where the social structure was too centralized to permit this, as in parts of the West African savannah zones where the Muslim brotherhoods were strong, in the form of large networks coordinated by these religious structures monopolizing the marketing.[37] But where the African social structure was too disintegrated or the settlers too strong for historical reasons or where concessionary companies were in a position to be momentarily very persuasive in the metropole, other modes of social organization emerged. From the point of view of metropolitan capitalist interests as a whole, however, it is probably true to say that these alternative forms (concessions which had a short life, and white settlement which survived longer) were less desirable than African land ownership. And this fact would in part explain some of the unexpected alliances in the later era of "decolonization."

If the first segment (1900-1913) of this second phase was a moment of a very favorable market for Africa's products, the world balance of trade would shift against Africa subsequently, very markedly in the period between the two world wars, less so but still so in the period following World War II. The reasons for these unfavorable balances in the two latter periods were however different. Between the two wars, the world market was basically depressed for all primary products. After World War II, at least until 1965 or so, demand for Africa's exports was expanding, but this fact was more than counterbalanced by a marked increase in imports.

That the first period 1900-1913/1920 was exceptionally favorable to African income levels and saw consequently greater *structural* change than later periods is attested to around the continent. Ehrlich notes:

> It was Uganda's good fortune that, at the very time [1903-1913] that the [British] Administration was becoming concerned with the development of a viable export crop, world market conditions were uniquely favourable for such experiments. [1965:399]

In the case of South Africa, De Kiewiet marks the change as coming between 1890 and World War I:

The Three Stages of African Involvement in the World-Economy 121

> With a speed that even the United States could hardly match, thriving towns sprang up where there formerly had been a struggling village or simply the bare veld. Between 1891 and 1911 the urban population increased by more than 200 per cent. In New Zealand, Australia, and Canada industry, commerce and the movement of population were stimulated by rising prices and an increased demand for goods. But in South Africa these world conditions were spurred forward still more emphatically by diamonds, gold, railway building, and the expenditures of war and reconstruction. [1957:195][38]

Szereszewski, whose discussion of structural change in Ghana between 1891 and 1911 we have already mentioned, explicitly notes how this period was different from the subsequent period:

> [T]he process of structural change lost its momentum after 1911, and after 50 years Ghana's economy retains a close affinity with 1911 Gold Coast, albeit at a level of roughly double per capita income. The pattern evolved between 1891 and 1911 almost froze for half a century. [1965:112]

Samir Amin, noting that one of the realities of colonial domination was the decline of the indigenous bourgeoisie, says that in Senegal the attempts of French merchants to liquidate the indigenous bourgeoisie succeeded only after World War I when it lost its independent status and its members either became employees of European firms or, if younger sons, went into the civil service (1969:20-29).[39] Finally, Merlier argues that this ecomonic transformation did not occur in the Belgian Congo before the 1920s, exceptionally because of the Leopoldian interlude (and presumably the outcome of its errors). "The colony of the Congo paid the price of its late conquest" (1962:74). Or, perhaps more relevantly, as Vellut indicates, the Leopoldian period was one in which the social basis for imperialist enterprise was unusual: it consisted of "speculators, military men seeking an escape from the mediocre boredom of Belgian garrisons" (1975:17), rather than the usual solid financial groups.

Leaving aside the perhaps special case of the Belgian Congo, how do we account for a slowdown in further structural change in the patterns of economic production after World War I? Very simply, it is that a pattern had been established which fitted within the parameters of the needs of the world-economy and which would be relatively stable until these parameters shifted.

The first half of the twentieth century is sometimes referred to as the "second industrial revolution," one based heavily on the automobile and petrochemical industries. The worldwide spurt in the forces of production required an expansion in industrial facilities and in global production of raw materials and foodstuffs, as well as an expansion of consumption income to provide markets. As to be expected, these expansions did not proceed evenly, as is reflected in both shifting global terms of trade and shifting loci of world unemployment. Basically the world curve of raw material production rose more rapidly at first than the curve of industrial production. This was because there was a demand pull coming from profitable sectors of new industries and because expansion of raw material production required relatively little investment on the part of the entrepreneurs of this production (as we have seen in the case of Africa). This relatively more rapid rise of raw material production took place before World War I. The period between the two wars was one of relative stagnation (or slow upward movement) of both raw materials and industrial curves. The period from 1945 to 1965 was one in which the industrial curve rose *more* rapidly than the raw materials curve, although both went up.

It follows from this general pattern that what went on in Africa from 1919 to 1965 was an expansion of total output, especially after 1945, but always facing a weak world market.[40] The one exception to this is the period immediately following the Korean War when there was a very sudden increase in world demand, which quickly however evened out.

The consequent political economy of Africa was composed of four main elements:

(1) Most production was primary production, but primary production was itself divided into three zones. The first zone produced for the world market. Its size was limited by the weakness of this market, but its fluctuating needs governed the other two zones. The second zone essentially produced food crops for workers in the first zone and in the allied urban zones and occupations. Both these zones added up to a small proportion of the total land area. The third zone produced manpower to export to the first zone (and to a very small extent to the second zone), sustaining itself largely on "subsistence" agriculture or pasturage.

The land of the first zone was controlled in different ways, as we have already seen: by white settler farmers, by companies (concessions), by African peasant farmers. The land of the second zone was controlled largely by Africans. The land of the third zone was controlled by the indigenous population, largely in the form of communal ownership.

(2) The manpower of the first zone (and even of the second zone) was largely migratory, which kept the cost of labor low in terms of world scales,

a corollary of being in a weak world market for the products. As a consequence, the vast majority of Africans were "semiproletarians," persons who earned part of their life family income in wage labor (whether contractual or forced) and the other part of it in so-called subsistence production. Such a system optimized the possibility of shifting any burden of reduced relative world demand onto the direct producers rather than the owners of enterprise. Nonetheless, the steady expansion of absolute production involved a steady increase in "proletarianization," the increase in the number of workers who obtained virtually their entire life income from wage labor, as well as in "peasantization," the increase in the number of Africans who moved into ownership status in the second (and even the first) zone.

(3) The administrative bureaucracy that was required for such a system was small and relatively inexpensive. There were two main functions for the administration. One was to construct the necessary economic infrastructure. This was done more or less on a cost basis. The taxes on African direct producers largely covered the costs of this infrastructure, but it brought in no profit as such. Needless to say, most of the owners of the first zone found this an admirable arrangement.[41]

The second function was to assure a proper *location* of African producers, getting them to move from one zone to the other as required. At first, force was widely used to get persons from the third to the first zone. Later, as the persons in the third zone became increasingly dependent on the cash economy, taxation or even temptation sufficed. In addition, workers in the third zone were often prevented from becoming owners in the first or second zones in order that they be available as wage workers (Arrighi, 1973). Finally, often the government intervened to force surplus workers back to the third zone.

Given the general lack of well-organized resistance in Africa, the bureaucracy needed to perform these two limited functions remained small until the rise of nationalist movements after the Second World War.

(4) The fourth aspect of the political economy was the slow growth of African middle classes. They remained few in number, given the limited urban and intermediary occupations for which they were required. Nonetheless, they grew, and over time the contradictions between their strength and their limited political and economic opportunities accounted for the rise of nationalist movements. Once these movements began to link up with mass protest, the potential cost of colonial administration rose drastically, both the direct costs resulting from the need to expand the bureaucracy for purposes of control and the indirect costs of investment in infrastructure required for purposes of political appeasement.

This provided the major impetus for "decolonization." This story is now quite familiar, and we shall not repeat it.

The second phase of Africa's incorporation into the capitalist world-economy would be brought to an end by the accumulated contradictions both of the world-economy as a whole and of Africa's role within it. On the one hand, the expansion of total industrial capacity in the world-economy had by the mid-1960s significantly outdistanced both the expansion of raw material production and more importantly the expansion of effective demand, given the world distribution of income. This led to the beginning of the world economic downturn whose first serious signs were the world monetary crises circa 1967.

The fact that the expansion of total industrial capacity had led to a diminution of the relative share of the United States, as well as a lowered relative efficiency of U.S. production, meant the end of undisputed U.S. world economic hegemony; and there ensued the uncertain transition of the 1970s when at least five centers of structural power (the U.S., Western Europe, the U.S.S.R., China, and Japan) maneuvered for optimal advantage in the prospective realignment of forces.

The fact that raw material production had fallen relatively behind accounted for both the energy and the food crises. The energy crisis made possible the improved terms of trade for petroleum via the politics of OPEC, with similar organizations of producers of critical raw materials in prospect. The food crisis, combined with transitory climatological shifts, led to the widespread famine, in Africa and elsewhere.[42]

This sudden shift in the patterns of the world-system accounted in large part for the sudden "decolonization" of Portuguese Africa, and the prospective decolonization of Zimbabwe and Namibia, thus completing a political process started in the 1950s, except for the case of South Africa. Phase two, that of colonialism, was passing into history.

PHASE III: 1975–

The third phase now starting will complete Africa's integration into the world-economy. In the coming 50 years this incorporation will take one of two forms: dependent development[43] or revolutionary transformation as part of a network of forces within the world-economy as a whole, which will further the transformation to a socialist world-system.

I will merely sketch very briefly the factors at play. The capitalist world-economy will probably now see a phase of contraction and depression, during which there will be a slowdown of expansion of industrial productive capacity and a reallocation of world income to increase effective demand and recreate the conditions for a further significant expansion of overall world expansion of the forces of production, probably to begin again circa 1990. This will be accompanied by a political realignment to reflect the new socioeconomic hierarchy of the world-system (Wallerstein, 1975a).

In the early period of contraction, semiperipheral areas of the world-economy will be in a relatively strong position. In Africa, this means areas with relative industrial and critical raw material strength: South Africa, Zaire, Nigeria, and possibly Algeria and Egypt. They will emerge as significant producers of industrial products not only for their home markets but for neighboring countries, and this increased income will represent part of the worldwide expansion of effective demand for the products of the core countries.

This same period will be one of acute suffering for truly peripheral areas, whose nonessential exports will find a very weak world market and whose internal food production may collapse further. They will bear the brunt of death from famine and major transfers of remaining populations from rural areas to bidonvilles. The corresponding political regimes will almost certainly be that of corrupt and repressive pretorians. The principal consequence for the social structure will be the disintegration of the third zone, the so-called subsistence sector, clearing the land areas of men and largely sounding the death knell for the concept of a semiproletarian labor force. The "reserve army of the unemployed" will thus become visible but also will have to be kept alive by some process of social redistribution of income.

The emptying out of the land areas will provide the space for an immense mechanization of African primary production, whether controlled by cooperatives, the state, multinational corporations, or some combinations thereof, permitting dramatic "development" of export crops when the new moment of world economic expansion begins.

The South African journal, *To the Point International*, caught the flavor of this prospect exactly in an article entitled "The Sahel: Today's disaster area...tomorrow's glorious garden?" (October 5, 1974, pp. 24-25). The article opened:

> Space-age farms, modern cattle ranches and lush market gardens in the middle of the Sahara...This is no mirage. It is what experts from six of the world's most backward nations have conjured up for the future. Their idea is to roll back the desert and turn their drought-

ravaged countries into a fertile green belt of productive crop land and pasture. The plan calls for giant dams to harness the Senegal and Niger rivers and provide power; advanced irrigation systems to water the dust bowls; and forest walls to check the southern march of the Sahara. It could eventually turn the rural subsistence economies of the west African nations of Chad, Mali, Mauritania, Niger, Senegal and Upper Volta into a vegetable garden for Europe and a vast beef belt. But to have a chance to succeed, the plan would require millions of dollars, take years to accomplish and need a spectacular social and political revolution within the countries.

It is clear that one version or another of this "revolution" will occur, but in whose interests? This will depend on the outcome of the class struggles both internal to Africa and in the world-system as a whole.

What the third phase of incorporation of Africa signals is the culmination of a long process of expansion of the geographic parameters of the capitalist world-system, and the approximation in reality, *for the first time*, of the model of this system, as outlined by both the classical economists and Marx. It thus constitutes a vital *political* turning-point, as it finally threatens to remove the veils that have obscured the functioning of the capitalist system and thus have sustained it.

The elimination of the African (and other) subsistence sectors and the corollary full proletarianization of world labor must in the coming period intensify the political conflict caused by contradictory interests, unless the capitalist classes can discover some new artificial equivalent of the subsistence sector and its semiproletarian labor force. The substitute, if one be found, would bound to be more expensive and hence only partially preserve the system; but for the tenants of privilege, every extra few decades of survival are worth it.

NOTES

[1] The now-classic exposition is Arghiri Emmanuel's *Unequal Exchange* (1972), a book that has given rise to a voluminous debate.
[2] See the forthcoming article by André Gunder Frank, "Multilateral Merchandise Trade Imbalances and Uneven Economic Development." Frank sees these imbalances as an element different from unequal exchange, each significantly reinforcing and aggravating the other.
[3] Amin is, however, talking of exchange within the capitalist world-economy, of

the periphery exporting essential goods and importing luxuries. I am talking of exchange in which both sides are exchanging luxuries, or preciosities. As I put it previously, it is a form of exchange in which "each can export to the other what is in its system socially defined as worth little in return for the import of what in its system is defined as worth much" (Wallerstein, 1974a). Compare the similar expression of Edward Alpers: "trade from which each side believed itself to be profiting" (1973). Alpers, however, asserts this is the pattern of all Euro-African trade prior to "direct colonial rule," whereas I argue, as shall be seen, that a shift in pattern occurred earlier, circa 1750.

[4]A.G. Hopkins (1973:90-91) said: "The eighteenth century was the golden age of prosperity for the West Indies, the time when the Islands became the chief suppliers of sugar to Europe...[A]bout two-thirds of all the slaves shipped to the Caribbean worked on sugar plantations...The expansion of sugar production was stimulated by a rise in demand in Europe following an increase in the consumption of tea and coffee; by a growth in the capacity of the sugar processing industry, which had caught up with supply by about the middle of the eighteenth century; and by government support, which underpinned the structure of Atlantic trade."

[5]Philip D. Curtin (1969:222) notes, "In the mid-[eighteenth] century, [slave] exports from both [West Africa and Central and East Africa] reached a plateau of relative stability." See also his Figure 15 and Table 63.

[6]Hopkins cites Benin, which developed without the slave trade, and the Niger Delta, where the trade did not lend itself to the creation of major states.

[7]Of course, this increased effort by the French government, it could be argued, only brought the French slave trade back to the level it was at before 1763, and from which it fell because of military defeat. See, for example, Pierre H. Boulle (1972:106-107): "It was the slave trade, the fastest growing sector before the war, which suffered the most serious impact, dropping below prewar levels until the last years of the Ancien Régime. Indeed, the figures of the 1750's when Nantes' slavers carried from Africa an annual average of over 9000 Blacks for five years running, were never again equalled."

[8]See Adu Boahen (1974:174, 178): "Finally, though the British had not abandoned their policy of Fante support, it is clear that their own position was so weakened by the turn of the nineteenth century, due mainly to the Seven Years' War, the American War of Independence and the Napoleonic Wars, that the policy could not be effectively enforced...The final conquest of Fante by Asante produced a situation the British had done everything to prevent in the eighteenth century, the domination of the entire coastline by Asante."

[9]Or perhaps they did not become peripheralized through the slave trade even to the limited extent suggested here. Dov Ronen makes the case that right up to the end of slave trading, it remained for Dahomey what I have called a trade in "luxuries," the exchange of a leftover accumulation (hence worthless in Dahomean terms) for European weapons and gifts. "It is suggested here, basically as an inference from a re-analysis of the role of the king, that the 'slave raids' were not carried out for the purpose of selling those captured but for the glorification and the aggrandizement of Dahomey (by means of sacrifice and absorption), the prime function of the king in

his ritual role in the society. The surplus captives were exchanged for weapons and gifts, and were then sold as slaves by the European trade, quite possibly together with others that the latter, with his own men, had hunted. The weapons he gave the Dahomeans were used in the Annual Wars and the gifts redistributed to Dahomeans at the Annual Customs. Dahomey was not a slave-trading state and slaves were not a trading item in the Dahomean economy, but Dahomey was a society dominated by the ancestor cult and had an economy based on agriculture" (1971:13).

[10] Boahen cites as evidence c.o. 267/24, Zachary Macauley to Lord Castlereagh, 6 May 1807.

[11] At first, the British West Indian planters pressed for protection. Later they pressed to enforce aboliton of the slave trade. In any case, the net effect of the ambivalence was to keep abolition an objective rather than a reality. See Christopher Fyfe (1974:44): "Despite the apparatus of enforcement the transatlantic slave trade went on undeterred. Large expanding markets for slaves opened in Brazil and Cuba, which were developed intensively for sugar production during the early nineteenth century. Supply met demand...By the late 1830's it was estimated that the slave trade, far from being 'abolished,' had doubled since 1807."

[12] See Curtin (1969), Tables 66 and 74 and Figure 18. Edward A. Alpers (1967:81) argues: "It is only in the last two decades of the eighteenth century, then, that the East African slave trade began to reach the proportions of the sixteenth century trade in West Africa. By 1810 the total East African trade was barely two-thirds of the average annual number of slaves exported from West Africa throughout the seventeenth century. It was not until after 1810 that the East African slave trade became anywhere near as voracious as the West African trade at its height in the eighteenth and first half of the nineteenth centuries."

[13] Alpers (1969:246) notes: "There is, however, another aspect of the [East African] slave trade [in the 19th century]: not only did it uproot people, it also encouraged the growth of larger political units."

[14] See the discussion of the consequences of these agricultural developments for the social structure of Zanzibar in J.M. Gray, "Zanzibar and the Coastal Belt, 1840-1884" (1963:217f.). The pattern of Indian Ocean trade changed as well, as explained by Alpers: "Gujarati textiles continued to dominate the Eastr African market into the early decades of the nineteenth century, when first American and then British cottons seized the East African market while decimating the Indian cotton textile manufacturing industry. Although Gujarati merchants continued to play a vital role in East Africa after this time, they no longer operated as independent merchant capitalists, but as compradors for Western industrial capitalism." See Alpers, "Gujarati and the Trade of East Africa, c. 1500-1800," *International Journal of African Historical Studies*, 9, 1, 1976: 22-44.

[15] See also George E. Brooks (1975:30): "Spurred by European and Eurafrican coastal traders, African agriculturists responded [in the 1830s and 1840s] to the new marketing opportunities [for peanuts] with remarkable swiftness."

[16] The latter phrase is that of Fyfe (1974:38-39). The former phrase is that of the Company, which Fyfe cites from Sierra Leone Studies, o.s., 1932, 18:42-77.

[17] See J.E. Flint (1974:399): "The *laissez faire* attitude to trade seemed in fact to have worked itself out, the trade seemed stagnant, competition too fierce, and African middlemen too strong. Increasingly some of the British traders began to turn to ideas of monopoly as a way out of their difficulties. From this time forward there were constant negotiations among the more powerful Liverpool traders, designed to secure price-fixing arrangements whereby African middlemen could be presented with a united front."

[18] Leonard Thompson (1971a:291) notes: "The growth of the diamond-mining industry in Griqualand West and the gold-mining in the Transvaal strengthened the previously tenuous arguments for territorial supremacy."

[19] "Now flourishing" may give a wrong impression. They were flourishing in the sense of expanding in numbers in response to a widening world trade. But obviously many of these merchants were unsuccessful, which may have been one of the motivations behind the Fanti Confederation. Edward Reynolds (1975:114) argues: "Although the merchant community of the Gold Coast was in sympathy with the objectives of the Confederation, it is significant that most of the leaders and advisors of the movement were ambitious literate Africans who had failed to make good in trade and other employment."

[20] Letter No. IX, to the Right Hon. Earl Granville, K.G., D.C.L., Secretary of State for the Colonies, on "The Fantee Confederation" from James Africanus B. Horton, *Letters on the Political Condition of the Gold Coast* (1870), reprinted in Henry S. Wilson (1969). The proposed Constitution of the Fanti Confederacy (1873) provided in Article 43 that "the officers of the Confederation shall render assistance as directed by the executive in carrying out the wishes of the British Government" (p. 218).

[21] Governor Pope-Hennessy of Sierra Leone (under whom the Gold Coast then came) urged the British government to seize upon the desire for change of "every educated native at Cape Coast" as shown in support for the Fanti Confederation by "extending the system of Colonial Administration," which however he would have combined with "a certain amount of native self-government in the towns, and of judicial power by chiefs in the interior, in concert with District Magistrates" (Wilson, 1969:221-222). The ultimate frustration of Horton's plans is described by Christopher Fyfe (1972, chap. 5). Far from getting self-government, what the Fanti got was the proclamation by the British of a protectorate over the Gold Coast in 1874.

[22] Colin W. Newbury (1969:77) noted: "Throughout the decades of the 'economic revolution' in the palm-oil and ground-nut trade there was an erratic upward progression in the value of exports between 1850 and 1880."

[23] "By the end of the seventies, limited colonial enclaves and consular jurisdiction were no longer felt to be enough where relations with African rulers were concerned" (Newbury, 1969:94). The motives for the accelerating desire by local whites for political authority over Africans in South Africa after 1870 is described by Leonard Thompson (1971b:251): "Chiefdoms were undermined from within and overwhelmed from without. Resident missionaries were a revolutionary influence, because they condemned African customs and institutions... Resident traders

pushed the chiefdoms more tightly into the network of British commerce and created a demand for European manufactures and the money with which to buy them. White farmers infiltrated inside the frontiers of African chiefdoms, often starting by asking permission..., but usually ending by claiming proprietary rights over farms. Recruiters sought labourers for railway construction and for the diamond- and goldmines. Speculators solicited all manner of industrial and mining concessions from chiefs."

[24]See Richard Wolff (1974:33-35): "The change in British policy [in East Africa between 1873 and 1887] was first and foremost a response to closely interconnected phenomena: the commercial interests of private European companies in East Africa, which had increased rapidly, and the simultaneous activity there of the major European powers...

"Facing this situation, the British government operating through Consul Kirk resorted to a strategy that had succeeded well for the previous half century. Put bluntly, the strategy involved the activation of serious anti-slave trade campaigns as a means of establishing British economic and political hegemony in an area....

"In the second stage [of the British campaign], from 1884 through the 1890's, the British finally subjected the slave trade to a systematic attack sufficient to stop it and to confront the traders with economic ruin. The coup de grâce followed, as Britain replaced both the Sultan and the Arab-Swahili aristocracy with the direct economy and political hegemony of the British colonial administration." Thus the last of the external arenas in Africa was being liquidated. Slavery had become definitely uneconomic.

[25]The term is found in an essay by C.R. Fay in the Cambridge History of the British Empire, 1940, 2:399.

[26]This argument is basically the same as that of Hla Myint, as Szereszewski recognizes (see p. 77, fn. 5), who argues that surplus land and labor is the basis of rapid development, thus applying Adam Smith's "vent-for-surplus" theory. See Myint's *The Economics of the Developing Countries*, London: Hutchinson, 1964, chap. 3.

[27]See S. Daniel Neumark (1964:151-152): "The essential point is that, given an export demand the whole development of agricultural products in Africa prior to World War I has depended upon the provision of bulk transport, equally for plantation production and for peasant production which predominates in Africa. In West Africa, river transport made accessible forest zones along the Niger, the Gambia, the Congo, and other rivers. New areas were opened later by railways, which not only make the effectiveness of river transport, as in the case of the Niger, the Congo, and the Senegal, but also make the savannas available for commercial crops. Similarly, the opening of railway communications with the East Coast led to the expansion of cotton, coffee, and sisal production in East Africa, and to the production for export of tobacco, tea, and cotton in Nyassaland."

[28]These correspond to the three categories used by Samir Amin (1973): Africa of the colonial economy (*économie de traite*), Africa of the concession-owning companies, Africa of the labor reserves.

[29] For a very brief history of the policy of concessions, see Catherine Coquery-Vidrovitch (1969), especially pp. 186-194.

[30] Coquery-Vidrovitch's figures for growth of imports and exports in French West Africa showed a 25-fold leap (1969:181).

[31] Why this was not so easy is explained in Merlier (1962:59-61). See also Robert Harms (1975:77): "Recent research on events in the concession of Abir, the most notorious of the Congo concession companies, has revealed that attempts at reform in the concession area were notably unsuccessful, and that the rubber system in the Abir territory had already broken down by 1906, when serious debate on the Congo question was just beginning in Europe. The cause of this breakdown had little to do with the reform movement or international diplomacy; the concession had run out of rubber."

[32] T.O. Ranger (1967:334-335) notes: "As far as [Cecil] Rhodes [the dominant figure in the British South Africa Company] was concerned, then, the [revolts in both Mashonaland and Matabeleland] in 1896 and 1897 merely decided him to move towards settler representation more rapidly...Finally, of course, there was the reluctance of the British government to become in any way financially responsible for Rhodesia which powerfully induced them to accept any reasonable looking settlement negotiated between Rhodes and [Lord] Milner [British High Commissioner in South Africa]. As Milner reminded them in December 1897, if further native troubles were to bankrupt the Company it 'will throw an impecunious, undeveloped country bigger than France upon your hands'." How the settlers pushed the African peasantry out of the food-crop sector as well is described in I.R. Phimister (1974).

[33] Between 1911 and 1913 there were "a series of court cases in South-West Africa in which settlers were charged with the murder or manslaughter of Africans.... Although the trials were concerned with social tensions on the farms, they were taken by the whole of the settler population and the administration as representative test-cases. Thus, the two major groups of the German population in SWA were in open conflict; on the one side the settlers, the dependents, their defense counsel, their witnesses and jurymen, the farming press, and the whole of public opinion in Windhock; on the other, the Civil Servants as judges and prosecutors, the police, and medical officers. The government intervened on behalf of the African victims and also called Africans as witnesses for the prosecution" (Bley, 1967:261).

[34] Rechenberg's "private opposition to the settlers was never concealed. 'Any settlement by Europeans on a large scale,' he wrote, 'must lead to a conflict with the natives, which could only be settled in bloody fashion.' He never forgot the danger of rebellion. Further, he believed that the proper goal of German settlement was Eastern Europe" (Iliffe, 1969:131).

[35] "The plantation sector, then, grew fairly slowly [in Tanganyika in the 1920s] and became really substantial only in the 1930's by which time...a rival African sector of cash crop production had emerged to balance it. Partly for this reason, the plantations never came to dominate the economy as did the European farms in

Kenya" (Iliffe, 1971:14).

[36] This is what Wolff suggests. He says (1974:135) that the British feared that Kenya in its "depressed economic conditions" faced only two alternatives: "To revert to an 'earlier, primitive' form of tribal, more or less subsistence economy or to implant non-African settlers in order to organize, invest in, and manage agricultural production of cash crops." As for the contrast of Uganda, Wolff argues (p. 177): "The geographic position of Uganda in the interior of the continent greatly reduced the economically damaging effects of the slave trade and its aboliton. Furthermore, the relatively strictly structured and 'stable' Buganda Kingdom offered the attractive possibility of organizing African peasant agricultural production managed at middle and lower levels by Africans already accustomed to workable hierarchical relationships."

[37] Amin points out (1973:191): "On the other hand, in the savannah, from Senegal through Northern Nigeria to Sudan, the Moslem brotherhoods permitted another type of colonial trading: the organization of production and export (groundnuts and cotton) in the context of vast areas subject to a theocratic political power—that of the Mourid brotherhoods of Senegal, the Sultanates of Nigeria and Ansar and Ashiqqa in the Sudan—which kept the form of a tribute paying social formation, but was integrated into the international system because the surplus appropriated in the form of tribute levied on the village communities was itself marketed. It was the Egyptian colonization in Sudan which created the most advanced conditions for the development of this type of organization, which in that country tended towards a pure and simple *latifundium* system. The British merely gathered the fruits of this evolution. The new *latifundia*-owners, who after 1898 accepted the colonial administration, had cotton grown for the benefit of British industry. Powerful modern techniques (large-scale irrigation in the Gezira) were made available to them. But the second transformation of Islam in West Africa, after the colonial conquest, opened the way to the same kind of evolution, although less definite and slower."

[38] Compare the discussion of the "mining revolution" of 1866-1918 offered by D. Hobart Houghton (1969). Figure 2 on page 18 of his essay shows how sharp the jump in exports were in the period of which we are speaking, doubling for example in the period 1906-1910 over the previous five years.

[39] Hopkins (1973:204) does warn against exaggerating the decline of the African bourgeoisie on the grounds that "the European firms already dominated the trade of the main ports in the period 1850-1880," that the decline was relative but not absolute, that Africans went into forms of commerce other than export-import, "being astute enough to realize" where their comparative disadvantage lay. But none of this undoes the basic point that a major structural change occurred at this point in time, what Hopkins calls "completing the open economy."

[40] See for example this comment on the presumably relatively prosperous group of white settlers in Kenya (Van Zwanenberg, 1972:8-10): "In the period up to 1939 the European settlers were struggling to establish their estates on a firm economic and technical base. The settlers suffered from an almost permanent shortage of labour, inadequate finances, and a lack of sufficient technical knowledge and, as a

result, the majority of estates were only able to use less than half the available land...The whole plantation system had been rocked by the great depression...In Kenya's case credit through the branches of the international banks was stopped for the duration of slump, while export prices dropped drastically [beginning in 1919]."

[41]E.A. Brett (1973:87) captures the flavor of this situation splendidly: "Commitment [of the colonial administration in East Africa] to the 'managed economy' did not involve any ideological doubts about the right of private interests to exploit resources when they could so profitably without excessively raising the costs of everyone else...What does emerge is the congruence between the interests of a bureaucracy committed to large-scale centralized administrative structures for reasons of simplicity of management and economy and those of private producing and trading groups that needed to have services provided at the cheapest possible rate...[Where there was conflict, it] was really about the relative advantages to different private interests of a state versus a private monopoly for the provision of essential services. In the cases detailed here the State solution was accepted because the most important of the capitalist groups were not prepared to pay subsidies to the incompetence or greed of others of their number."

[42]The socioeconomic roots of the African famine are well discussed in Comité Information Sahel, *Qui se nourrit de la famine en Afrique?* Paris: Ed. Maspero, Cahiers Libres 292-293, 1974, and two articles in *Review of African Political Economy, No. 1*, 1974: Claude Meillassoux, "Development or Exploitation: Is the Sahel Famine Good Business?," pp. 27-33; Lionel Cliffe, "Feudalism, Capitalism and Famine in Ethiopia," pp. 34-40.

[43]I am using the phrase of F.H. Cardoso and Enzo Faletto, which emphasizes the fact that increased dependency and increased development (in terms of increase in industrial capacity and more generally in the forces of production) may go hand in hand. See their *Dependencia y desarollo en América Latina,* Mexico: Siglo XXI, 1965.

BIBLIOGRAPHY

ALPERS, E. (1967). The East African slave trade (Historical Association of Tanzania Paper no. 3). Nairobi: East African Publishing House.
⎯⎯⎯(1969). "The nineteenth century: Prelude to colonialism," in B.A. Ogot and J.A. Kieran (eds.), Zamani: A survey of East African history. Nairobi: East African Publishing House.
⎯⎯⎯(1973). "Rethinking African economic history." Ufahumu, 3 (winter).
⎯⎯⎯"Gujarati and the trade of East Africa, c. 1500-1800," *International Journal of African Historical Studies,* 9, 1, 1976: 22-24.

AMIN, S. (1969). Le monde des affaires sénégalais. Paris: Editions de Minuit.
_____(1973). "Underdevelopment and dependence in black Africa—Their historical origins and contemporary forms." Social and Economic Studies, 22(1).
_____(1974). "Accumulation and development: A theoretical model." Review of African Political Economy (no. 1).
ARRIGHI, G. (1973). "Labor supplies in historical perspective: A study of the proletarianization of the African peasantry in Rhodesia." pp. 180-234 in G. Arrighi and J.S. Saul (eds.), Essays on the political economy of Africa. New York: Monthly Review Press.
BARBER, W.J. (1964). "The movement into the world economy." In M.J. Herskovits and M. Harwitz (eds.), Economic transition in Africa. Evanston, Ill.: Northwestern University Press.
BEAN, R. (1974). "A note on the relative importance of slaves and gold in West African exports." Journal of African History, 15(3).
BLEY, H. (1967). South-West Africa under German rule, 1894-1914. Evanston, Ill.: Northwestern University Press.
BOAHEN, A. (1974). "Politics in Ghana, 1800-1874." In J.F.A. Ajayi and M. Crowder (eds.), History of West Africa (vol. 2). London: Longmans.
BOULLE, P.H. (1972). "Slave trade, commercial organization and industrial growth in eighteenth-century Nantes." Revue française d'histoire d'outre-mer, 59(214, ler trimestre).
BRETT, E.A. (1973). Colonialism and underdevelopment in East Africa. London: Heinemann.
BROOKS, G.E. (1975). "Peanuts and colonialization: Consequences of the commercialization of peanuts in West Africa, 1830-70." Journal of African History, 16(1).
COQUERY-VIDROVITCH, C. (1969). "French colonization in Africa to 1920: Administration and economic development." In L.H. Gann and P. Duignan (eds.), Colonialism in Africa, 1870-1960 (vol. 1). Cambridge: University Press.
CURTIN, P.D. (1969). The Atlantic slave trade: A census. Madison: University of Wisconsin Press.
DAAKU, K.Y. (1968). "The slave trade and African society." In T.O. Ranger (ed.), Emerging themes of African history. Nairobi: East African Publishing House.
DAVENPORT, T.R.H. (1969). "The consolidation of a new society: The Cape Colony." In M. Wilson and L. Thompson (eds.), The Oxford history of South Africa (vol. 1). New York: Oxford University Press.
DE KIEWIET, C.W. (1957). A history of South Africa: Social and economic. London: Oxford University Press.
EHRLICH, C. (1965). "The Uganda economy, 1903-1945." In V. Harlow and E.M. Chilver (eds.), History of East Africa (vol. 2). Oxford: Clarendon Press.
EMMANUEL, A. (1972). Unequal exchange. New York: Monthly Review Press.

FIELDHOUSE, D.K. (1971). "The economic exploitation of Africa: Some British and French comparisons." In P. Gifford and W.R. Lewis (eds.), France and Britain in Africa. New Haven, Conn.: Yale University Press.
FLINT, J.E. (1963). "The wider background to partition and colonial occupation." Pp. 350-390 in R. Oliver and G. Mathew (eds.), History of East Africa (vol. 1). Oxford: Clarendon Press.
_____(1974). "Economic change in West Africa in the nineteenth century." In J.F.A. Ajayi and M. Crowder (eds.), History of West Africa (vol. 2). London: Longmans.
FYFE, C. (1972). Africanus Horton. New York: Oxford University Press.
_____(1974). "Reform in West Africa: the abolition of the slave trade." In J.F.A. Ajayi and M. Crowder (eds.), History of West Africa (vol. 2). London: Longmans.
GALLAGHER, J., and ROBINSON, R. (1970). "The imperialism of free trade." In A.G.L. Shaw (ed.), Great Britain and the colonies. London: Methuen. This is a reprint which originally appeared in Economic History Review (2nd ser.), 1953, 6(1).
GRAY, J.M. (1963). "Zanzibar and the coastal belt, 1840-1884." In R. Oliver and G. Mathew (eds.), History of East Africa (vol. 1). Oxford: Clarendon Press.
HARMS, R. (1975). "The end of red rubber: A reassessment." Journal of African History, 16(1).
HOPKINS, A.G. (1973). An economic history of West Africa. London: Longmans.
HOUGHTON, D.H. (1969). "Economic development, 1865-1965." In M. Wilson and L. Thompson (eds.), The Oxford history of South Africa (vol. 2). New York: Oxford University Press.
ILIFFE, J. (1969). Tanganyika under German rule, 1905-1912. Cambridge: University Press.
_____(1971). Agricultural change in modern Tanganyika (Historical Association of Tanzania Paper no. 10). Nairobi: East African Publishing House.
JOHNSON, M. (1974). "Cotton imperialism in West Africa." African Affairs, 73(291).
JULIEN, C.A. (1964). Histoire de l'Algérie contemporaine (vol. 1). Paris: Presses Universitaires de France.
LEWIS, W.A. (1952). "World production, prices and trade, 1870-1960." Manchester School of Economic and Social Studies, 20(1).
LOW, D.A. (1965). "British rule, 1895-1912." In V. Harlow and E.M. Chilver (eds.), History of East Africa (vol. 2). Oxford: Clarendon Press.
MERLIER, M. (1962). Le Congo de la colonisation belge à l'indépendence. Paris: Ed. Maspero.
NEUMARK, S.D. (1964). Foreign trade and economic development in Africa: A historical perspective. Stanford, Calif.: Food Research Institute.
NEWBURY, C.W. (1969). "Trade and authority in West Africa from 1850 to 1880." In L.H. Gann and P. Duignan (eds.), Colonialism in Africa, 1870-

1960 (vol. 1). Cambridge: University Press.
OMER-COOPER, J.D. (1966a). "The Mfecane and the Great Trek." In J.C. Anene and G.N. Brown (eds.), Africa in the nineteenth and twentieth centuries. Ibadan: Ibadan University Press.
──── (1966b). "South Africa at the dawn of the nineteenth century." In J.C. Anene and G.N. Brown (eds.), Africa in the nineteenth and twentieth centuries. Ibadan: Ibadan university Press.
PATTERSON, S. (1975). The last trek. London: Routledge and Kegan Paul.
PHIMISTER, I.R. (1974). "Peasant production and underdevelopment in Southern Rhodesia, 1890-1914." African Affairs, 73:291.
RANGER, T.O. (1967). Revolt in Southern Rhodesia, 1896-97. Evanston, Ill.: Northwestern University Press.
REYNOLDS, E. (1975). "Economic imperialism: The case of the Gold Coast." Journal of Economic History, 35(1).
RODNEY, W. (1968). "European activity and African reaction in Angola." In T.O. Ranger (ed.), Aspects of Central African history. London: Heinemann.
RONEN, D. (1971). "On the African role in the trans-Atlantic slave trade in Dahomey." Cahiers d'études africaines, 11(1).
SCHUMPETER, J. (1939). Business cycles. New York: McGraw-Hill.
SRAFFA, P. (1972). Production of commodities by means of commodities. Cambridge: University Press.
STENGERS, J. (1969). "The Congo Free State and the Belgian Congo before 1914." In L.H. Gann and P. Duignan (eds.), Colonialization in Africa, 1870-1960 (vol. 1). Cambridge: University Press.
SURET-CANALE, J. (1964). Afrique noire occidentale et centrale (vol. 2). Paris: Edition Sociales.
SZERESZEWSKI, R. (1965). Structural changes in the economy of Ghana, 1891-1911. London: Weidenfeld and Nicholson.
THOMPSON, L. (1971a). "Great Britain and the Afrikaner republics, 1870-1899." In M. Wilson and L. Thompson (eds.), The Oxford history of South Africa (vol. 2). New York: Oxford University Press.
──── (1971b). "The subjection of the African chiefdoms, 1870-1898." In M. Wilson and L. Thompson (eds.), The Oxford history of South Africa (vol. 2). New York: Oxford University Press.
UZOIGWE, G.N. (1974). Britain and the conquest of Africa. Ann Arbor: University of Michigan Press.
VAN ZWANENBERG, R. (1972). The agricultural history of Kenya to 1939 (Historical Association of Kenya Paper no. 1). Nairobi: East African Publishing House.
VELLUT, J.L. (1975). "Le Zaire à la périphérie du capitalisme: quelques perspectives historiques." Unpublished paper delivered to the Canadian Association of African Studies, Toronto, February 19-22.
WALLERSTEIN, I. (1970). "The colonial era in Africa: Changes in social structure." In L.H. Gann and P. Guignan (eds.), Colonialism in Africa, 1870-

1960 (vol. 2). Cambridge: University Press.
———(1972). "Social conflict in post-independence black Africa: The concepts of race and status-group reconsidered." In E.Q. Campbell (ed.), Racial tensions and national identity. Nashville, Tenn.: Vanderbilt University Press.
———(1973). "Africa in a capitalist world." Issue, 3(3).
———(1974a). "The rise and future demise of the world capitalist system: Concepts for comparative analysis." Comparative Studies in Society and History, 16:387-415.
———(1974b). The modern world-system: Capitalist agriculture and the origins of the European world-economy in the sixteenth century. New York: Academic Press.
———(1975a). Old problems and new syntheses: The relation of revolutionary ideas and practices. Saskatoon: University of Saskatchewan Press.
———(1975b). "Class-formation in the capitalist world-economy." Politics and Society, 5(3).
WHEELER, D.L. (1971). "Part one." In D.L. Wheeler and R. Pélissier (eds.), Angola. New York: Praeger.
WILLIAMS, E. (1964). British historians and the West Indies. Port-of-Spain, Trinidad: P.N.M. Publishing.
WILSON, H.S. (1969). Origins of West African nationalism. London: Macmillan.
WOLFF, R. (1974). The economics of colonialism: Britain and Kenya, 1870-93. New Haven, Conn.: Yale University Press.

Peripheralization of Southern Africa:*
Changes in Household Structure and Labor-Force Formation

The incorporation of an area in the capitalist world-economy means first of all, and most importantly, the integration of its production processes into the interdependent network of production processes that constitute the world market. As the capitalist world-economy has expanded historically, new zones have been regularly thus incorporated.

The process of incorporation may be thought of as a transformation that normally takes at least fifty years to complete. It can be measured by the restructuring successively of production processes, household structures, and political institutions. Since the physical loci of these three institutions are not normally identical, it is an analytically confusing process, but this does not make the links less real.

In southern Africa, *latu sensu*, the process of incorporation began circa 1800 in terms of changes in production processes. And in some interior areas, the process is only being completed today. Responsive changes in household structures began much later. The political consequences are of course the most familiar in terms of the creation of colonial states (and today of so-called "decolonization").

Peripheralization of an area means turning the use of local resources—in land, in subsoil resources, and in labor—toward the production of items that maximize the process of overall capital accumulation within the world-economy. This involves not only the production of cash-crops, ores, or

---

*Co-authored with William G. Martin.

transformed products for sale on the world market, but production of the foodstuffs necessary to sustain the work force, and production (or reproduction) of the labor to work in market-oriented production organizations.

Peripheralization is a process which individuals act to promote. It does not occur of its own accord. There are two major stumbling blocks that must be overcome if an area is to be incorporated in the network of world production processes. The first is resistance by any efficacious political institution for whatever reason to this transformation of production processes. The second is the real availability of labor for the (new) production processes.

Political resistance to incorporation is overcome in many ways. One is outright foreign military intrusion, that is, colonization, in which the resisting, or potentially resisting, political authorities are simply eliminated from the scene. The second involves an internal replacement of resisting with cooperating political authorities, which is of course the whole political history of the capitalist world-economy. On occasion this process of replacement is brusque, that is, "revolutionary."

However that may be, and this process is not itself our subject, it does not necessarily occur at all—indeed, often the contrary—at the beginning of the process of peripheralization. In order for peripheralization to proceed, the key element is the availability of labor. Now, in one sense, labor is always (or almost always) "available." People usually live in the zones that are being peripheralized, and these people normally work. Hence, it is theoretically merely a matter of transferring the locus, and perhaps the technical methods, of work.

But it has never been so easy. Labor in a capitalist system is a different social process from labor in a redistributive tributary system (and *a fortiori* different from that in a reciprocal lineage mode of production). For the vast majority, labor under the imperative of capital accumulation is longer, harder, and less rewarding. This being the case, it is usually rather difficult simply to persuade an individual by oral argument to "enter" the labor market of the capitalist world-system.

Yet, unless an adequate number of persons (eventually *most* persons) of an area are in fact both willing to work according to the imperatives of world production processes and willing to locate themselves near the place of work, it is not possible to operate the production institutions profitably. This willingness to work has never been, is not now, taken for granted by those who control productive institutions in the capitalist world-economy.

The use of force has been central to the acquisition of a labor force. Individual willingness has been ignored. Force of course has come in two extreme versions. One is direct, overt force, legitimated by state authorities (or at least tolerated), when these authorities are not themselves the agents of coercion. The costs of overt force can be high. The other is mediate force operating via the market, that is, the process of proletarianization. The latter mode is however even more expensive—for the world-system as a whole, for particular state machineries, for individual entrepreneurs. Hence direct force (in all its many variations) has been the normal first recourse of employers in areas that have been undergoing peripheralization.

Availability of labor requires of course location of labor—mobility to the work zone, and immobility once there. When overt force is employed, there is little question about location. Getting and tying the worker to the work place becomes simply one of the first elements on the agenda. Proletarianization, by contrast, leads to increased mobility—not merely legal, but real—which further adds to the real cost of labor.

In fact, the "extreme" versions of force—overt and direct, mediate and market-based—are *both* expensive. Whether the costs are augmented via the mechanism of supervision (in the case of overt force) or real wages (in the case of mediate force), they give rise to the search for other forms of labor control, which will permit reproduction of labor at lower real costs for the owners of produced commodities (that is, the world bourgeoisie).

Those modes of labor control which are in the middle of the formal continuum from forced labor to proletarian labor turn out in fact to be least costly over the long run. It is no accident, therefore, that what we shall call part-life-time wage-laborer households are the primary way of organizing consumption (reproduction) units, and hence the pools of available labor, in the world-economy. These are households in which of the total income of the "household" over a "life time," *part* of the income comes from direct wages (whether in cash or in kind) and the other parts come from subsistence production, sales of commodities on the market, subsidies (transfer payments), and "gifts."

The wage-labor component of the income may be received as returns for work done in part of every week, or part of every year (seasonal work) or a discrete part of a life cycle (target working). The sums expended by employers on such part-life-time wage-laborers can be and are less than those paid either fully coerced workers (e.g., slaves) or full-life-time wage-laborers, since employers can in fact push the worker into accepting "below-subsistence wages," which are then supplemented out of the alternative sources of income.

Such a system can however only operate provided there exists a particular type of household structure in which money is pooled over time and space over a flexible unit not necessarily the same as the formal family (whether nuclear or extended). The institutionalization of such a flexible household community would seem to be one of the prime consequences of (and indicators of) peripheralization.

If this process has gone unnoticed, it is not only because of the glamorous isolation of "primitive" and "tribal" peoples, but also due to the objectification of the *individual* male laborer as the historical subject of proletarianization. It takes but a brief moment's reflection to perceive that this is questionable, for under capitalism (and indeed in most precapitalist societies) the social organization and reproduction of labor takes place through processes that bind individuals together into primary social units, often called households. In a capitalist system, these households are, in economic terms, income-pooling units, whose boundaries may or may not be formed along purely kinship lines. We are interested in the process by which part-life-time proletarian households are in fact created and sustained. Creation of such households has involved the gradual alteration of the production, consumption, and reproduction patterns of the precolonial household, the fundamental unit of precapitalist production. As long as the internal social and production relations of indigenous households remained untouched, African participation in the colonial labor and commodity markets could not be guaranteed.

The difficulties colonial and settler agencies faced very early in their occupation of southern Africa attest to the problem of creating an African labor force. Not only was slave labor imported to the Cape, but even in the first half of the nineteenth century the labor requirements of settler agriculture, including wine and wheat plantations, were met largely by irregular methods, including the direct plunder of labor. The Mfecane and Xhosa cattle killing led to an injection of impoverished laborers into the colony, laborers subsequently tied to white agriculturalists by acts such as Ordinance 49 of 1828.

As British and Afrikaner expansion continued in the nineteenth century, such methods became inadequate, and colonial authorities were confronted with the need to secure African labor services in ever-increasing quantities. The basic solution to this problem was to ensure that Africans could no longer exist outside the market and production processes of the world-economy. And this in turn meant the curtailment of the ability of African households to meet their own needs, ensuring the linkage of African producers to the commodity chains of capitalist accumulation.

The "gun and ivory" frontier was in fact the first form of capitalist penetration of the countryside and the alteration of household structures. The transition from barter, or the exchange of preciosities, to colonial (and hence world) market values that this process induced often led to the revaluation of the central elements of the social reproduction of the household (lobolo, cattle, etc.) in colonial currencies, a reallocation of the labor time of household members toward the pursuit of commodities demanded by traders, and the decline of handicraft production. By the last quarter of the nineteenth century travelers and missionaries throughout southern Africa continually reported the sway of the pound sterling.[1] This slowly corrosive process was unable by itself, however, to ensure a steady labor supply to the wide range of capitalist production processes that emerged in the course of the nineteenth and early twentieth centuries. Colonial and settler agencies thus turned to more direct measures to limit the ability of African households to reproduce themselves outside the nexus of colonial production processes.

It was here that the reduction of the consumption level of indigenous households *below* the minimal levels needed to ensure the reproduction of the household was critical. This was not an easy task, as African resistance was great to such efforts. A primary instrument was of course the introduction of head and hut taxes after conquest, as colonial authorities extended their control over African communities. Such measures were most effective where the sale of surplus product was diminished to the extent that part-time wage labor was necessary, and necessary not only in the slack agricultural season. That this was well realized by colonial authorities is indicated by the precise calculations of the tax levels necessary to produce sale of cattle, as in Natal;[2] the elimination in many areas, such as Katanga, Zimbabwe, and Zambia,[3] of the ability to pay taxes in kind; and the loss of cattle due to tax levies, as Phimister has documented in the case of the Victoria district in Zimbabwe.[4] In these, as in myriad of other cases, the basic intent was clear: the eventual elimination of control by African households over the means of production.

In this endeavor the loss of cattle and land through conquest proved to be ultimately of more importance, even if it did not figure on the balance sheets of the Colonial Office. And conquest only prefigured more complex mechanisms by which household productive capabilities were diminished. These mechanisms through which household transformations were promoted varied widely according to the resources and policies of colonial and settler state agencies, the precolonial organization of the household (about which we know far too little), and the labor requirements of the different production processes that arose with the incorporation of successive areas of southern Africa. The pattern is thus not unidimensional. The result of colonial and settler penetration was however quite clear: the disruption of the agricultural and life cycles of the precolonial household.

In some areas this process began even before conquest,[5] as the decline of wild game reserves in response to barter and subsequently market opportunities resulted in the loss of a central source of subsistence reproduction. As Sherilyn Young has noted for southern Mozambique: "By the end of the nineteenth century not only had the elephants been destroyed for what might be termed 'cash-cropping,' but antelopes and wildebeest, which were mainly 'subsistence' crops of hunting, were seriously depleted."[6] The loss of cattle by successive pastoralists, through both conquest and "natural" disasters such as drought, bovine pleuro-pneumonia in mid-century, and the continentwide rinderpest of the late 1890's (which resulted in extremely heavy cattle losses approaching 90% in some areas)[7] both further devastated the productive capabilities of the African household and tore the very social fabric of the community. As R. Moorsom notes: "The loss of hunting and particularly of cattle robbed men of the object of a substantial proportion of their labour-time: the loss of cattle was sudden and total, and a severe material and social shock."[8]

Equally important to the loss of husbandry was the pressure on African access to land, another result of the expansion of settler pastoralism. Wherever settlers were weak however, either in numbers or in organization, African households were able to maintain their agricultural activities, often by occupying speculators' and Crown lands in nineteenth-century Natal, the northern Transvaal, and parts of Zimbabwe. This phenomenon was prevalent in areas where mining was absent; in such areas colonial authorities even on occasion encouraged peasant cash-crop production. An early period of flourishing peasant cash-crop production has been documented for the Cape region by Colin Bundy,[9] but it also occurred in parts of Zimbabwe,[10] and even Zaire.[11]

Often promoted by missionaries, the emergence of peasant production marked one form of the creation of part-life-time wage-labor households, as household production, consumption, and reproduction became directly oriented to, and dependent upon, participation in the colonial (capitalist) market. In its most developed form this represented a transition from the sale of surplus product based upon precolonial household structures to true simple commodity production. This meant not only integration with the exchange process, but also transformations in the productive process of the household, as is indicated by the emergence of new crops, the use of new agricultural implements, and the alteration of male and female tasks within the household.[12] Such a system most often occurred where colonial authorities, backed by merchants, foresaw this as the most rewarding use of available land and labor resources. As large-scale capitalist enterprises emerged in the last quarter of the century, and as settlers intensified their agricultural production by shifting from pastoral to cereal crop production, even this option was foreclosed.

Within the period under consideration it was indeed in the long expansion of world economic activity, roughly from 1897 to 1920, that the full transformation of African households began to be completed in the region. This period was marked by the completion of the conquest of southern Africa. It was also the period of the introduction of new production processes, both in the mining and the agricultural sectors. Mechanisms of control became far more complex, as is illustrated by the plethora of legislative acts, promulgations, and schemes of the period aimed at regulating the use of labor and land in colonial territories. These included the 1913 Natives Land Act in South Africa, the Decrees of August 1910 and January 1912 in Katanga, the introduction of labor control systems in the Transvaal and the Orange Free Colony through the Natives Passes Proclamation of 1901, the 1897 *Regulamento* in the Portuguese colonies prescribing mandatory labor service, and the Regulations of 1906-07 in Southwest Africa, all of which were designed to curtail African access to land and cattle in order to ensure a labor supply for non-African enterprises. State assistance to white agriculture, closure of markets to peasant producers, networks of credit indebtedness whose outcome was contract labor, and even more brutal and hidden activities such as the *shibalo* system in Mozambique, round out the activities circumscribing African participation in agricultural production and colonial markets. Under such pressures not only was peasant production severely curtailed, but households only just being incorporated felt the full force of the acceleration of demands for labor.

One result of such activities was the emergence of true coerced cash-crop production in areas far removed from mining and settler agriculture, as in the forced cultivation of cotton in northern Mozambique. Of far greater import however was the effect of the establishment of large mining houses in the Transvaal after 1886, and the successive opening up of new mines in the next twenty years in Zimbabwe, Zambia, Zaire, and Namibia. Not only did these production processes require very large numbers of African laborers, but the establishment of railway systems lent an impetus to settler agriculture and even to the import of cheaper foodstuffs from abroad. These developments not only lessened colonial and settler interest in allowing African agricultural production to continue, but also provided the financial means by which colonial and settler states could enforce the new mechanisms of control outlined above. It involved the alteration of household structures such that male labor could be procured at ever lower real costs. And the condition upon which this rested was the institutionalization of a lower level of well-being for Africans than had existed prior to European penetration of southern Africa.

Further details of the processes and mechanisms by which African households' control over production and labor were diminished as land and labor became commodities may be gathered from the existing literature.[13] What remains much less known are the actual dimensions of the reorganization of internal household dynamics as a part-life-time wage-labor force was created. From the description above of the processes leading to the emergence of a part-life-time wage-labor force, it should be evident however that the reproduction patterns of households that became integrated into the world-economy were significantly transformed. The domination of exchange value alone suggests that the expenditure of household labor and capital funds in the form of cattle and land (where these existed) was placed on a fundamentally new basis. To take but one example, the production and consumption patterns of newly emergent "peasant"—or, more properly, petty commodity producer—households reflected the development of more technologically advanced methods of production attuned to the (world) capitalist market. Accounts of peasant households attached to mission stations[14] thus remark upon the exchange of hoes for ploughs, the rise of new agricultural commodities, and the consumption of goods produced outside the household. As reflections of the transformed social relations, these changes often meant the subordination of the household to merchants, the reorganization of production relations internal to the household, and an alteration of the foundation of the sexual division of labor. The emergence of male agricultural field activity, in the case of oxen-drawn ploughs, and emergence of new forms of *lobolo* are but two examples of this process of transformation.

The decline of male productive activities in migrant labor households may in fact be the most striking and widespread alteration of household reproductive patterns. This was of course the intent of colonial mining authorities, as wages were predicated upon the assumption that they did not provide the means of subsistence for a whole family, but were supplemented by returns from agricultural production, returns that were however less than the amounts needed to sustain all household members. And the South African Native Affairs Commission of 1903-05 stated the objective quite clearly in its preface to measures designed to compel male labor service:

> Natives have had access to the land on terms which have enabled them to regard work for wages as a mere supplement to their means, and not as it is regarded in the older industrial communities, namely, as the urgent condition under which the majority of mankind earn their daily bread.[15]

In South Africa the President of the Transvaal Chamber of Mines indicated the solution:

> What is wanted is surely a policy that would establish once and for all that outside special reserves the ownership of land must be in the hands of the white races and that the *surplus of young men*, instead of squatting on the land in idleness and spreading out over unlimited areas, must earn their living by working for a wage, as every white man who is not a landowner has to do.[16]

As these comments suggest, a low-wage labor force was created through the separation of adult males from productive household tasks. As Arrighi has noted for Zimbabwe,[17] and as others have subsequently demonstrated for other regions, the loss of cattle at the turn of the century led to a period of male underemployment. Where this occurred the creation of male migrant labor entrenched what may have been only a temporary phenomenon. In addition to the decline in consumption goods from animal husbandry, there was thus also the loss of adult male labor, including in some areas even male child labor.[18] This naturally affected not only the care and feeding of animals but also foodstuff production, if we recognize that male agricultural activities had hardly been nonexistent, as colonial authorities so often claimed. Thus as males left their villages more frequently and for longer periods, the heavy proportion of tasks associated with the production of agricultural goods—often cash crops that needed to be sold in order to buy consumption goods, as in the case of cotton cultivation in northern Mozambique—fell on the shoulders of women. As Sherilyn Young has noted in the case of southern Mozambique at the turn of the century:

> Labour migration and internal forced labour of men kept more than half of the adult males away from home at most times. Drought and flood brought frequent famines while Portuguese alienation of land and imposition of taxes placed unusual demands on cultivators. ... [W]omen were thus increasingly expected to fulfill all home duties and supply food without the assistance of men.[19]

More recent studies of southern Mozambique have confirmed in greater detail the historical pattern by which households became dependent for their reproduction upon women's agricultural activity *and* returns from male wage labor. In areas where approximately 90% of miners represented the second and even third generations of male migrant labor, returns from both agricultural activities and migrant wage labor were necessary to fund the reproduction needs of households in the area. Even the replacement of agricultural implements and cattle had come to depend upon wages remitted by miners.[20]

While the predominant form of labor supply throughout the region, the oscillating migration found in southern Mozambique, along with the scattered emergence of "peasant" households, were neither the sole forms of labor service nor the sole manners in which part-life-time wage-labor households were formed. In areas of settler agriculture, as in the Transvaal, Natal, Orange Free State, and parts of Zimbabwe, tenantry arrangements emerged whereby access to land was controlled through the provisioning of labor, or in early periods of crop-shares, to the settler proprietor. And in areas of plantations and estates, as in Mozambique north of the Savé River, labor service was required for African males as well. Despite differences in these forms of labor utilization, the consequences for African households were much the same: the creation of a new pattern of household reproduction that necessitated multiple sources of income based on the engagement of at least some household members in wage-remunerated productive activities.

In these areas much further research remains before us. It may well be that the examination of household members' multiple productive roles will unveil the varied constellations of internal household dynamics that are still hidden from view. In this endeavor evidence constructed along four dimensions regarding households may prove especially fruitful: (1) source of consumption funds, (2) changing allocation of labor time, (3) shifting boundaries, size, and mobility, and (4) the sexual division of labor. Such investigations would, furthermore, shed considerable light on the differentiation of households into new classes—a process that accompanied the emergence of new production processes and their attendent forms of labor control. Studies based on similar premises, such as *The Mozambican Miner*,[21] indicate the promise that such an approach holds. As we move toward clearer and more distinct understandings of the history of southern Africa, such conceptual guides will be of ever greater importance.

It is for reasons such as these, then, that the emergence of the part-life-time wage-labor household remains so central to the process of peripheralization, as the concomitant process of the full penetration of low-wage, peripheral production processes. Whereas the precolonial household had previously formed a unit of production and consumption, with the integration of an area into the capitalist world-economy, such households lost their full productive capabilities and came to depend upon returns from labor service for a significant proportion of their consumption needs. Incorporation on these terms meant a decline in the well-being of Africans. And as more and more households reached this position, a substantial labor force was indeed created. By the 1930's, both mining capitalists and settler agriculturalists alike were able to proclaim the success of their policies.

This did not however represent full proletarianization, if by that term we mean the creation of a labor force dependent for its reproduction solely upon the wage mechanism. Households did not in our period (and we think this is still the case for the large majority of African households in the region) meet their consumption needs *solely* through wage-labor. This was quite explicitly ruled out by both colonial and capitalist agencies, for it was well recognized that full proletarianization would require higher levels of wage payments. Proposals to meet the labor shortages of the early twentieth century by stabilizing families near mining sites, such as Phillip Wrey's scheme in Zimbabwe[22] and Creswell's attempt in South Africa, met with little success. Even the stabilization of a skilled core of the mine labor force, as by the Union Minière du Haut-Katanga, depended upon the return of miners and their families to rural areas after their period of service.[23] Combining remuneration from both labor service and production internal to the household, the part-life-time wage-labor household was critical to the maintenance of a low-wage labor force. And as elsewhere in the peripheral areas of the world-economy, the emergence of this form of household was only the result of a long period of struggle. It was in this sense the product of capitalist domination of the countryside, a central indicator of the development of rural poverty, and the fundamental operating premise of the reproduction of the labor force and peripheral enterprises as a whole.

NOTES

[1] See Junod (1962, I, 276).
[2] See Robertson (1934, 415).
[3] For Katanga, see Perrings (1976, Ch. 1); on Zimbabwe, see Arrighi in Arrighi and Saul (1973, 194); on Zambia, see Heisler (1974, 6).
[4] See Phimister (1974).
[5] For an indication of how far this could proceed without pacification by colonial powers, see Clarence-Smith and Moorsom in Palmer and Parsons (1977).
[6] Young in Palmer and Parsons (1977, 72-73).
[7] For a survey of the impact of rinderpest, see van Onselen (1972).
[8] Moorsom (1977, 35).
[9] See Bundy (1975).

[10] See Arrighi (1973).
[11] See Perrings (1976).
[12] See Bundy (1975, 66, 84-86, 137).
[13] Palmer and Parsons (1977).
[14] See Bundy (1975) and Wilson (1971).
[15] South African Native Affairs Commission (1903-05, I, 80).
[16] Transvaal Chamber of Mines (1911, 1xxi); emphasis added.
[17] See Arrighi (1973, 187).
[18] See van Onselen (1976, 125).
[19] Young in Palmer and Parsons (1977, 75).
[20] See Universidade Eduardo Mondlane, Centro de Estudos Africanos (1977, 55, passim).
[21] Ibid.
[22] See van Onselen (1976, 76).
[23] See Perrings (1976, 344ff).

BIBLIOGRAPHY

Giovanni Arrighi, "Labor Supplies in Historical Perspective: A Study of the Proletarianization of the African Peasantry in Rhodesia," in Giovanni Arrighi & John S. Saul, *Essays on the Political Economy of Africa* (New York: Monthly Review Press, 1973), 180-234.

Colin Bundy, "African Peasants and Economic Change in South Africa 1870-1913," unpubl. D. Phil. dissertation, Oxford University, 1975.

Gervase Clarence-Smith & Richard Moorsom, "Underdevelopment and Class Formation in Ouamboland, 1844-1917," in Robin Palmer & Neil Parsons, eds., *The Roots of Rural Poverty* (Berkeley: Univ. of California Press, 1977), 96-112.

Helmuth Heisler, *Urbanization and the Government of Migration* (New York: St. Martin's Press, 1974).

Henri Junod, *Life of a South African Tribe* (New York: University Books, 1962), 2 vols.

Richard Moorsom, "Underdevelopment and Class Formation: The Origins of Migrant Labor in Namibia, 1850-1915," in T. Adler, ed., *Perspectives on South Africa* (Johannesburg: African Studies Institute, University of Witswatersrand, 1977), 3-50.

Charles Aubrey Perrings, "Black Labour in the Copper Mines of Northern Rhodesia and the Belgian Congo," unpubl. D. Phil. dissertation, University of London, 1976.

Ian Phimister, "Peasant Production and Underdevelopment in Southern Rhodesia, 1890-1914," *African Affairs*, 73, 29, Apr. 1974, 217-28.

H.M. Robertson, "150 Years of Economic Contact Between Black and White," *South African Journal of Economics*, II, 4, Dec. 1934, 403-25; III, 1, Mar. 1935, 3-25.

South African Native Affairs Commission 1903-1905, I, 80.

Transvaal Chamber of Mines, *Twenty-Second Annual Report*, 1911.

Universidade Eduardo Mondlane, Centro de Estudos Africanos, *The Mozambican Miner* (Maputo, 1977).

Charles van Onselen, *Chibaro* (London: Pluto Press, 1976).

Monica Wilson, "The Growth of Peasant Communities," in Monica Wilson & Leonard Thompson, eds., *The Oxford History of South Africa* (New York: Oxford Univ. Press, 1971), I, 49-103.

Sherilyn Young, "Fertility and Famine: Women's Agricultural History in Southern Mozambique," in Robin Palmer & Neil Parsons, eds., *The Roots of Rural Poverty* (Berkeley: Univ. of California Press, 1977), 66-81.

Race Is Class?
Some Reflections on South Africa Inspired By Magubane*

South Africa today is not only the locus of a key contemporary geopolitical conflict, one that will have a lasting impact on the world transition to socialism; it is also the locus about which a key intellectual debate rages, one that is intimately linked with both the immediate geopolitical conflict and the wider worldwide struggle for socialism. Magubane's book is a statement in this intellectual debate, his contribution to the geopolitical conflict.

The story is in the title: *The Political Economy of Race and Class in South Africa*. Race *and* class—that is Magubane's theme; not race or class. Indeed, he comes near to arguing that race *is* class or, more accurately if less elegantly, that under certain conditions race is the equivalent of class, and under those same conditions what seems to be class may not be class. Lest this seem obscurantist, let me explain.

Magubane states in his preface that: "Today, black and white have irreconcilable claims to the South African state." (xi-xii) To Magubane the reason for this is clear. "The white settlers today are the descendants and defenders of those who forcibly robbed the African people of their land three centuries ago." And, at this point, he stops and makes his central point in a footnote:

> Throughout the book I refer to the whites as settlers and not as white South Africans; there is a philosophical reason for this. Before the

---

*Review essay of *The Political Economy of Race and Class in South Africa* by Bernard Magubane (Monthly Review Press, 1979).

Africans became "Kaffirs," "Natives," "Bantus," and now "Blacks," they were citizens and owners of the land later usurped by their European conquerors. Both the statelessness and degradation of the African people emerged in one and the same historical process—in the act of conquest, the forcible robbery of their means of subsistence. Their indigence today is a result of the most cruel lawlessness known to human history. Having taken this into account, the whole meaning of being called Kaffir, Native, Bantu, or Black, rather than being called African, changes the moral and legal status of the white settlers' claim to the South African state.

And what is for Magubane the way out? "[S]hould [the white settler] be driven into the sea? Certainly not." No. "Only the restructuring of the entire economic and social system, as spelled out in the Freedom Charter...could create the social climate in which a new start could be made..." The Freedom Charter, adopted in 1956 by the African National Congress and three other organizations (representing Indians, coloreds, and whites), opens with the famous and controversial sentence: "We, the People of South Africa, declare for all our country and the world to know: that South Africa belongs to all who live in it, black and white, and that no government can justly claim authority unless it is based on the will of all the people..."

To justify his position theoretically, Magubane places on page 1 this quote from Oliver C. Cox:

> Our hypothesis is that racial exploitation and race prejudice developed among Europeans with the rise of capitalism, and that because of the worldwide ramifications of capitalism, all racial antagonisms can be traced back to the policies and attitudes of the leading capitalist people, the white people of Europe and North America.

Or, in Magubane's words: "To study the development of capitalism is...the best way to study race inequality, for to do so places socioeconomic relationships at the heart of the problem, and shows how underdevelopment and racial inequalities developed together." (p. 3)

Perhaps readers are now merely nodding their heads. Is this not obvious? No, it is not obvious at all, and indeed in terms of certain "classical" versions of "Marxist theory," Magubane is a heretic, as we can see when he spells out the corollary of his approach to racism in terms of the political economy: "The history of the [native] reserves demonstrates that capitalism can *never* totally eliminate the precapitalist modes of production nor, above all, the relations of exploitation which characterize these modes of production." (pp. 97-98; italics added) Racism and the maintenance of "precapitalist" forms are not therefore for Magubane an anomaly, due to be eliminated soon. They are "structural" and the heart of the political economy of capitalism. The political strategy of socialists must start from this understanding if it is to be consequential.

This is the old debate about the ways in which socialists should respond to the "national question." It has divided socialists from the beginnings of the movement, and the debate has, if anything, grown far more intense since the Second World War. On the one hand, there is the fear, most recently expressed in an article by Eric Hobsbawm that, if we "change the terms" of the debate towards greater support of nationalism, "it puts Marxism at the mercy of nationalism." Hobsbawm reminds us of Zinoviev's warning at the Baku Congress of 1920: "Do not paint nationalism red."* On the other hand, there is the reality that nationalism is and has been central to every major successful socialist struggle. After all, the slogan of the Cuban Revolution is: "¡Patria o muerte! ¡Venceremos!"

Our collective problem is not how to take a "balanced" position on the national question—non-socialists can also do this and have done so—but to understand why so much of the class struggle takes on the rhetoric of "national" claims, and therefore the ways in which "nationalism" is a class concept.

There are two basic conceptual issues that we must confront: What is a "people," and what is "race"? We all belong to "peoples." We think of our "people" and that of others as a fundamental category—in formal terms, an ascribed and not an achieved status. We are born into the category. Of course, we are aware of individual problems. If the parents of an individual are of two different "peoples," of which is the child? The answers (the rules) vary. We even conceive that when an individual changes legal citizenship, he or she up to a point changes peoplehood—except that we also know that when a "minority" member seeks to pass (the light-skinned Black who claims to be White, the Jew who changes names and nominal religion), he or she may be "caught out" and "correctly designated" by others.

But our usual discussion centers around how the individual (variable) relates to the people (constant). We almost never discuss how constant is the constant. But "peoples" are not a given, a group that has always been there from time immemorial. The "peoples" that exist today have come into existence as a result of the development of the capitalist world-economy,

---

*E.J. Hobsbawm, "Some Reflections on 'The Break-up of Britain,'" *New Left Review*, no. 105 (September-October 1977), pp. 22-23.

through which some groups (names) that were in existence before have become molded into peoples, other groups (names) have disappeared from our vocabulary, and some entirely new groups (names) have been invented. Furthermore, this *creation* of "peoples" is not a once-and-for-all happening. It is a matter of constant, if somewhat slow-moving, flux, as we can tell if we look at a list of U.S. ethnic groups of African nations found in newspapers or official documents of 1980 and compare it with a similar list of 1930. The assertion of peoplehood is, as we know, a major political act, often violently resisted (even at the level of concept) by others: Palestinians for Begin, Québécois for Trudeau, Kurds for Khomeini, Algerians for Guy Mollet—and Africans of South Africa for the Afrikaners. For Begin, the Palestinians are Moslem Arabs; for Trudeau, the Québécois are French-speaking Canadians; for the Afrikaners, the Africans of South Africa are a congeries of largely Bantu peoples, not a single people.

To define a given people, inclusively or exclusively, obviously has great political (and economic) consequences. In the argument, much appeal is made to "history," but many of the historical claims are, for a disinterested observer, a bit stretched. The truth of these historical claims is relatively unimportant—there has been an incredible mobility within the world's population in the last 2,000 years. What matters is how groups define themselves today, and why. Creating a people, or remolding its definition of boundaries is an important mechanism in shaping the world market, and in the "assignment" of different "peoples" as specific work-forces in the production processes that are integrated through that market. To create and recreate peoples is to mold and remold class boundaries, and to strengthen or weaken particular processes of accumulation of capital (appropriation of surplus value). People-formation is an integral *part* of class-formation.

Where does "race" enter this picture? Let us return to Magubane's suggestion that "capitalism can never totally eliminate the precapitalist modes of production." Global unequal exchange, the structural antinomy of core and periphery, is integral to the ongoing functioning of capitalism. Racism is then the ideological legitimation of this mechanism. Racism has nothing to do with physical anthropology, and skin color is only marginally useful as a defining characteristic, even symbolically. "What is a Black? And first of all, what is his color?" asked Genêt. Indeed, what is his color? The Blacks, the "coloreds" are the oppressed peripheral peoples. A Chicano (whose skin is white) or an Iranian both are "black" in terms of real social definition. And under the appropriate conditions, a black-skinned person may be whiter than an Irishman. W.E.B. Du Bois tells us about his childhood in Great Barrington, Massachusetts, in the late nineteenth century: "The colored folk were not set aside in the sense that the Irish were, but were a part of the community of long-standing; and in my case as a child, I felt no sense of difference or separation from the main mass of townspeople."* The great "color line" of the twentieth century, of which DuBois spoke in 1900, is a variable line, which has something to do with skin color and a lot to do with the world class struggle.

When, therefore, Magubane tells us that "black and white have irreconcilable claims to the South African state," he has not forgotten that there are persons of white skin who are his comrades-in-struggle in the African National Congress, nor has he forgotten his enemies of black skin. He has merely drawn the political line in terms of the *primary* class contradiction of the South African state. What distinguishes Magubane's views from those of so-called cultural nationalists is that he has analyzed race in class terms. This is the crucial difference, as noted by Agostinho Neto in his lecture "Who is the Enemy? What is Our Objective?" given in 1974. Neto argued that the identification of the white man as the "enemy" in Africa was a confusion, but one which was "to a certain extent logical and emotionally valid." But, said Neto, the African must remember that "today we are all linked in solidarity in a liberation struggle against oppressors who have the same color, but tomorrow there will certainly be different social personalities to be preserved."

The struggle against racism, the struggle for national rights, is an inescapable centerpiece of the struggle for socialism, precisely because the capitalist system is one in which men and women have been grouped economically and politically into "peoples" as a mode of legitimating and facilitating their exploitation. Socialists cannot wish away these categories on the ground that they are "superstructural." The superstructure is an element of the totality, or in Magubane's words: "We must recognize the role of ideas or illusions in history." (p. 118) In the "struggle against oppression and exploitation in South Africa," a struggle that has, as Magubane says, "many fronts" (p. 330), to debate the primacy of race or class is not merely to be scholastic; it is to mislead us politically in a critical way. Magubane's book therefore is of the utmost political relevance to socialists in South Africa, in the United States, and elsewhere.

---

*The Autobiography of W.E.B. DuBois (New York: International Publishers, 1968), p. 83.

The Integration of the National Liberation Movement in the Field of International Liberation

One of the great virtues of Amilcar Cabral was that he tried very hard to theorize praxis in order thereby to understand the real historical alternatives before us which might permit us to move in the directions we truly wish to move. Cabral led a struggle for national liberation of a colonized people, and his whole adult life was absorbed as a militant in that struggle. Yet I would contend that the problem that preoccupied him and puzzled him was not how to conduct that struggle (which seemed to him a rather clear and straightforward question) but what to do in the postindependence period.

It is in this connection that he developed one of his most controversial ideas, the prospective or possible "suicide" of the petty bourgeoisie as a class. As he saw it, there was in African colonies only one stratum "capable of taking control of the state apparatus when the colonial power is destroyed"—the petty bourgeoisie. It followed that: "the moment national liberation comes and the petty bourgeoisie takes power we enter, or rather return to history, and thus the internal contradictions break out again."[1] Once these contradictions would "break out again," he argued, this petty bourgeoisie would find itself before a historic choice: becoming more bourgeois, and thus negating the revolution, or strengthening its revolutionary consciousness.

This means that in order to truly fulfill its role in the national liberation struggle, the revolutionary petty bourgeoisie must be capable of committing suicide as a class in order to be reborn as revolutionary workers, completely identified with the deepest aspirations of the people to which they belong.²

It is easy to criticize this concept as faulty and self-contradictory. If a stratum is a conscious class, it is highly unlikely to commit suicide since its consciousness is defined by the pursuit of its class interest. This being the case, the formulation by Cabral is an unhappy one, and probably an unhelpful one.

However, if we are to use theory as a weapon, as Cabral adjured us, we must not content ourselves with easy debater's victories. For behind Cabral's unhappy formulation, we can see that he was wrestling with the central problem of the world revolutionary movement in the 20th century. This central problem is not how to make the enemy retreat (a process we often call "revolution") but how to keep the resilient enemy from regaining power in new guises, thereby aborting the very long process of the revolutionary transformation of the capitalist world-economy into a socialist world order that is egalitarian and democratic.

Cabral had a sure sense of the components of successful strategic action—patient preparation, bold assault, tactical maneuvers, sure-footed advance, and the struggle to consolidate position. If we are to honor him, we must try to emulate this mode of analysis and of action.

In the 20th century, in a long series of countries, revolutionary antisystemic movements have come to power, usually but not always under the aegis of a revolutionary party which had conducted a protracted struggle in a period prior to the actual coming to power. The period of prior struggle, if protracted, was usually one that mobilized popular consciousness, in itself a revolutionary phenomenon.

I do not intend here to trace the complicated histories of all the postrevolutionary states. I wish merely to underline two elements that it seems to me have been common to all of them. One is that each revolutionary party, once in state power, has discovered that control of the state machinery gave it a good deal of political power to be sure, but less than it had hoped or expected to achieve. That is to say, each party discovered the limits of state sovereignty: the fact that all states, including postrevolutionary states, continue to be part of an interstate system that places very real constraints on the actions of any single state and of a world-economy whose dynamic strength has forced each state, no matter what its ideological commitments, to conform (at least up to a point) to the unpleasant imperatives of the law of value.

The various postrevolutionary states reacted in different ways to this discovery, and indeed their internal histories can be said to consist of debates about how one reacts to this discovery. War Communism and NEP, not as temporary tactics but as long-term strategies, are two of the main (but not the only) modes of action in the face of the realities of the world-system.

The reactions to the discovery, and indeed the seesaw of the national policies of postrevolutionary states, thereupon produced the second common element of all the postrevolutionary states. The atmosphere of heightened collective revolutionary consciousness, of politicization, normally so important in all these states at the moment of revolutionary seizure of power, has tended to decline, to dissipate itself, even to disappear. If one reads the statements of the parties, of the governments, and of the leaders of the postrevolutionary states, one sees a constant effort to revivify ideology, to renew enthusiasm, to combat cynicism and fatigue, to maintain the sense of struggle. Disillusionment is widespread inside these countries, and outside them, about them.

If one reflects on why each state seems to go through one or another variety of "depoliticization" of the working classes, one notices that the essential complaint is that the social transformations the working class had hoped for did come about, but not as completely as they had hoped. The old evils of unequal allocations, of corruption, of arbitrariness persist, to degrees that are not acceptable in postrevolutionary states. No doubt, as the parties constantly say when they acknowledge the complaint, this is because of the first common factor: the insertion of these states in a world-system they do not control, and whose negative pressures they are feeling. But it is also a reality that the working classes are not readily persuaded that this is the whole explanation. They have become suspicious and have often retreated into depoliticization.

It is this depoliticization of postrevolutionary states that has offered the most hope to the defenders of the world capitalist system, who have seen in it the crucial weapon with which to deflect the growing strength of world antisystemic forces in the world class struggle. Furthermore, as we know, "depoliticization" is never "apoliticism." Rather, it is a tactic of the politically weak, who are biding their time, until the conditions for political explosion arise once again.

Is there something that the world's revolutionary movements can do to make it more likely that the explosion of angry workers will be directed primarily against the world capitalist system and not be deflected into negative feelings about postrevolutionary states and revolutionary movements? This is the question I think Amilcar Cabral would address today, were he here. Let us do it for him, in his stead, and in his honor.

I think the clue lies in the title of my talk, which was formulated by the organizers of this Symposium: "the integration of the liberation movement in the field of international liberation."

The capitalist system is a world-system. If we are to understand it, we must start with that fact. If class struggle is to be efficacious, it has to be a world class struggle. It cannot be defined as a series of national struggles, linked by a vague sense of international solidarity. This does not mean that the national liberation struggle is not a meaningful focus of our efforts. It is, but the national liberation struggle is meaningful precisely because it is a form, a modality of world class struggle.

Let me suggest a number of controversial propositions about this world class struggle, which I offer not as a finished analysis but as a basis of discussion among us.

1) We are presently in the transition from the still-existing capitalist world-economy to the socialist world order which does not yet exist. We have been in this transition for more than 50 years already and we shall be in it for at least 100 more. We are *all* in this transition, not merely those living in postrevolutionary states. The transition is a phenomenon of the whole world-system, which is in structural crisis.

2) The world class struggle has never been more intense than now, during this transition. We are all involved in this world class struggle, which is going on in every geographical corner of the world. No country is outside this struggle, or beyond it.

3) The forms that this world class struggle takes are varied, since the modes of appropriating surplus value are various. This is because the composition of the world's bourgeoisie and proletariat has become complex and disparate and can in no meaningful sense be reduced to the early 19th-century English model of the private industrialist versus the male wage-earning factory worker.

4) The world class struggle is conducted by the various elements of the world proletariat organized in movements. It is these movements and never the states which conduct class struggles. Class *struggle* involves politicized movements with active militants. It is in the struggle of the movements that political power is achieved.

5) The organizing issues of these multiple movements have been many—national oppression, oppression in the workplace, the oppression of socially weaker groups (women, the aged, and the young, ethnic and racial "minorities"). The themes have varied and will continue to vary in different concrete circumstances. The decisive factor is whether a particular struggle is in fact antisystemic; that is, the particular movement in fact constrains the real power of the world bourgeoisie and augments the real power of the world proletariat.

The Integration of the National Liberation Movement 163

6) The control of state machineries is a tactic in the world class struggle, and never an end in itself. It is only one tactic among many, and not always necessarily the one that deserves priority.

7) The most urgent political need for the movements individually, whether the movements are located in postrevolutionary states or in other states, is to create a truly trans-state alliance of the multiple forms of movements, which would be based on a clear distinction between the movements and the states.

8) "Economic development" is a double-edged sword. As long as a capitalist world-economy exists, and we are part of it, the "economic development" of all zones simultaneously is inherently impossible, since the operation of the law of value requires that surplus be unequally distributed over the globe. The development of any one zone is therefore always at the expense of some other. World socialism cannot be defined by the phenomenon of less "developed" zones "catching up" or by the universalization of the law of value under the claim of the development of the forces of production. It involves rather the construction of a radically different mode of production, centering on production for use in an egalitarian, planned world, in which the states individually and the system of states collectively have both "withered away."

9) The measure of the construction of a world socialist order is the steady increase during this transition in the real effective power of the working classes to direct their own lives at the workplace, in their homes, and in their communities. Self-direction is not direction by the representatives of the working classes but by the working classes in their own right. It is this last issue which Cabral was talking about when he envisaged the "suicide" of the revolutionary petty bourgeoisie, in Africa as elsewhere. Only of course, we we know, they will not commit suicide. The workers must impose it on their representatives in social reality.

10) The crisis of the capitalist world-economy is also the crisis of the world's antisystemic movements, which are—let us remember—children of the present system and not of the future. We need to rethink our strategy, our mode of organization, and our categories of thought, all of which were molded in the 19th-century period of a capitalist system at its most self-confident. We need to reflect on whether our present strategy, mode of organization, and categories of thought serve us well for this period of crisis, of intensified class struggle, and above all of clever adjustment by the world's bourgeoisie who are seeking to survive as privileged strata under entirely new guises. The real danger is that, 30 years from now, everyone may call himself a Marxist or a socialist, and private property may be reduced to a minor role in world production. We will still then be in the

midst of the transition and the world class struggle. Such an "ideological triumph" may itself serve as one of the most serious impediments for the achievement of a world socialist order.

Let us remember that nothing is inevitable. We are before a historical choice. The existing capitalist world-system is surely doomed. But a socialist world order is only one possible outcome. A second is the creation of a new class-based (but noncapitalist) system. A third is imagining. *A luta continua* is not a mere slogan; it is an analysis that we must bear in mind precisely when we look at postrevolutionary states and at antisystemic, revolutionary movements.

NOTES

This article was written as a paper offered at Simpósio Amilcar Cabral, Praia, Cabo Verde, January 17-20, 1983.

[1]"Brief Analysis of the Social Structure in Guinea," in Amilcar Cabral, *Revolution in Guinea* (New York: Monthly Review Press, 1969), p. 69.

[2]"The Weapon of Theory," in op. cit., p. 110.

Africa, 100 Years After the Berlin Conference

The Berlin Conference of 1884-85 is far more a political than an economic turning-point in modern African history. That is, it can be argued that the economic incorporation of various parts of Africa into the capitalist world-economy started since 1750 and was well along by 1815,* and that the Berlin Conference was a consequence, not a cause, of this involvement. This can be seen quite easily by viewing Africa from the perspective of the core-states of the world-system throughout the nineteenth century.

The period from 1815 to 1873 constituted more or less the era of British hegemony in this world-system. The definitive defeat of France in the Napoleonic wars entailed not merely a political and military triumph for Great Britain, but a real setback economically to its only immediate economic rival of scope and strength. This permitted Great Britain not merely to dominate the European market for a half-century but to preside over the consolidation of (as well as to be the prime beneficiary of) the expansion of the peripheral zones of the capitalist world-economy that had been going on since circa 1750.

Various parts of the African continent, mostly coastal areas (in the north, west, and south in particular), began to transform their productive processes in ways that involved them in the integrated production network

---

*See my article, "Africa and the World-Economy," forthcoming in *Unesco General History of Africa*, VI: J.F.A. Ajayi, ed., *The Nineteenth Century Until the 1880's*.

of the world-economy. This transformation of production processes did not require systematic political colonization. What it did require was two things: First, it required the abolition of the slave trade. The development of any form of cash-cropping was basically incompatible with the kinds of political structures necessary to maintain a slave-trade. For one thing, slavers and cash-crop producers were competitors for the same labor force.

Secondly, it required the creation and/or reinforcement of political authorities who were ready to guarantee the economic flows that were the definition of involvement in the world-economy. In some areas, existing state-structures became ready to play this role. In other areas, new state structures arose for this end. And in still other areas, outside colonizers created the structures.

From Great Britain's point of view, who it was that controlled these local state structures set up in areas being incorporated into the world-economy did not matter very much. Nor was the expansion of overall productive capacity very urgent, since the role reserved for African areas in the ongoing economic operations of the world-economy was still rather small. The total of economic productive processes elsewhere was about all the world-system could handle at that stage of its development.

Thus both Great Britain and those who controlled the various regions involved in some way in the capitalist world-economy were willing to allow the relations to develop in a relaxed way. This is what later was designated by the name of "informal imperialism." The imperialism was real in terms of flows of economic surplus, but it was "informal" in that it tolerated a great deal of political autonomy in Africa. From an African perspective, by and large, the European impact was insufficient to curtail significantly the strength of competing socio-political forces in their ongoing historical trajectories, or so they thought.

If this "relaxed" atmosphere disappeared after 1873, it was not because of developments internal to Africa but because of structural changes in the world-system as a whole. Great Britain had lost its hegemony. It was to be sure still the strongest power in the world both economically and militarily, but it was no longer so strong as to be the unquestioned arbiter. Germany and the United States had emerged as major industrial competitors in the leading industries, with France remaining strong as well. The Pax Britannica thus came into question.

Furthermore, in 1873 the world-economy had entered into one of its recurrent phases of stagnation which periodically reinforce the harshness of direct economic and political competition among the core powers. It was quite clear to everyone that the continued economic advance of other states vis-à-vis Great Britain required the elimination of the virtual monopoly

Great Britain maintained over commercial and financial flows between core and periphery.

Where peripheral states were politically already well-established as functioning members of the interstate system, as for example, in South America, the intercore competitive struggle was fought out largely in the economic arena. But many other weapons were available to core powers in this intensified competition: encouragement of the break-up of bureaucratic empires (the Ottoman Empire, China) the "temporary" occupation of sovereign states (the U.S. in the Caribbean), the forced reform of existing state structures to make them perform as members of the interstate system (Japan, Thailand, Persia, Ethiopia). For the rest, there was the alternative of direct colonization.

Direct colonization recommended itself for most of Africa (but also for Southeast Asia and Oceania at this time) for several reasons. The existing political structures in Africa were on the whole militarily weak and, in many areas, because of the turmoil created in the wake of the continuing slave trade, there were conditions of instability which made cash-cropping difficult to launch. Above all, direct colonization appeared to France and Germany as ways in which they could "preempt" zones of potential economic flows and close them to Great Britain.

That is to say, colonization was for some European powers part of a mercantilist strategy of the kind which recurrently arises as a mechanism by which the medium strong states attempt to eat away at the economic strength of the strongest state. This is only politically possible once the economic primacy of the leading state has begun to decline. This latter condition was met after 1873. The "scramble for Africa" was a logical consequence.

In this sense, the "scramble" must be seen as a tactic, primarily of France and Germany, directed against Great Britain. Great Britain would have been quite happy to allow the pre-1873 status quo to develop slowly as it had been doing. However, once Great Britain no longer had the strength to stop a "scramble," it had no choice but to join the scramble. And once it joined the scramble, since it was still the most powerful state, it won it, in the sense that Great Britain emerged from the scramble with the majority of African territory under its control. Furthermore, one must add to this calculation the Portuguese zones, which Great Britain helped keep for Portugal, because it knew that it could be an indirect economic beneficiary. One must also add the Congo Free State, which was maintained as an "open" area. Thus by 1900, Great Britain was closed out only of the French, German, and Italian zones (and after the First World War, it won access to about half the German zones).

Suddenly, in a short period, virtually all of Africa was constituted into a set of mutually-bonded "colonies." In itself, this did not change much in terms of the economic processes, but it did change things enormously in terms of the interstate system, of which all of Africa now became an integral, functioning part. Africa's multiplicity of political structures, almost none of which were involved previously in the interstate system nor constrained by its rules, were replaced by circa 50 entities, all of which asserted sovereign authority within the juridical and political framework of the interstate system. To be sure, in almost every case, this sovereign authority was non-independent, that is, a colony of a European state. But it was "sovereign" nonetheless. That is, it was an internationally, juridically-recognized entity with relatively accepted boundaries and clearly-defined legal responsibilities.

We know today how persistent a social reality was thereby created. The boundaries of these entities as of 1885-1900 are with extraordinarily little modification the boundaries of the independent African states as of 1984. Furthermore, it is more than a matter of juridical definition of boundaries. These state boundaries have become the framework within which national consciousness has been defined for the governments of these states and for ever larger percentages of the citizenry. The very concept of "citizen" in the African context is a function of the actions that flowed directly from the decisions of the Congo Conference of 1884.

While in itself this process of boundary-definition did not derive from economic transformations within Africa, they would have of course economic consequences for Africa. One must distinguish at this point between the economic-financial concerns of the imperial governments, and the concerns of capitalist strata throughout the world (and of course particularly those located in the imperial states).

The governments might have some medium-run concern with advancing the interests of capitalist strata in their countries, but their short-run concern was the maintenance of order in the colonies at the lowest possible expense to metropolitan taxpayers. Colonies are an expense. Someone has to pay the costs of administrators, armies, and at least minimal infrastructure. The easiest solution, or at least the one that placed least financial burden on the metropole, was to have the colonized themselves pay these expenses. Thus arose the widespread policy that some kind of local taxation be introduced that would "cover" the costs of colonial administration. Such a need pointed towards the extension of commodification, if only to enable persons to pay taxes in money.

This need of the colonial administrators coincided, after 1900, with a different but convergent need of European capitalist strata. In the economic upturn of the period 1897-1920, the expanding level of world production required a considerable expansion of the production of a long list of primary goods. Africa provided a variety of soils and climates which permitted many of these goods to be cultivated. Furthermore, because of the relatively low level of commodification in Africa at that time (by world comparison), it was possible by and large to remunerate a part-lifetime labor force at relatively low levels (again by world comparison). The products were thus needed, and the prospective rate of profit was relatively high, whether the mode of production was plantations or peasant commodity production.

Hence both the administrations and the capitalist strata sought to commodify labor in various ways, in order to "develop" the economy. In fact, the French locution for this was extraordinarily accurate. The French spoke of the "mise en valeur" of the colony. The dictionaries translate that as the "increase in value" but it literally means "putting (something) into a form such that it has value."

The "mise en valeur" of Africa was not a simple straightforward proposition. First of all, African laborers (including in this term so-called independent peasant cultivators) resisted the increased exploitation in time, energy, and distortion of lifestyle, that the new cash-cropping and mining export-oriented activities involved. They rebelled openly in many ways and places, and they sabotaged passively almost everywhere.

Secondly, the colonial administrations and the capitalist strata may have had generally convergent interests in the initial period of economic transformation, but after 1920 for one set of reasons, and after 1950 for another set, their short-term interests often diverged.

Thirdly, the term "capitalist strata" includes at least two quite different segments, those large firms in the metropoles directly or indirectly concerned with the flows of production and capital and those much smaller European firms or individuals operating in the colonies themselves. Their interests—economic and political—regularly diverged and were the source of much consequent hesitation in colonial policy.

What we can say about the whole period 1900-1945 was that economically it resulted in a very limited "mise en valeur" of the continent, in terms of an integration of its production processes with that of the world-economy as a whole, with the exception of some mining areas.

Sociologically, the consequence was a similarly limited amount of commodification of labor (almost none of the land), and a limited amount of urbanization along with the creation of transport and communications facilities. Politically, the consequence was the politicization of a small African educated stratum. But as yet (except possibly in South Africa), African nationalism was not yet a mode of political organization.

It is really in the post-1945 period that all the most dramatic changes occurred. It is only then that Africa's productive activity expanded to the point where it began to matter as a producer of world surplus-value. (No doubt this was already true for South Africa in the interwar period, but even there the post-1945 years saw a significant expansion of export of surplus-value.) The post-1945 years were also the period of so-called decolonization. The two phenomena were not unlinked and certainly not contradictory.

The period running from 1945 to circa 1970 was that of unquestioned U.S. hegemony in the world-system. Periods of unquestioned hegemony (relatively rare) are normally periods of decolonization, since the hegemonic power does not need mechanisms of political control for economic advantage, and secondary powers (who do) find themselves unable to resist the two-pronged assault (from below by the colonized, and above by the hegemonic power) against the monopolistic constraints which are incarnated in colonial rule.

Furthermore the period 1945-1970 was a period of expansion in the world-economy, and indeed of greater expansion than had been known in any previous A-phase. This meant that there was need for the "mise en valeur" of considerable additional African production for the world market. Expanding an export-oriented production base requires not merely effective demand (which existed) and capital investment by someone, whatever the true source of the capital (which was there in sufficient quantity, in fact) but a structured and low-cost labor supply.

Obtaining the latter is far more a socio-political question than an economic one. It is an old truism that if one wishes to press people into doing things they are reluctant to do, it is better to have intermediaries who can bring to bear pressures other than brute force than to try to do this directly. The colonial powers in the pre-1945 period were still using one or another form of very direct coercion in Africa to obtain a labor force (poll taxes, corvées, etc.). The early stirrings of nationalist movements in the post-1945 years often centered their mobilization around popular resentment of such practices.

It is thus no surprise that the decolonization of British, French, and Belgian Africa was so relatively swift and so relatively bloodless. The combination of African mobilization, Asian example, U.S. quasi-complicity, and western European weakness was very potent. After some early resistance by the colonial powers, the dam burst between 1956 and 1960, and suddenly Africa was sovereign. This was of course not true of Algeria, of Portuguese Africa, or Southern Rhodesia, and South Africa. But in each of these cases, the difference was/is the presence of other pro-status quo interests who had much to lose from decolonization and therefore were/are tenacious. Still even there, resistance finally crumbled, except in South Africa where the struggles promise to be long and hard.

What is the significance of this massive transfer of sovereignty? Both much and little. Let us start with the little. It is probably not the case that collectively Africa has improved its relative economic position within the world-economy. Pessimistic appraisals of the last 10-20 years' performance are widespread, even if the policy implications drawn therefrom vary widely (from say the World Bank Berg report to the OAU's Lagos Plan of Action). Indeed, if anything, one could argue that Africa is relatively worse off precisely because African decolonization has permitted a significant deepening of its participation in the production networks of the world-economy (even if the World Bank complains this deepening is far from enough).

The "development" plans of the independent African states have all moved in that direction, even when "self-reliance" was an ideological motif, and *a fortiori* in its absence. There is nothing in the political and economic conjuncture of the 1980's to make us expect any early reversal of this historical tendency. "Neo-colonialism" may be regularly deplored, but it is a depressingly powerful reality of contemporary Africa.

Yet the picture of post-independence Africa is of course not merely a picture of economic gloom. Independence has strengthened the African collective political hand in the world-system, despite the constant coups d'état and weak states. Julius Nyerere may speak, as he has, of a "second scramble for Africa" but the wholesale political disregard of African claims which the Berlin Conference of 1884 represented is past history and unrepeatable today. Africa may be weak but not defenseless.

The reason that 1884 cannot be reduplicated in 1984 has to do with the political impact that popular mobilization through anti-systemic movements had—and continues to have, for it is a continuing phenomenon Africa-wide if discontinuous in any one state. These movements, which as elsewhere in the peripheral areas of the world-system, have combined nationalist and socialist themes—this is almost the definition of a "national liberation movement"—have altered consciousness, thereby organizational potential, thereby the world political *rapport de forces*. One does not need to exaggerate the extent of this to realize that this is a significant variable now and in the coming years.

In this respect, Africa is not alone. The political transformations are occurring in the world-system as a whole, which is one of the main factors that accounts for their strength in any particular region. The question is where this is heading.

There are three principal variables to take into account in discussing the prospects for the coming 20 years. (I think it would be foolish to try to foresee a longer period.) The first variable is the evolution of the interstate alliance system among the principal powers. Given the acute and prospective economic rivalry in this present world economic stagnation of the U.S., western Europe, and Japan and given the breakdown of ideological constraints in both the U.S.S.R. and China, a major reshuffling of economic (and hence implicitly of political) alliances is occurring. I have argued elsewhere* why I expect the ultimate outcome will probably be a Washington-Tokyo-Peking axis versus a Paris-Bonn-Moscow axis. This makes economic but not ideological sense. I will not debate this here. But should such an alliance system crystallize, it would probably serve Africa well, as an area "in dispute" and therefore to be "counted" by both sides.

Secondly, and quite differently, there is the prospective evolution of the world family of antisystemic movements, which at the moment is in great disarray. In the core countries, the old dominant IInd International movements are under assault by the various expressions of the so-called New Left. In the socialist countries, the IIIrd International movements in power are under assault from a variety of movements, of which Solidarnosc is merely the most prominent. In the Third World, traditional national liberation movements are still pursuing their objectives in countries which have not yet had their "revolution"—from the ANC in South Africa to the FDMR in El Salvador.

There is a veritable crisis in antisystemic activity which revolves around the now five-fold split structurally and a growing skepticism about the long-range efficacy of the classical strategies. The question is whether in the next twenty years there occurs (a) the beginning of a new synthesis on strategy and consequently (b) the beginning of a new trans-state alliance of movements. This is far from certain, as the activity has barely begun. Still, were it to proceed any distance, it could affect Africa's situation enormously.

The third and last variable is what will occur directly in Africa. Africa is the poorest periphery and the last to decolonize. With the crucial exception of South Africa and Namibia, all African states have now gone through a first round of mobilization and political change. The results have been unsatisfactory. It is clear that a second round is brewing. It is less clear what form this will take. In fact it is so unclear one hesitates to foresee anything precise.

What one can say is that probably the greatest single variable in Africa's immediate future is the nature and direction of anti-systemic mobilization

---

*See my "Crisis as Transition" in S. Amin, G. Arrighi, A.G. Frank and I. Wallerstein, *Dynamics of Global Crisis* (New York: Monthly Review, 1983).

Africa, 100 Years After the Berlin Conference

within African independent states themselves, upon which the South African struggle may have a crucial impact. Nkrumah may have come along too soon. A new pan-Africanist, anti-capitalist thrust is certainly a real possibility. I speak of a real thrust and not the mere mouthing of slogans. But it must be constructed from within to succeed. That is in fact the challenge of the next twenty years. And if it occurs, it will change the givens of the world-system profoundly. It is certainly not to be ruled out.

PART TWO

The U.S. Role in Africa: Kissinger, Carter, and Southern Africa

Kissinger's African Mischief
Worse Than An Error

Henry Kissinger says he went to southern Africa to seek a peaceful solution. Whatever his claims, he has dangerously escalated the level of conflict there and has set the United States on a road that is likely to lead within a few years to sending troops to South Africa, there to fight on the side of its white government against its Black majority and perhaps against neighboring African governments as well. Kissinger's mission is more than a gamble or an error in judgment; it is a negative act which should be opposed outright by anyone who purports to stand for majority rule in southern Africa.

This, however, is not an *ad hominem* argument. I am not calling Mr. Kissinger a bad apple in an otherwise fine barrel. His actions are merely an *escalation* of long-standing American policy toward Africa, an escalation that, if not inevitable, was predictable; in fact many of us have been predicting it for some time.

First let me clear up some phony issues. It is not a matter of whether or not "race war" can be prevented, or a "peaceful solution" found. The war, whatever one wants to designate it, began long ago and in a serious way. And *all* solutions are by definition peaceful. If Messrs. Vorster and Smith were to announce tomorrow that they favor one man, one vote, the solution would be peaceful. Asking whether a "peaceful solution" can be found really means: will the African majority be willing to accept something less than their rights—"peacefully"? And the answer is no, *for which we should all be grateful*. Every time, anywhere, people defend their rights, the rest of us are better off.

A second phony issue is Zimbabwe (Rhodesia) and Namibia. The peoples of these countries are oppressed and struggling to be free, but they are not what brings our Secretary of State to southern Africa. The name of the game is *South* Africa, and Mr. Kissinger hasn't breathed a whisper about doing anything about majority rule there. The reason is very simple. Zimbabwe and Namibia are, for Kissinger and Vorster, the ballast to be thrown overboard to save the sinking ship of South Africa—and to save it more or less as it is.

To see where we are today, we must go back as far as 1940. The United States "assumed its world responsibilities" on a very simple principle. It did *not* decide to become the world's policeman, as an oversimplified rhetoric would have it; it decided to police its own world interests, whenever and wherever somebody else could no longer do the job as Washington wanted it to be done.

The United States entered Europe when France and Britain could no longer handle it; that was in 1940. It entered Southeast Asia in 1954 when France was forced to retire. It entered the Middle East when Britain could no longer handle it after 1956 and escalated that intervention when Israel was outpaced in 1973. In each of these cases, "entering" meant more than expressing some political concern with developments in the particular region. It meant assuming the *principal* responsibility for the West's *tactical* decisions.

Before 1940, the United States had assumed tactical responsibilities only in Latin America and to some degree in East Asia. Of all the regions of the world, the one which required least direct responsibility was Africa. Thus, it has often been said that the United States had no interest in Africa and no policy toward Africa. That was not true, but at least up to 1960 the United States felt, correctly, that its interests were, by and large, well protected by the tactical decisions of the four major colonial powers (Great Britain, France, Belgium and Portugal), plus South Africa.

That does not mean that the U.S. Government approved every policy of every colonial government. It means that, overall, nothing was seriously enough wrong from a U.S. point of view to warrant *direct* intervention. Now and then, the United States would make quiet suggestions about "changes"; these were most often ignored. Now and then, spokesmen for the administration in office would make a public declaration of liberal ideology which no one took seriously, as well they ought not to have done. But that was it. Otherwise the motto was: hear no evil, see no evil, speak no evil.

What changed this quiet content? As usual in history, the complacency of the powerful was undone by the refusal of the oppressed to acquiesce. The "peaceful" decolonization of Africa "downward," that is from north to south, had been launched well enough by Great Britain and France in the 1950s. Things got a bit sticky for France because of Algeria, but General de Gaulle got the train back on the track. The political objective was simple. The claims of the African middle classes to local political power and a share in the world economic pie would be granted in return for two things: no substantial change in the nature of economic ties to the Western world, and internal policing by these middle classes of their potentially radical peasants and workers.

Although one or two of the new African governments were a bit rambunctious (notably Kwame Nkrumah's Ghana and Sékou Touré's Guinea), the "peaceful transfer of power" was seen by Great Britain, France *and* the United States as a splendid success—until July 1960, when the newly independent Congo/Leopoldville, now Zaire, "exploded."

The Congo exploded for two reasons: Belgium, which was running the tactical show, had no previous experience with decolonization and made fearful errors. But even more important, for the first time decolonization had touched the "sensitive" zone of southern Africa. It was like a dentist finally getting near the nerve.

The Congo was part of Africa's mineral-rich area and it had a significant contingent of white settlers. Of course, it could have been "decolonized" without danger to Western political and economic interests; Britain's successful operation just four years later in Zambia—also mineral-rich and with settlers—proved it could be done. But the Belgians lacked Britain's acquired talents. So in the Congo, Katanga "seceded" and Patrice Lumumba ran around aggressively asserting Congolese interests and actually dared to ask the Russians for some transport planes to fly his troops into Katanga to put down the Belgian-protected rebel forces. Panic bells rang in Washington, London, Lisbon and Pretoria. And the United States stepped in.

It took the United States—operating both directly and via the United Nations—four to five years to pull the chestnuts out of the fire. But in 1964, United States (not Russian) transport planes flew Belgian paratroopers to jump near Stanleyville (now Kisangani) and join South African mercenaries already on the ground. Together, they liquidated the National Liberation Council, the heirs of Lumumba's nationalist movement.

The fact that an American ambassador was at that very moment negotiating in Nairobi with the NLC's Foreign Minister, Thomas Kanza, under the auspices of Kenya's President Jomo Kenyatta and the Organization of African Unity, didn't seem to make anyone in Washington blanch. When the Japanese pulled much the same thing before Pearl Harbor in 1941, Franklin Roosevelt called it "a day that will live in infamy." But what is infamous when done by Japanese to Americans is "humanitarian" when done by Americans to Congolese.

In any case, U.S. intervention worked. Within two more years General Mobutu was securely ensconced in the Congo, Nkrumah was ousted in Ghana and Ben Bella in Algeria, and the Angolan revolution ground to a temporary halt. From the point of view of African liberation, the decade from 1964 to 1974 was ten long years of frustration, stagnation, and a deteriorating status quo. The United States had done what needed to be done in the Congo and could leave Angola to the Portuguese, Zimbabwe to the British, Namibia to the South Africans, and everyone else to the local boys.

The spurt of Kennedy liberalism—a vote here and there denouncing the Portuguese at the United Nations; some scholarships to political refugees—died down. Mr. Johnson was preoccupied with Vietnam and the Dominican Republic. Mr. Nixon began to consider even more open support of the white regimes in southern Africa with National Security Staff Memorandum 39 (a product of Mr. Kissinger's staff).

What a shock it was, then, on April 25, 1974, when the Portuguese Government fell—or rather crumbled from within as the result of a decade of patient, painful corrosion of its power and internal legitimacy by the PAIGC in Guinea-Bissau, the MPLA in Angola, and FRELIMO in Mozambique. Despite prescient warnings from General Spínola and others, the United States was caught unawares.

It took the United States, with Vietnam and Watergate on its mind, about sixteen months to realize how far things had gotten out of hand, and to comprehend that the new "reformed" Portuguese Government would be unable to arrange one of those harmless little decolonizations in Angola. When Kissinger did finally wake up, it was too late. The United States tried to do something in Angola, directly and via South Africa, but it was abortive.

The alarm bells went off again—both in Washington and in Pretoria—as they had in the summer of 1960. It took four to six years of hard work last time to get Africa back under Western control. Can it be done again? Not as likely, but neither Mr. Kissinger nor Mr. Vorster are the kind to give up easily.

Of the two, Vorster is the more knowledgeable and the more suave. He is also the more desperate. He has seen the menace of revolution coming for a long time now, even before Portugal's collapse. And he has been trying to head it off by "détente." To understand the Kissinger mission one must know what Vorster meant by détente.

Pending the ability of the oppressed Black majority to shake the regime from within, independent nations had been trying to undermine South Africa's international legitimacy and respectability by formal condemnations and practical isolation. Hence they sought to pass resolutions in the U.N. and to achieve diplomatic, economic and cultural boycotts. Bit by bit, this was working. The United Nations passed ever more militant resolutions and more and more Western nations voted for them. An arms embargo was theoretically enacted under international law. Diplomatic, transport and economic ties were broken, at least by most Third World and Socialist countries. One after another, international sports organizations barred South Africa from participation.

All this involved only pinpricks in material terms, since arms flowed in anyway, and trade and industry flourished, thanks to open and covert Western cooperation. But the moral isolation was beginning to have its effect—on the morale of the white regime, on the collective consciousness of the Black majority, and on "liberal public opinion" in the West.

From 1964 to 1974, the international anti-apartheid campaign represented a growing bother to the regime. It wasn't a crisis, but to sophisticated analysts (including Vorster), it boded no good. The way to handle a campaign to de-legitimize a regime is to launch a counter-campaign to re-legitimize it. This was Vorster's "détente." The idea was to get at first tacit, then open, support for "normal" relations between independent African nations and white South Africa.

Vorster started with the easy states—weak neighboring countries with conservative regimes: Malawi, Lesotho, Swaziland. Then he started after bigger fish among the ex-French colonies: the Malagasy Republic, the Ivory Coast, Gabon. He was working his way to still bigger fish like Zaire, Zambia and Kenya. And somewhere out on the horizon, he hoped maybe Nigeria could be persuaded to join the list.

It must be said that Vorster was a very prudent and patient fisherman and he was doing quite well. To be sure, he had behind-the-scenes backing from Paris, London and Washington; but he was making the decisions. He had even been involved *since 1966* in a quiet effort to decolonize Rhodesia. He couldn't say this too loudly, since his own voters were not sophisticated enough to understand the tactic, but Harold Wilson knew what was going on, and so did Ian Smith.

Vorster was a good enough tactician that even the Portuguese coup did not slow him down. He was in fact merely emboldened to try to draw Mozambique into the net. What undid Mr. Vorster therefore was nothing he did or failed to do. Vorster was undone by Kissinger's false start in Angola.

Nothing is worse in war and politics than starting an aggressive action and not going through with it. Kissinger started to overthrow the MPLA in Angola in the summer of 1975, persuaded the normally more prudent South Africans to commit their troops to sustain UNITA, and then pulled back. Nothing as disastrous as that had happened to the West since the Suez operation of 1956.

And Vorster had to pay the cost. The carefully constructed emergent arrangements for "détente" were suddenly abandoned by many of the prospective adherents. Even worse, the war of liberation that had been underway since 1966 in Zimbabwe and Namibia finally spread into South Africa itself. Readers of *The New York Times* commenced to hear of Soweto, and Soweto turned out to be only the start of a continuing and organized action.

Mr. Vorster said to Mr. Kissinger: do something. You undid years of my careful planning. And there's no time to lose. It was at this point, and only then, that Kissinger began to engage in "shuttle diplomacy." When for the first time the South African regime was seriously and imminently threatened from within, the United States "entered" the region—not to achieve a "peaceful solution" but, quite the opposite, to struggle to contain the movement for African liberation.

The scheme is very simple. (1) Dump the Rhodesian whites quickly. Buy them off. These whites stole the land from the Africans, and made a handsome profit for twenty-five to seventy-five years on the stolen property and underpaid African labor. But never mind. Use some U.S. taxpayers' money to reward these whites one last time; give them a hefty start on their new life in Canada or Argentina. (None of them would want to go to Britain; the standard of living there is too low.) (2) Create a puppet independent state in Namibia with a large political role for the white settlers, and a semi-permanent invitation to the South African armed forces to station troops there. (3) Do a minor cosmetic job in South Africa, eliminating so-called "petty apartheid." Buy off the Coloureds (those of "mixed" ancestry). (4) Get international recognition for Transkei, a Bantustan scheduled to become "independent" this year. Thus, set the stage for the ultimate partition of South Africa with the 20 percent of whites retaining 80 percent of the land area (including all the mines and factories). (5) Re-legitimize Vorster and the white regime by getting the so-called "front-line Presidents" (Tanzania, Mozambique, Zambia, Botswana and Angola) to meet with Vorster and "trade" the rights of Blacks in South Africa for concessions to Blacks in Zimbabwe and Namibia.

It is this noble program that President Ford is presenting to the American voters as a great contribution to world peace. It is this noble program that

Carter and Mondale and Senator Clark (the official Democratic "liberal" on southern Africa) are afraid to criticize. They all wish Kissinger well. And if they come into office, do they propose to do more of the same?

The United States is in southern Africa now in a big way. Vorster no longer is in tactical command. No doubt he liked it better before. But U.S. tactical leadership is a price he has had to pay to preserve privilege for his voters. And he is a sensible man. Kissinger's mission is a setback for the liberation movements. They know it, and are saying so loudly. The "front-line Presidents" know it too. But the United States can wield a mighty big stick when it wants to, and they are being careful.

Just recently I went down to Washington to participate in a conference called by the Methodist Church on southern Africa. At lunchtime a lot of Congressmen showed up and I happened to be sitting across from a rather prominent liberal Republican Senator. He asked me what the conferees thought of Mr. Kissinger's mission. I told him not much, and I explained why. He then asked me that old liberal question: "What can the United States do to make sure that it doesn't end up this time on the side of the wrong people?" I gave him the only answer I know: Get on the side of the right people.

Luanda Is Madrid

Angola has become the focal point of world political conflict in the 1970s in exactly the way Vietnam was in the 1960s and Spain in the 1930s. It is the story of a localized war which is nonetheless the meeting point of world forces. It is a long and extended war. Despite all the complexities and confusions, the sides are clear, and those who will not choose have thereby chosen. Its outcome will have a major effect not merely on its immediate neighbors, but on political struggles everywhere in the world.

For all these reasons it is extremely important to get the facts straight, to pull apart the multiple strands which, by now, have a complicated history. I therefore propose to recount in some detail the prehistory of the present struggle, what occurred before the Portuguese coup of 1974. It is only thus that one can appreciate the implications of the present war for southern Africa and the world as a whole.

We start with two particularities that have largely determined the particular evolution of Angola's movement of national liberation: Angola was a colony of Portugal; Angola is located in southern Africa. To have been a colony of Portugal in the 20th century rather than a colony of the other European colonial powers, notably Great Britain or France, meant primarily two things. First, the metropole was itself "underdeveloped," a semi-colony, and the prospective economic losses from decolonization were greater for powerful interests there than they would have been for similar groups in other countries. Hence the resistance to "decolonization" as a political strategy was exceptionally strong. Second, the metropole was, until 1974, a Fascist state in which all opposition (which included all

Portuguese even mildly sympathetic to African aspirations) was underground. Hence the possibility for Africa to follow a policy of what might be called "parliamentary anti-colonialism" was nonexistent.

From this pair of pincers many things followed. The freedom movements in the Portuguese colonies were among the last to be formed in the colonial world. The movements were from the beginning clandestine and oriented to armed struggle. Not only did it require a major institutional upheaval in Portugal (how much of a revolution it is seems in doubt) for a policy of decolonization to become legitimate there, but it can truly be said that the struggle of the African movements is what made it possible to overthrow the Fascist regime. Thus the government of Portugal today, and especially the now-dissolved Armed Forces Movement, owed a particular debt to the African movements. Finally, the fact that movements in Portuguese Africa were among the "last" was not entirely negative. It enabled these movements to profit by the experiences of others, a circumstance that has served the Angolans well today.

The Portuguese component of the background is Portugal's historically structured relative poverty. The southern African component is the opposite. Angola lies astride a mineralogical belt which makes it one of the richest areas in natural resources in the world today—to which was added in the 1960s the fortune of the discovery of oil. Angola is a prize worth seizing, not merely as one more pawn in a world power struggle, but quite literally for itself as an economic entity. And the fate of Angola is intimately tied up with the fates of Zaire and South Africa, two other economic "prizes." So the world is playing for high economic stakes in the narrow sense, in a way that was never true, for example, in Indochina.

These two components—Portugal's poverty and southern Africa's wealth—account for much of the history of Angolan nationalism, which I shall try to summarize briefly before coming to the present situation. In the 20th century, three social changes of some significance occurred in Angola, each of which evolved slowly but at an accelerated pace after World War II.

(1) Portuguese policy led to the creation of a very thin segment of educated Angolans who were given the legal status of *assimilados*, a status which accorded access to white-collar and professional positions and, for a few, a university education in Portugal. Some, but by no means all, of this group were mulattoes.

(2) The push to escape forced labor in Angola (which was not abolished, even legally, until 1961) and the pull of economic development in Leopoldville (today called Kinshasa), capital of the neighboring Belgian Congo, led to a steady emigration from northern Angola, especially by the Bakongo, since that tribe was also the "host" ethnic group in Leopoldville

and its environs. The migrants "assimilated" well, and many came to speak better French than Portuguese.

(3) The push of agricultural poverty in Portugal and the desire of the authorities to encourage small cash-crop plantations in Angola led to a steady migration of Portuguese colonists, who grew in number to a point that Angola could be placed in the category of white settler colony (along with Algeria, Kenya and Southern Rhodesia, for example).

Three emergent social groups, three political thrusts. The urban-educated African cadres in Luanda (and in Lisbon) gave birth in the 1950s to the Movimento Popular para a Libertaçao de Angola (MPLA). The migrant Bakongo living in Leopoldville gave birth in the 1950s to the Uniao da Popoulaçoes de Angola (UPA). The white settlers in Angola grew restive as settlers tend to do, flirted for a while with Left opposition to the Salazar regime, and finally fell back for the most part into their logical stance as bulwarks of resistance to any form of "decolonization."

Both the MPLA and the UPA followed paths in their early days which resemble those of many other movements. The MPLA was founded by "intellectuals." It had to carve its nationalism out of the larger entity, greater Portugal, and the latter's ideology of "luso-tropicalism." Thus, it was forced to define itself first of all vis-à-vis the Portuguese Left. In the 1950s the African students in Lisbon (who included Amilcar Cabral, Agostinho Neto, Marcellino dos Santos, Mario de Andrade) were engaged in a little-known ideological debate with the Portuguese Left, including the underground Communist Party. Both sides were opposed to the regime, but whereas the Portuguese Left defined the evil it opposed as "fascism," the African students insisted that the evil was "fascism *and* colonialism." The founding of the MPLA, the first truly "nationalist" movement in Portuguese Africa, meant the rejection of a view that the internal class struggle in Portugal should take priority over the national liberation of Angola.

The UPA was founded by uprooted urban migrants who came together on their ethnic identity. It started life in 1954 as the UPNA, the "N" standing for North. It was at first nothing but an ethnic association, and its leader was a migrant with some education and links to a traditional chief named Holden Roberto. The UPA tried to create its nationalism by attaching other ethnic groups to its Bakongo base. The first step was the initial change of name in 1958 to UPA. The second step was an alliance with some other neighboring ethnic groups in 1962, which produced the Frente Nacional de Libertaçao de Angola (FNLA).

The problem of the MPLA was to enlarge its base vertically in terms of popular support. The problem of the FNLA was to widen its base horizontally in terms of ethnic support. In the 1960s the MPLA was to show itself far more successful than the UPA-FNLA in resolving its problem. The key point to remember, however, is that the present split in Angola of two competing forces had already crystallized by 1960.

The split might conceivably have been overcome in the common nationalist struggle against Portuguese colonialism, had it not been reinforced and sharpened in the larger southern African scene. For it must also be noticed that not only Portuguese Africa but southern Africa as a whole was "late" in decolonizing. And the overall explanation can be stated in two phrases: white settlers and mineral wealth. Here enters the United States Government in the role of long-term protector of the interests of the multi-national corporations which controlled this mineral wealth.

In West, Central and East Africa, the United States could afford to be relatively relaxed about the fact of decolonization; indeed, even benignly "liberal." Few investments were at stake, and if these states were decolonized "gracefully" one could expect the resulting independent African governments to be "moderate." And that, by and large, has turned out to be the case. But southern Africa was a major resource area and, largely because of the white-settler element, a more politically volatile one.

The so-called Congo crisis or crises of 1960-64 was the opening phase of what promises to be southern Africa's Thirty Years' War. For the province of Katanga in the Congo (since renamed Shaba in Zaire) was the northern tip of the mineral belt and had a white-settler population. The sudden decolonization of the Belgian Congo in 1960 was, for the multinationals, a risky "gamble," and for the white settlers of southern Africa a disastrous breach in their fortress. When an authentic and irrepressible nationalist like Patrice Lumumba came to power in the Congo, the risk turned sour and the United States decided to intervene. (Those who followed the situation closely knew this in 1960, but for the doubters quite detailed revelations have recently emerged from the U.S. Congress' investigations into the covert operations of the CIA.)

This is not the place to review the enormously intricate ups and downs of the Congolese crisis. For present purposes, three facts must be kept in mind:

(1) The Congolese divided not into two but into three camps: the Lumumbists, incarnating progressive nationalism; the Katangan secessionists, led by Moise Tshombe; and a politico-military coalition, including Joseph Kasavubu (Bakongo ethnic leader and first President of the Congo), Cyrille Adoula (the United States' favorite son) and Gen. Joseph-Désiré Mobutu (the man on horseback and ultimate military victor).

(2) Faced with this triple split, the independent African states also split into the so-called "revolutionary" Casablanca group backing the Lumumbists, and the so-called "moderate" Monrovia group backing the Kasavubu-

Adoula-Mobutu coalition (the Congo-Brazzaville regime of Abbé Youlou was almost alone in supporting Tshombe). Outside Africa, the USSR backed the Lumumbists (but rather feebly); the United States, the multinationals, the United Nations Secretariat and Great Britain backed the Kasavubu-Adoula-Mobutu forces (and rather vigorously); South Africa, Portugal, Rhodesian whites, Belgian white settlers and to some extent France backed Tshombe (while Belgian mining interests were ambivalent).

(3) As the split in the Congo hardened, so did the corresponding split in Angola. Holden Roberto and the UPA-FNLA were linked politically (and personally) to the Kasavubu-Adoula-Mobutu coalition, while the MPLA was linked in spirit to the Lumumbists. Hence the destruction of the Lumumbist forces in 1964 and the installation of a strong regime by Mobutu in 1965 was a major setback for the MPLA. Conversely, after 1965 it was clear to Mobutu and to the United States that any success for the MPLA would threaten the internal order they had imposed in that part of the Congo now called Zaire.

The military struggle of Angolan nationalists against the Portuguese divides into two phases: 1961-65 and 1965-74. In 1961, spurred on by Congo's independence and the confusion of the Congolese "crisis," both the MPLA and the UPA launched open attacks on the Portuguese. That of the MPLA started on February 4, and took the form of an urban uprising in Luanda, the capital. The only "outside" support at that point was the cooperation of a handful of Portuguese Left elements. The uprising was a military failure, and was followed by an internal crisis in the MPLA that almost caused it to disintegrate by 1963.

The attack of the UPA started on March 15, and took the form of a peasant revolt of Bakongo in the two northern provinces adjoining the Congo. This outburst was sudden, ferocious and anti-white, a number of small white coffee proprietors and their families being slaughtered. The UPA received arms from their Congolese friends, as well as from Tunisian forces (who formed part of the United Nations contingent in the Congo). The UPA received some encouragement (via Tunisia, particularly) from certain liberal elements in the Kennedy regime. Because the uprising was located in deep forest areas where roads and communications were difficult for the Portuguese, and because the Congo border served as a backstop, the UPA-FNLA forces could survive in what the Portuguese called the "rotten triangle."

In all this period, attempts to bring the UPA and MPLA together foundered on the mutual ideological suspicions of the two groups. The MPLA leadership, university-educated and politically immersed in European Left traditions, saw the UPA as tribally based, essentially conservative, manipulated by the United States, racist, and incapable of conducting a long war against the Portuguese. The UPA leadership saw the MPLA as urban intellectuals, privileged mulatto *assimilados*, pro-Communist (despite the fact that the honorary president of the MPLA was a Catholic priest), and incapable of rallying peasant support. That such a split was in principle neither inevitable nor irreparable is demonstrated by the ultimately different histories of nationalism in Guinea-Bissau and Mozambique, where at the moment of independence in each country there was a clearly dominant, united national liberation movement. The difference lay not in the will of the Angolans but in the crucial interest of the governments of Zaire and the United States in preventing such a unification in Angola.

In 1963, the MPLA was beset by internal difficulties while the UPA-FNLA seemed to be leading an effective struggle. The latter formed the Govêrno Revoluçionario da Angola em Exil (GRAE), and was able to convince the newly formed African Liberation Committee of the Organization of African Unity (OAU) to recognize it as both a government and the *sole* legitimate representative of Angolan nationalism. With only a few exceptions, the GRAE was formally recognized by most African states and admitted to meetings of the OAU.

Hence in 1963 the GRAE was not in the least interested in the united action for which the MPLA was crying. It proclaimed itself *the united movement*, recognized by all Africa. The then Adoula regime in the Congo even expelled MPLA from its territory, thus denying it a base for action in Angola. Yet within one year it was to tumble from this height, showing thus that the base of its strength was in fact very fragile.

On the one hand, the MPLA was patiently restructured and rebuilt by Agostinho Neto. And it prospered from two changes in African government. Congo-Brazzaville had a coup in July 1963, which brought to power a regime sympathetic to MPLA, which thereupon established its headquarters there. This was particularly useful since Congo-Brazzaville bordered on Cabinda, an Angolan enclave separate from the main territory of the country, and thus gave access to a part of Angola. And in 1964 when Zambia became independent, its government, whose country bordered the eastern edge of Angola, was also willing to let MPLA operate from its territory.

Precisely as the basis for a future military revival was opening up for the MPLA, the GRAE suffered a crucial setback. In Congo (Zaire), there was a short period beginning in 1964 when Tshombe was Prime Minister. And Tshombe, who had received support from the Portuguese in the days of Katangan secession, returned the favor by closing the frontier to the UPA-

FNLA-GRAE. At that point, the latter rapidly collapsed militarily, never to revive again significantly in the period before the Portuguese coup.

As if to jump off a sinking ship, the "Foreign Minister" of the GRAE, one Jonas Savimbi, resigned dramatically at an OAU meeting in Cairo in July 1964. Savimbi publicly accused Holden Roberto, president of the GRAE, of acting as an agent of the Americans. Soon thereafter, the OAU withdrew its "exclusive recognition" of the GRAE, and agreed to restore the MPLA to equal status as a legitimate national liberation movement meriting support. Individual governments then began to withdraw recognition of the GRAE until, by 1971, the OAU would no longer even tolerate the label, and Roberto had to return to the earlier "nongovernmental" initials of FNLA.

A word about Savimbi, who now enters the scene as a third actor. Who and what was Savimbi? He had been a student in Switzerland when the wars began in 1961. Holden Roberto, looking for some way to overcome the reputation of UPA-FNLA as tribally based and without intellectual support, discovered Savimbi and his friends and saw in them two advantages. They were Ovimbundu, that is, tribesmen from the south of Angola; and they were "intellectuals," but had not been exposed to the "Marxist" infested atmosphere of Portuguese universities. Rather, they were mission-trained anti-Communists. Roberto offered Savimbi the post of Foreign Minister and that was one more factor making possible the ephemeral triumph of 1963. And where did Savimbi go once he quit the GRAE? Within a year he had created a third movement, the Uniao Naçional para a Independençia Total de Angola (UNITA).

In general, 1965-66 was a bad year for Africa. Nkrumah and Ben Bella were overthrown. So was the Nigerian Government, a coup which led eventually to a civil war and placed Africa's largest country *hors de combat*. Mobutu consolidated the anti-revolutionary regime of Zaire. Elsewhere in the world, the United States invaded Santo Domingo, the generals took over Indonesia, and the Americans began their massive participation in Vietnam.

In Africa, as elsewhere, progressive forces seemed very much on the defensive, and the Portuguese looked forward to an end of an unpleasant interlude in their 500 years of imperial luster and thirty-odd years of corporatist tranquillity. In 1965, with three different movements in Angola, none of them engaged in much activity, the Portuguese seemed to be in good shape.

What Lisbon had not counted on was the tenacity of three allied, anti-Portuguese movements in Portuguese Africa: the MPLA; in Mozambique, the FRELIMO; and in Guinea-Bissau, the PAIGC. As it turned out, all three movements conducted a steady campaign on three distinct fronts—political, diplomatic and military—that led to control of more and more territory by all three movements, and to more and more support abroad, until their combined strength so strained Portuguese moral and economic resources that the captains revolted in 1974.

In this period, 1965-74, the Portuguese spared no effort to wipe out the movements. And they received ample military assistance from both the United States and other Western powers on the one hand and from South Africa on the other. They tried to split movements and assassinate leaders. In the case of Mozambique and Guinea-Bissau, they succeeded in killing the leaders, Eduardo Mondlane and Amilcar Cabral, but despite this, the movements in those two colonies held together. In Angola, as always, the situation was more complex. The FNLA built up its army in Zaire under the protection of Mobutu, but left the Portuguese in Angola largely untouched. UNITA followed every available wind. For a while, it talked an ultra-Maoist language, then a Black Power line (which seduced a few Black Americans), and all the while it "organized" peacefully in its southern ethnic base with the complicity (as we learned after the Portuguese coup) of the Portuguese armed forces.

During this period, the MPLA alone fought a continuous guerrilla action, alone sought to be a national rather than a regional movement, and alone resisted the temptations of anti-white racism, insisting always on *political* criteria for identifying friends and foes. It did not, however, have an easy time.

First of all, the fact that the Zaire border was *always* closed to the MPLA and that the Zambian border lay astride open, semi-arid plains several hundred miles deep meant that the logistical problems of the MPLA were enormous and hindered the intensification of guerrilla activity. Hence MPLA never achieved the degree of relative military success of FRELIMO or the PAIGC.

This indeed accounts for the fact that in December 1972 when the FNLA was at a political, diplomatic and military nadir, the MPLA was willing to enter into a never-to-be-implemented unity pact with it. The MPLA hoped, in vain as it turned out, that the pact would open the Zaire frontiers for its men and arms. The only one who gained from the pact was Holden Roberto, to whom it gave renewed legitimacy. Shortly thereafter, the Portuguese again tried their assassination tactic. This time the leader (Neto) escaped, but they succeeded in splitting the movement, in the form eventually of the break away of a faction headed by Daniel Chipenda, who commanded strength in the southern part of the country. Like Savimbi before him, Chipenda wandered from camp to camp, and ideological position, until today he has joined the FNLA as its Secretary-General, although still holding his forces geographically and militarily separate from the rest of the FNLA.

The assassination attempt on Neto and the schism with Chipenda occurred just before the April 1974 Portuguese coup. Once again, at a critical turning point (as in 1963), the MPLA was internally split. Once again it washed dirty linen in public. Once again, by the strength and stubbornness of Agostinho Neto (both his virtue and his weakness), the MPLA regrouped forces and pulled through.

The struggle however was far from over. Indeed, with the Portuguese coup ("Our victory," cried Neto in Montreal where he was on the day it happened), the struggle became more acute, the ideological options became clearer, and the fear of an MPLA victory by the Zaire, South African and American Governments more intense.

As with the Congo crisis of 1960-64, it is not to the point to review in detail the politico-military maneuvers in Angola since April 25, 1974, but rather to summarize the broad lines up to the present.

(1) The three main Angolan groups (or three and a half, if one adds the Chipenda forces) have distributed themselves *de facto* in different geographical areas: FNLA in their northern Bakongo bastion near the Zaire border; UNITA, and the Chipenda forces in Ovimbundu areas in the south; and MPLA in the capital, Luanda, as well as a broad central belt running across the country, plus the enclave of Cabinda.

(2) The successive Portuguese Governments have been internally split over Angola. Indeed, Angola has been a key issue of the internal debate. The result has been waffling which, as time went on and the Portuguese Governments slipped to the right, became a neutrality that hurt MPLA more than it did the others.

(3) The South African Government, immediately following the Portuguese coup, played the game of so-called détente in southern Africa with great flexibility, thus preventing any immediate domino effect. As the day of Angolan independence came nearer, they moved more and more openly to the support of the two "southern" anti-MPLA forces, UNITA and the Chipenda forces (technically now FNLA), by sending in arms, mercenaries and even troops.

(4) Zaire and the United States have been openly supporting FNLA with arms, money and, in the case of Zaire, probably men. Zaire has also tried to promote a secessionist movement in Cabinda (called FLEC).

(5) MPLA has received unreserved support from the governments of the four other independent African states that were formerly Portuguese colonies: Mozambique, Guinea-Bissau, Cape Verde Islands and Sao Tomé

e Principe. Mozambique has sent some troops to help. Samora Machel, President of Mozambique, has stated unambiguously:

> In Angola, there are two parties in conflict: on the one side, imperialism with its allies and its puppets; on the other side, the progressive, popular forces who support the MPLA. That's the whole story. It is not Spinola, Holden [Roberto], Savimbi or anyone else who matter to us. They are only instruments of imperialism. It is imperialism that is the danger and the true menace. (*Interview in Afrique-Asie, October 20, 1975.*)

MPLA has also had strong support from African progressive states, such as Congo-Brazzaville, Guinea (Conakry), Algeria, Tanzania (after a moment of hesitation), and (a bit unexpectedly) Nigeria.

(6) MPLA has received very strong material assistance from the USSR. It should be noted that this support was not always unreserved, but that it is at present considerable. MPLA also has had strong support in arms and material from Yugoslavia and Cuba, and the latter has also sent men. And from Vietnam: the place of honor at the independence celebrations in Luanda was given to the representative of South Vietnam. Romania has supported MPLA after initial hesitation.

(7) The Chinese seem to have adopted that old slogan of John Foster Dulles: If the USSR supports a movement, it can't be any good. The Chinese ambivalence about MPLA has a long history. In 1963, they welcomed to Peking Viriato da Cruz, leader of a small break-away faction of MPLA. When da Cruz joined FNLA, at least momentarily, Chou En-lai in 1964 invited Holden Roberto to visit. (Roberto didn't go because Tshombe, then in power in Leopoldville, warned him that if he did he would never be allowed back in the Congo.) The Chinese played footsie with UNITA for several years. In between, from time to time, under the pressure of progressive forces around the world (including of course FRELIMO and PAIGC who had, however, their own difficulties with them), the Chinese acted in a more friendly fashion toward MPLA. Then in 1973 they entered into an agreement with FNLA to train their soldiers. When MPLA protested, the Chinese offered a stance of neutrality vis-à-vis all *three* movements, which MPLA rejected as unacceptable.

On November 11, 1975, the date when the Portuguese had agreed Angola would become independent, the MPLA pronounced the establishment of the People's Republic of Angola. On the same day, FNLA and UNITA agreed on a last-minute coalition counter government with temporary headquarters in Huambo in the south (a region under UNITA control). As of December, some thirty governments had recognized the MPLA government. No one has formally recognized the counter regime. But, *de facto*, it has very active support from the trio that have consistently opposed MPLA: Zaire, South Africa and the United States. China is in a most uncomfortable position, which it finds difficult to explain to forces sympathetic to it around the world.

What may we expect in the near future? The civil war promises to be long. Zairois forces plus South African mercenaries are clearly insufficient to destroy MPLA, given the arms it is now receiving from various friends. The great unknown is whether or not the United States will intervene more directly *à la* Vietnam. It is not impossible, despite the real counter pressure that is coming from within America—after Vietnam, Watergate and CIA revelations.

Mr. Kissinger is saying these days, with shameless hypocrisy, that any intervention would only be a response to Soviet actions. The fact is that the United States has been intervening in Angola and Zaire *since 1960—continuously, flagrantly and never on the side of progressive forces*. Angola might have been independent ten years ago, and under an MPLA government, were it not for U.S. support of the Portuguese, of Holden Roberto, of Mobutu against anyone who threatened the structures of dominance in southern Africa.

Let those who find moral solace in self-deception remain neutral. No doubt Léon Blum still does not confess his sins. But the Basque nationalists who were hanged in Spain in October 1975, over the protests of European social democrats and the pleas of Pope Paul, should be on the consciences of those who preached nonintervention in Spain while Franco's Fascists marched on Madrid and the *Luftwaffe* strafed Guernica. Luanda is Madrid. And the moment to choose is now.

Luanda is Madrid, but 1975 is not 1936. There is a good side to South Africa's invasion, the malice of Mobutu and the machinations of Kissinger. The Angolan war will ignite a hinterland that has been dormant too long. Lumumbism, in far more sophisticated and explicit ideological armor, will now rise from the cinders of Mobutu's scorched earth. The South African revolution will see its long-awaited explosion. South Africa's adventures abroad will turn against it exactly as did those of Portugal in Angola, the United States in Vietnam, and France in Algeria. The solidarity of the whites will become brittle while the solidarity of the oppressed will become more firm. During 200 years of worldwide revolt against the capitalist world-system, the Left has made countless errors and engaged in egregious misadventures. But it has at least learned from them. Whereas the Right declines, it becomes both more brutal and more stupid.

One year ago, I thought to myself that things looked bad, that Vorster might put across his notion of détente, that the West might tame the national liberation movements in Angola and Mozambique, and that an historic moment might pass. But the powers that be were too greedy and too frightened. And they have roused Africa, as the world will soon see.

Yankee, Stay Home!
South Africa and Liberal Interventionism

The Carter administration has been asserting of late, through Andrew Young, Walter Mondale and even Cyrus Vance, that it is seeking to bring about majority rule in southern Africa. It has put forward an image of liberal interventionism—on the side of the Africans. It has even suffered attacks by Ian Smith and John Vorster for excessive pressure on them.

Yet Joshua Nkomo, co-leader of Zimbabwe's Patriotic Front, has publicly asserted, not once but many times, that he does not want the United States to take any initiatives, alone or jointly with Great Britain, to bring about a Rhodesian settlement. And Sam Nujoma, president of Namibia's South West Africa People's Organization (SWAPO), has called the sending of a mediating mission to Namibia by the five Western powers (United States, Great Britain, France, West Germany and Canada) " a very unfriendly act," and a defiance of United Nations resolutions.

Nonetheless, the Carter administration continues to proffer its "assistance" to the African movements, who continue to insist that all they want is for the United States *not* to help the white regimes. Is this not a strange situation? On the surface, yes; but on closer inspection, not at all. "Liberal interventionism" stands forward today as the most dangerous enemy of African liberation movements in southern Africa, and the Africans know it.

Exactly what is at stake in southern Africa? The answer depends on the perspective. In one sense, it is simple. For the two groups most directly involved in the social conflict—the African majority and the white minority—the stake is clear: the destruction or the preservation of a social structure in which acute socioeconomic inequality and political oppression are built on a foundation of racial division. The Africans wish to liberate themselves; the whites want to maintain the essentials of the status quo. Or at least most of them do.

Few would disagree with this analysis, although the words in which it was expressed might differ according to one's ideology. But wherein lies the interest of the governments of the Western world, most particularly of the United States and of the multinational corporations? On this question, there is less agreement and less clarity. Indeed, one might argue there is deliberate obfuscation. Furthermore, the lack of clarity—or obfuscation—has become greater, not less, with the coming to office of President Carter.

To comprehend what considerations govern the policy making in Washington, one should look at both the geopolitics and the world economic role of southern Africa. Geopolitically, southern Africa has become, and promises to remain for some time, a world node of acute political conflict. The ending of the war in Vietnam brought into being a new and relatively stable situation in that region. The Middle Eastern conflicts seem to be winding their way, however slowly, to an arrangement that may or may not turn out to be stable. But southern Africa promises most clearly to be a center of *increasing*, not decreasing, armed conflict. The long-predicted "explosion" has occurred. But why there, and why now?

One could answer somewhat metaphorically that the present world-system is based on the likelihood of constant "explosions," but that it has "energy" only for one or two at a time. Hence, it was precisely the conclusion of the struggle in Southeast Asia that made possible the eruption of the struggle in southern Africa. This metaphor turns out to be not so implausible if one looks closely at how the *internal* dynamics of southern Africa have been affected by the shifting world political and economic situation.

To expose the roots of this situation we must go back a good many years. Parts of Africa were being incorporated into the capitalist world-economy as peripheral producing areas from the beginning of the 19th century. By and large, this was done by means of so-called "informal empire," that is, without setting up formal colonial rule. In southern Africa, the incorporation was accompanied by white settlement.

During the last third of the 19th century a world economic crisis brought about the decline of Britain's aboslute hegemony in the world-system and led to the "scramble for Africa"—the replacement of "informal empire" by colonial rule. This coincided, not accidentally, with the "discovery" and exploitation of southern Africa's vast mineral wealth.

Mineral wealth had two major consequences that set this region off from other parts of Africa. First, the exploitation of Africans was more intense—

both in terms of work load and working conditions, and in terms of uprooting the people from the land. And, second, it created an intense conflict on the white side of the equation as to who would reap the primary benefits—local white settlers, largely farmers, or the "counting houses" of London, that is, the newly emerging international corporations that "owned" or controlled the mineral wealth. This latter conflict—sometimes summarized as Boer versus Briton—for a long time so dominated world perception of southern Africa as to make many outsiders forget that both Boer *and* Briton were building their privilege on African sweat.

World War II was a turning point for Africa, as it was for so many areas of the world. The achievement of world economic (and politico-military) hegemony by the United States was what made possible the rapid "decolonization" of Africa. Hegemonic powers seldom appreciate the fact that lesser powers (like Great Britain and France) have colonial "empires." Hegemonic powers do not want others to have *chasses gardées*. They much prefer free trade and "informal empire." They also know that if one wants to increase significantly the production and productivity for the world market of a region like Africa, one must enlist the collaboration of local cadres, and that the price of this collaboration is a cut of the pie. Political independence is the easiest package to insure such an arrangement.

So when African nationalist movements began to assert themselves, and then to find moral and political support from the Soviet Union, it was not long before the United States began to lend a sympathetic ear to their complaints about "old Europe." Of course, the United States was concerned about "communism"—that is, about the degree to which these nationalist movements would align themselves politically and economically with the Soviet bloc.

Hesitatingly under Eisenhower, and then with a flourish under Kennedy, the United States's position on African nationalism took clear form. The United States would encourage Britain, France, Belgium and even Portugal to "decolonize," provided the resulting African regimes were pro-Western or at least "nonaligned," and provided—even more important—that economic links with the West were not cut. Indeed, it was proposed that such links be reinforced by means of "economic development." First the British, then the French under de Gaulle, bought this line and, with minor self-serving amendments, implemented it.

The so-called "downward thrust of African liberation," starting in the mid-1950s and lasting a decade, took on the overtones of a gigantic deal. On the one side and moving south, one African colony after another was granted independence, and without bloodshed. (The French press often spoke of this independence as being *octroyée*, that is, dispensed as a favor.)

On the other side, the new African regimes curbed internal radicalism, and their new governing bourgeoisies took with a vengeance to "development," that is, more intensive participation as peripheral producers in the capitalist world-economy.

It seemed a very workable deal, but there was one fly in the ointment. As liberation thrust downward, it hit the southern region which had a special pair of characteristics—mineral wealth and white settlers. Mineral wealth meant there was a lot more at stake for the Western world, and fewer "risks" could be taken; white settlers meant that there was involved a powerful political element that had little to gain from the "deal" of decolonization.

The northern tip of the "southern African" region is the Congo (Zaire) or more specifically, Katanga province (now renamed Shaba). In 1960, decolonization reached the Congo, and there was a "crisis." The white settlers resisted decolonization, the Congo "exploded," the multinationals and the Western governments were ambivalent, and the United States engaged in "liberal interventionism" under Kennedy. After five years the dust settled, with the following result:

> Zaire found itself with a strongman, Mobutu, installed in power and leading an openly neocolonial regime. Patrice Lumumba had been murdered and indigenous "Left nationalist" forces had been militarily suppressed. Governments in independent Africa that were reluctant to respect the "deal" of decolonization in full (Nkrumah in Ghana, Ben Bella in Algeria, Keita in Mali) had been overthrown. The "downward thrust" of African liberation had been stopped. (Whereas in 1961 the United States had seemed inclined to extend the arrangements of decolonization to Portuguese Africa, by 1965 it was emphatically behind Portugal's attempt to wipe out the national liberation movements.) The white settlers of Southern Rhodesia, led by Ian Smith in November 1965, made a "unilateral declaration of independence" which Great Britain bewailed but did nothing about. In short, the lid had been put on African liberation, and would stay on for a decade.

The difficult years for African liberation (1965-74) were precisely the years of intensive U.S. involvement in Vietnam. The United States quite clearly felt it could not "afford" another major trouble zone. It did its best to bottle up the genie in the Middle East. (See its attempts in 1967 and 1973 to cut off the wars.) It took a hard line in Latin America and the Caribbean (from the invasion of the Dominican Republic in 1965 to the many coups from Brazil to Chile). In southern Africa, it threw its weight behind the status quo.

But the United States lost the war in Vietnam. The quite extraordinary resistance by the Vietnamese turned U.S. intervention into an *economic* nightmare, which hastened (even if it didn't cause) the world economic crisis that began about 1967 and in which we are all living today. This crisis took on many faces: currency floats, the rise in the price of gold, the end of United States "free trade" policy, the rise in world petroleum prices, the world famines of the early 1970s.

The United States had to quit Vietnam. And, more immediately relevant to our story, there was a coup in Portugal in 1974—the direct consequence of the economic drain of ten to fifteen years of warfare the Portuguese had been forced to wage in Guinea-Bissau, Angola and Mozambique. With the Portuguese coup, the lid was off again. The "downward thrust" of African liberation could resume its onward movement.

But now the situation in two important ways was different from what it had been in the 1950s. The African movements in southern Africa, having learned the lessons of history, were no longer mere nationalist movements. They were now national liberation movements—that is, movements concerned with the socioeconomic content of political independence. This caught the United States Government somewhat unawares (though why it should have done so is beyond me) and suddenly Angola loomed as a new symbol. Furthermore, the world-economy was now not expanding as in the 1950s but stagnating or contracting, which meant that the economic stakes in southern Africa were suddenly even higher.

The significant action taken by Henry Kissinger was not the adoption of National Security Study Memorandum 39 in the first Nixon term. That memorandum represented merely the culmination of our "status quo" option from 1965 to 1974. It was rather Kissinger's meteoric emergence as a "mediator" on the southern Africa scene in 1976. Basically, Kissinger sought to revive the earlier United States option of a "deal" of decolonization, of an independence that was *octroyée*, and apply it to the remaining non-African-controlled areas of the continent. As said above, the earlier policy had been initiated hesitatingly under Eisenhower, then with a flourish under Kennedy. Its revival was hesitating under Kissinger, and it is continuing with a flourish under Carter.

Thus, when Andrew Young or Walter Mondale or British Foreign Secretary David Owen speaks of a "last chance" for a "peaceful transition," he means it is a last chance to install relatively tame African governments in Zimbabwe and Namibia, governments that would hold their own radicals in check and would continue to permit the same steady flow of products and profits as has historically been the case. Of course, the "deal" would provide a cut for local African politicians and businessmen. But this is no skin off the back of the large corporations. The "cut" for the African cadres would simply substitute for the "cut" now taken by the white settlers. What Mr. Carter and his advisers hope to see are some more replicas of Zaire or Kenya—perhaps "at worst" of Zambia.

They would be perfectly happy to make this "deal" with the Patriotic Front in Zimbabwe, with SWAPO in Namibia (and one day maybe even with the African National Congress in South Africa). But, as we have seen, the leaders of these movements are not buying any such "deals" at the moment. They represent movements that are both dynamic and politically educated, and they are aiming for independence on better terms.

To be sure, Ian Smith is also *not* interested in the proffered "deal," and John Vorster would be interested in a deal for Zimbabwe and Namibia only if it guaranteed exemption for the deal for the South African white regime. But Smith, even Vorster, are rapidly becoming secondary factors in the equation. The fact is that Carter, and behind Carter the multinationals, do want the deal. If they can't have it with the leaders of the national liberation movements, they will seek (are already seeking) to by-pass them for more amenable types like Bishop Muzorewa or Clemens Kapuuo. For Carter is not merely *offering* a deal, he is seeking to *impose* one. He is trying to persuade both Nyerere of Tanzania and Vorster to help him impose it, but the United States is ready to go it alone, if need be.

The "aid" programs are being drafted; the agents are being planted all over the place; the pressures are being felt in Congress and the foundations and the press to "cooperate"—all in the name of African majority rule—for the good of the African movements, whether they like it or not.

Why the haste and why the pressure? The answer there seems very simple too. Southern Africa will not be another Vietnam, but a Vietnam ten times worse. Vietnam was politically important; southern Africa is politically *and economically* important. The use of U.S. troops in Vietnam caused a major social crisis at home, whose fallout is still with us, even though the "worst" was contained as a result of the withdrawal from Vietnam. But picture a "race war" (for so it will popularly be defined) in South Africa, with U.S. troops essentially on the side of the whites. Could it lead to anything but a parallel "race war" at home? It's a nightmare for the makers of U.S. policy.

But is it plausible that the United States would ever send troops into South Africa, and on the side of the whites? There are two reasons to think it might well happen. First of all, the U.S. administration is repeating all the "preparations" made under Eisenhower and Kennedy for an involvement in Vietnam: particularly the ideology of "liberal interventionism." But even more fundamental is the matter of options. The Carter administration is right: nonintervention now does mean a continued escalation of the violence. It also probably means a rapid coming to power of the Patriotic Front and SWAPO. It means open warfare in South Africa. It means radical upheavals in Zaire and probably elsewhere in the "northern" two-thirds of the continent. It means in short the steady working through of an African revolution. And the United States is simply not yet ready to contemplate that with equanimity.

Of course, U.S. mediation might reduce "violence" now, only to insure even more of it eventually. The issue is not whether or not violence but what the substantive outcome will be. Nixon may meet Mao Tse-tung twenty years after the establishment of the Chinese People's Republic and C.L. Sulzberger may find virtues in Hua Kuo-feng's pragmatism today, but these are signs of resignation, or of manipulation, not of wisdom, even belated wisdom.

What can Americans do who think that African liberation in southern Africa is part of human liberation? They can support the African movements. They can demand that their own government *cease* supporting the white regimes. But above all they can avoid being lured into the trap of supporting liberal interventionism. The siren song is sweet, but the shoals are very sharp. And the game is for keeps.

Why We Said No To AID*

In 1977, Congress authorized the expenditure of one million dollars for "the preparation of a comprehensive analysis of development needs of southern Africa to enable the Congress to determine what contribution United States foreign assistance can make." AID was instructed to present specific proposals on how to spend this one million dollars. AID seems to have approached several groups of scholars heretofore critical of U.S. policy in southern Africa on the possibility of serving as "consultants" to draft this analysis. AID in late November approached the four of us as scholars in contact with persons knowledgeable about the region (and not ostensibly because of our links to the Association of Concerned Africa Scholars) to meet with them to discuss what kind of work ought to be done, could be done, and might be done by us. We agreed to meet with them in December in Washington.

The project was presented to us as one on "Constraints to development of greater self-reliance within and among the economies of the independent states in the southern Africa region." AID said it wished to identify and analyze these constraints in such a way as "to permit derivation of action policies and projects." AID said it wished a genuinely new approach which utilized African and Africanist scholars to articulate African aspirations. In this connection, they said they were discussing a proposal to develop a consortium of universities and scholars in the majority-ruled states of southern Africa as the major locus of such research.

---

*Co-authored with Sean Gervasi, Ann Seidman and David Wiley.

We discovered in talking with some of them that there were, however, some constraints imposed on how one could discuss constraints. One could not "politicize the analysis" (although one could "recognize the political context"). One could not discuss policy-making or policy goals of the U.S. or other governments towards the evolution of southern Africa. One was supposed to assume a majority-rule government in Zimbabwe and Namibia, *however that were achieved*, and of whatever political groups that might be composed. One was *not* supposed to talk about the role of transnational corporations, but only about the flow of factors of production.

In the course of the presentation by AID, we learned that it is likely that during an anticipated interim government, but *prior* to the elections, a large World Bank mission will be sent to Rhodesia to prepare a plan to be implemented by the "transition government" and presumably afterwards by the government of a majority-ruled Zimbabwe. We were told that our task would be to present an analysis of "development needs" for the entire region that was so persuasive that whoever was in power (in southern Africa, or the U.S.) would wish to adopt an action program based on this analysis, and that this would be a major contribution to an ongoing dialogue and debate within the U.S. government.

We rejected the proposal categorically on the following grounds:

(1) We could see no way of discussing "development needs" in the absence of discussing the political arrangements that are probable and preferable.
(2) As far as we could tell, present U.S. government policy in the National Security Council and the State Department was moving in a direction contrary to the aspirations of the liberation movements, and we could not work within such policy assumption.
(3) We felt we were far more likely to affect U.S. policy along lines we favored by laying bare its premises and mobilizing opinion than by "working from within," *a fortiori* since we doubted that any AID analysis would affect policy decisions at the level of the National Security Council; and that "working from within" would hamper our credibility as fundamental critics of present U.S. policy.
(4) We rejected any effort to *conceal* the nature of the debate by pretending to "depoliticize" it.
(5) We rejected the assumption that development aid was necessarily *per se* a good thing, and that more aid is always better than less aid.
(6) We rejected the assumption that the United States should be planning strategies of development for southern Africa, even if the parties concerned were not making such plans, since it might be for good

reason (but of course we believed the leaders of the Patriotic Front and SWAPO were indeed making plans in the light of their own political perspectives).

Let us elaborate briefly on each of these points:

(1) We asserted our view that the political economy is an integrated whole and that it was absurd to discuss development strategies, especially for the entire region, in the absence of political premises and choices. We cited an elementary example. The present Rhodesian government has an open border with South Africa and a closed one with Mozambique. How can anyone analyze what a Zimbabwe government could or could not do unless we had some idea if the borders were to remain as is, or if both borders are to be open, or if the situation will be inverted (open with Mozambique and closed with South Africa)? In short, it is not plausible to make an analysis (not to speak of its not being desirable) without knowing if we are talking of a Patriotic Front government, or a government arrived at by "internal settlement" (and presumably still coping with the offensives of the liberation movements).

We further said that we could not possibly leave out the role of the transnational corporations (TNC's) from an analysis of the "causes" of underdevelopment (as was suggested), when we believed that the TNC's were one of the prime causes. We said that inviting the World Bank to make proposals was itself a political decision of the greatest importance, since the World Bank represented a particular (and highly contested) view of political economy. And how could one discuss solutions to southern African economic dilemmas, including Mozambique and Angola, in the face of present Congressional strictures on U.S. aid to these two countries? In short, we felt it was not true that there were technological analyses that were ideologically "neutral." We were not neutral, nor could AID be, nor did we think it ever had been.

(2) We emphatically did not believe the U.S. government was presently being neutral. We were in fact appalled by the recent developments in U.S. policy towards southern Africa. We saw the U.S. government as breaking away from its prior commitments to the frontline states to support the Patriotic Front. We saw the U.S. government as acquiescing in, if not taking a lead in, the creation of the so-called "internal settlement." We saw the U.S. as preoccupied by the creation of "moderate" regimes, the criterion of moderation being

primarily how little such a regime proposed to tamper with the social and economic status quo. We saw the U.S. as having failed to take any serious measures against U.S. corporations (like Mobil and Union Carbide) that have systematically violated the Rhodesian embargo. We noted that the U.S. was taking no serious measures against the enrollment of U.S. citizens as mercenaries for Ian Smith. We were deeply concerned with the recently-confirmed transfer of Cessnas to Rhodesia from France, as well as their continued sale to South Africa. This was the type of U.S.-origin, dual-use, strategic material President Carter precisely promised would no longer be delivered, directly or via third parties. In short, the political context which we saw for this study was one of a U.S. effort *not* to promote the well-being of southern Africa as represented in the aspirations of the liberation movements of southern Africa. We remembered all too well the creeping involvement of the U.S. in Vietnam and we chose not to be party to repeating a similar kind of involvement in southern Africa.

(3) We were told, in response, that we could best affect policy by doing such a report. In was implied we were letting down those who agreed with us within the Executive Branch or in Congress. We felt, however, that we could not in any way lend support to present policy objectives, and it seemed quite clear that consulting with AID in such a context would in fact do this. We could see no way in which our report would affect real policy; instead it might simply provide window dressing for continuation of current directions. We were not impressed by the receptivity of the Administration to critical views. Earlier in 1977, a petition concerning U.S. southern African policy signed by 600 African scholars had been presented to officials of the State Department and the National Security Council. Thus far, there has not even been the courtesy of a substantive response. Nor has there been a significant change in policy; if anything, U.S. policy has deteriorated since.

(4) The proposed emphasis of the consultative study was to be on the *regional* plans for development of southern Africa, and on economic and social constraints within each nation, without reference to either the nature or the constitution of these governments or the goals they set or will set for development. We were warned that if we insisted on "politicizing" the discussion on southern African aid, there were others equally eager to "politicize" it, but in ways we would not like. It was implied that groups like those opposed to ratifying the Panama Canal Treaty were sympathetic to Rhodesian white settlers as people who had "built up" their country. We said that we were very aware of

such views and that the very best thing for all of us was to move the discussion out into the open, with options clearly drawn. At the present, the discussion is often clouded in Aesopian language. A "depoliticized" discussion of development is inevitably Aesopian. Hence if we wrote a report in this form, it would only assist those within government who wished to push U.S. policy in the direction of maximally maintaining the status quo to get away with it.

(5) We were told that it was the friends of Africa who had sought, and with some difficulty, to increase the size of aid to southern Africa, and that if ways to spend this money were not forthcoming, it might be reduced. Here we took the position that spending money on aid is not a virtue in itself, and that badly-spent money is far worse than unspent money.

(6) Finally, we said, if there is to be planning for the future of southern Africa, obviously southern Africans should do it. It was one thing for the U.S. to respond to the requests of independent majority-rule governments like Mozambique and Angola (and we noted the U.S. is precisely failing to do this), and quite another for the U.S. to make plans for not-yet-created majority-rule governments in Zimbabwe and Namibia. It was our view that the liberation movements would probably reject the whole idea of pre-planning by outsiders, not only on the grounds that it was a diversion, but even more strongly on the grounds that it was a *negative* political act. (At this point, we were astonished to be told that this was more or less what one of the AID planners had recently heard from Tanzanian officials about this very same project.) We also discovered that the plan to involve southern African scholars through a consortium of African universities was no longer being actively pursued. We said that nonetheless, if appropriate groups of African scholars associated with the liberation movements and the frontline states were to engage in such a study, and thought our help might be in any way useful, we would be ready to do what we could. But to presume that this analysis should be done *for them*, for their own good, was part of the dangerous atmosphere that had infected U.S. policy since the Second World War. We did not think it was morally or intellectually tenable.

We concluded by saying that we were very concerned with the well-being of southern Africa and with the lack of fit between U.S. foreign policy and the aspirations of the liberation movements. We would continue to do research on southern Africa, and continue to speak publicly in criticism of the liberation movements. That, it seemed to us, was the most relevant immediate contribution we could make.